Make A Joyful Noise Unto the Lord

MAKE A JOYFUL NOISE UNTO THE LORD: HYMNS AS A REFLECTION OF VICTORIAN SOCIAL ATTITUDES

by

SUSAN S. TAMKE

OHIO UNIVERSITY PRESS
ATHENS, OHIO

ISBN 0-8214-0371-0 cloth
0-8214-0382-6 paper
Library of Congress Catalog Number 76-05193
Printed in the United States of America by
Oberlin Printing Co., Inc.

DEDICATION

For Sandy and Monty,
whose patient (and sometimes impatient)
forbearance gave me the time to write.

ACKNOWLEDGMENTS

THIS book has been a long time in the writing. It began as a doctoral dissertation and I should like to thank my committee for their corrections, suggestions and encouragement: Daniel Callahan, John Hurt, Gerald Straka, and especially Raymond A. Callahan, whose continued support has propelled the book from first rough draft to final copy.

The hymnbooks used in this study came from many sources, but I should particularly like to thank the Speer Library at the Princeton Theological Seminary and its director, Charles Willard, for generously granting me the use of their facilities and books, especially those in the Louis Benson Collection. Librarians are special people; I have met many in the course of this research and they have invariably gone out of their way to be helpful. I should like to thank the staffs at the Speer Library of the Princeton Theological Seminary, the British Museum Library, the Institute of Historical Research, London, and the Victoria and Albert Museum Library.

A very special debt is owed to colleagues and friends who read and reread, suggested, corrected, and criticized, but always encouraged: David Vaughn, Elaine Mayo Paul, Gerald Cavannaugh, Roberta and Gordon Jacobs, and Ross Miller.

Portions of the Introduction and Chapters III and IV have appeared in different form in, respectively: *Journal of Popular Culture*, IX, 3 (Winter, 1975), 702-709; *Albion* (Fall, 1976), 255-273; and *Victorian Newsletter*, 49 (Spring, 1976), 18-22.

Finally, for the preparation of the manuscript I should like to thank Mae Thompson and the women who did the manuscript typing at George Mason University, and Rosemary Pye and Lee Meiser of Bowling Green State University.

TABLE OF CONTENTS

INTRODUCTION

HISTORIANS and students of literature have long recognized that literature, properly interpreted, reflects some, at least, of the values and ideas of a society. In his study of the early Victorian period, Walter Houghton, for instance, relied almost entirely on literature:

> For my data I have turned to literature in the full faith that "if we hope to discover the inward thoughts of a generation," as Whitehead once remarked, "it is to literature that we must look." But literature in the broad sense that includes letters and diaries, history, sermons and social criticism, as well as poetry and fiction. It is there that "the concrete outlook for humanity receives its expression."[1]

Although Houghton obviously intended to expand the traditional definition of literature to include as many literary sources as possible in his survey of "the inward thoughts of a generation," he neglected one source, a source which is particularly fertile for the Victorian period—hymns. For an age that was distinguished by its profession of Christian ideals,[2] church literature would seem an obvious source for the social and intellectual historian, but until recently it has been neglected as a poor stepsister of belles-lettres. Hymns are still suffering from this neglect.[3]

The number of hymns available to the nineteenth-century hymn singer is simply astounding. Although in the early years of the century all churches did not accept congregational hymn-singing as a valid expression of man's praise to God, during the course of the century the practice became increasingly widespread, so that by 1900 all major denominations published their own hymnals. When Dr. John Julian produced his first edition of the *Dictionary of Hymnology* in 1891, he examined more than 400,000 hymns in various languages. That hymn-singing was popular is evident from a glance at some publication statistics: sales of the official Union-sanctioned Congregational hymnal were so large (40,000 copies of the first edition sold in the first three years) that they provided the Congregational Union with a major part of its revenue. John Keble's *The Christian Year* (1827) went into forty-three editions, but children's hymns were even more popular—Cecil Frances Alexander's *Hymns For Little Children* (1848) went into more than a hundred editions during the century. Within seven years of the publication of the first edition of *Hymns Ancient and Modern* (1861), 4 1/2 million copies had been sold. The British publishers of the Sankey hymnbooks claimed to have sold more than 90 million copies in less than eighty years.[4] Between 1800 and 1820, when many Anglican clergymen still opposed congregational hymn-singing, nearly fifty different hymnbooks were used in the Church of England alone.[5] By 1872 the *Literary Churchman* stated that about 200 hymnals were used in Anglican churches.[6] In addition to the denominational hymnals, there were hundreds published by individuals.

It seems indisputable that quantitatively the effect of hymns on the Victorian public was more profound than the literary works which traditionally have been mined so assiduously by cultural historians. In sheer volume, the writing of hymns far outweighed the writing of poetry in the nineteenth century. More important, the people whose lives were affected by hymns far outnumber those who were affected by poetry. Only a small percentage of Victorian society read the Greek and Latin poets, or even the more popular contemporary writers such as Southey or Wordsworth. But hymns were sung everywhere —on streetcorners, at secular meetings, in the nursery, as well as in the churches and chapels. For instance, when Hippolyte Taine traveled through the English countryside, he noted that hymn-singing was a common way to release excess religious energy: "I saw, at forty miles from London, on the village green, two men in frock coats and top hats, singing hymns. I am told that this is not unusual when the afternoon sermon has been a good one—they bring away a surplus of religious fervour from the service and seek an outlet for it."[7] W. T. Stead also remarked on the widespread use of hymns in everyday life: "It was a sight to see and not to forget,—a string of cabmen at a north-country station sitting on a fence, singing the hymns of the Salvation Army in the intervals between the trains."[8]

The effect of hymns was one of great depth as well as breadth. Little work has been done on the psychology of hymn-singing, although the subject demands examination if we are to understand religious experience. Among regular churchgoers hymns seem to have been absorbed into the deepest recesses of the memory. The personal experiences of two of my acquaintances affirm this belief. In the first case, a woman who was terminally ill with cancer, slipped into a state of unconsciousness. She failed to respond to voice or touch. She thrashed about restlessly in her bed, despite hospital restraints. A friend tried to calm her by talking to her and holding her hand. When that failed, she sang hymns, at which the patient became calm. When the friend finally stopped singing, the patient squeezed her hand and whispered, "more, more." In the second instance, a woman who became progressively enfeebled mentally finally failed to recognize even her closest family members. But until the end of her life, she responded to familiar hymns.

Hymn-singing is a vital part of the communal aspect of public worship. The act of rising (or sitting) as one body and singing as one voice creates a bond of community within the congregation. It is a palpable confirmation of the idea that the church is the faithful gathered together. If the hymn is a familiar one, if the music is not so difficult that the singers become individually self-conscious, if the congregation throws itself into the singing—if, in other words, the hymn-singing successfully creates a feeling of shared experience—this part of the worship service can be most affective. It creates a bond of community that implies strength and comfort to the individual who is an integral part of a greater whole. Emotionally, hymn-singing is probably the most important part of the worship service. The feeling of togetherness in unison-singing comforts. The act of standing and singing releases. Performed again and again, this ritual act of hymn-singing has the power to tap emotional wellsprings that are not wholly conscious or rational.

For many Victorians the memory of hymns in later life recalled an associated memory of joy and security in community. The Victorian journalist W. T. Stead summed up this deep emotional response in his book, *Hymns That Have Helped.* It was a response, he thought, particularly common to the colonist, for whom "the sound of some simple hymn tune will . . . call from the silent grave the shadowy forms of the unforgotten dead, and transport the listener, involuntarily, over land and sea, to the scene of his childhood's years, to the village school, to the parish church."[9] This evocation of lost worlds must have been poignantly memorable not only for colonists far from home but also for the many Victorians who had been transplanted from rural to urban communities, and for the many Englishmen who simply felt that the uncomplicated world of childhood had been replaced in their adulthood by a less comprehensible industrialized, urbanized world.

Hymns were learned and sung by families at home as well as in church and because of this, for some Englishmen, hymns recalled the comforts of childhood, the love and warmth of the family circle, and, no doubt, parental approval at having mastered the words of a particularly difficult hymn. If we can take an example from nineteenth-century fiction, we can see the deep psychological impact which hymns could have on young minds. In the novel *Heidi*, the young girl Heidi cures a learned doctor of an emotional malaise by repeating a familiar hymn to him; the doctor's response is profound:

> Heidi stopped suddenly, for she was not sure that the doctor was still listening. He had laid his hand over his eyes and was sitting motionless. She thought perhaps he had fallen asleep. . . . Everything was still. The doctor said nothing, but he was not asleep. He had been carried back to days of long ago. He stood as a little boy beside his dear mother's chair; she had placed her arm round his neck and was repeating the hymn which Heidi had just repeated, and which he had not heard for so long. Now he heard his mother's voice again and saw her gentle eyes resting on him lovingly, and when the words of the hymn had ceased, the kind voice seemed to be speaking still other words to him; he must have enjoyed listening to them and have gone far back in his thoughts, for he sat there for a long while, silent and motionless, with his face buried in his hands. When he finally rose he noticed that Heidi was looking at him in amazement. He took the child's hand in his. "Heidi, your hymn was beautiful," he said; and his voice sounded more cheerful than it had been before. "We will come up here another day, and you shall repeat it to me once more."[10]

The doctor's cure is begun by his returning to a remembered state of childhood, where he relives momentarily his comforting relationship with his mother. The whole scene is triggered by a familiar hymn.

It is probable, of course, that in some families hymns had the opposite effect of reminding children not of familiar comfort but of a bleak and forbidding religion. It is interesting, for instance, that Janet Courtney, the daughter of a Lincolnshire vicar whom she describes as "a God-fearing but timorous father," connects hymns, subconsciously perhaps, with fear and death. In a brief memoir of her early years, she associates her childhood with a series of gloomy images: the fierce weather of a Lincolnshire winter, hymns about the "last Trump," and the dead in the churchyard cemetery.[11] The emotional response which hymns evoked in many churchgoing Englishmen was profound, whether positive or negative. Because hymns recalled unconscious associations of childhood, family, school, and community, their emotional impact was greater than their explicit message would necessarily indicate. The commands embodied in the hymns, then, were reinforced by powerful emotional associations.

Hymns were important not only among the churchgoing population, but also among the unchurched—those people unaccustomed to listening to or unwilling to endure sermons could often be lured by music. The curious who were drawn to the Moody-Sankey meetings recalled the effects of Ira Sankey's solos as long as, in many cases longer than, they remembered Dwight Moody's sermons. This effect was why the revival and home missionary services made such prominent use of hymns. In the great wave of missionary outreach after mid-century, a new type of hymn became prominent—the catchy tune with a simple verse and rousing chorus, the type of song which in form and often in vocabulary resembled popular secular songs and therefore attracted more readily the unchurched masses. General Booth, the founder of the Salvation Army, staunchly defended the use of such secular music in missionary work. "I rather enjoy robbing the Devil of his choice tunes," he wrote, "and after the subjects themselves, music is the best commodity he possesses."[12] Booth freely used the catchy "gospel songs" which more conservative churchmen disparaged on aesthetic and doctrinal grounds. In answer to criticism about the religious value of this kind of gospel hymn, Catherine Booth, William's wife, wrote "To whom does all the music of earth and heaven belong if not to Him? I contend that the devil has no right to a single note and we will have it all away from him yet."[13] The Salvation Army attempted to speak to the unchurched in their own idiom, whether in sermons or hymns. This use of the common idiom in church work was evidently very popular with many among the working classes and the very poor. One Victorian observer in Finsbury Park reported hearing several working men gleefully shouting a Salvation Army hymn chorus after the Army had marched through:

There may be some on me and you
But there ain't no flies on Jesus.[14]

The influence of hymns on individuals was obviously great but the social scientist inevitably asks the question, "How great?" To this demand for quantification of the effect of hymns, I can only answer that measuring the psychological impact of hymns on Victorian individuals is at present a difficult task, fraught with uncertainty. Until psychologists, sociologists, and historians develop an appropriate methodology qualitatively and quantitatively to analyze the impact of a medium of popular culture on individual consciousness, such measurement will have to be done by impressionistic methods. Our impressions are that hymns had a great effect on the singers. Certainly, many Victorians felt that hymns were an important cultural medium for shaping thought and behavior. R. W. Dale, a nineteenth-century Congregational minister, thought that hymns were most influential: "Let me write the hymns of a Church," he wrote, "and I care not who writes the theology."[15] Recognizing the effect that hymns could have on the hymn singer, many nineteenth-century hymn writers used hymns as a didactic vehicle. The enthusiasm with which the teetotal societies adopted hymns as a propaganda device in the last half of the century is a pertinent example. We have only to look at hymns like Frederick Faber's *Faith of Our Fathers* (1849) and S. J. Stone's *The Church's One Foundation* (1866) to see the genre used as ammunition in theological battles. When W. L. Alexander exhorted the Presbyterian churches to adopt the practice of singing nonscriptural hymns, he listed their effectiveness in inculcating lessons as a point in their favor:

> And first among these [incidental benefits] I would place the opportunity afforded by the psalmody of the church for instilling, in an attractive and memorable manner, religious truth into the minds of the people. In every proper hymn or psalm, there is an embodiment of some great principle or idea of a devotional kind; this is set forth in a poetical or at least rhythmical form, and the words thus put together, being sung to an attractive tune, the idea not only comes to be familiar to the mind, but what is of more importance, it comes to be surrounded with agreeable associations, which tend to make us love it, and cling to it. . . . In regard to the younger and less instructed part of our congregations, especially, may this beneficial result be expected to display itself.[16]

More recently David Martin, in *A Sociology of English Religion*, concludes that "there is no doubt that the hymn provides the most resonant evocation of religious feeling in Britain: far more so than the liturgy. The Bible itself hardly rivals it even among the most biblicist of believers." In support of this contention, Martin cites the traditional singing of the hymns *Abide With Me* at the Cup Final and "Jerusalem" at the last night of the Promenade Concerts.[17]

In light of these strong impressions that hymns were an important element in the lives of many Victorian Englishmen, it seems strange indeed that they have been so neglected. We are confronting here a historiographical bias and a methodological challenge involved in the problem of popular culture. Our own century is the first in which historians have taken a serious interest on a wide front in popular culture. As Lucien Febvre wrote so pointedly in 1938, "Being aristocratic in its origins, history has been for centuries now, and often still is, solely concerned with kings, princes and the leaders of peoples and armies—the men 'who made history.' "[18] For the last seventy years social historians in particular have attempted to resurrect the faceless masses from historical anonymity, but elitism still dominates the field of cultural history and aesthetics and in no area is this more true than in the study of literature. Cultural historians have traditionally looked at culture with an elitist bias. Trained in a classical conception of culture—that is, that a given society's culture is defined in terms of the best that has been created—the cultural historian defines an historical period by a synthesis of artifacts which are valued largely according to elite aesthetic principles. The "culture" of the nonelite, the majority, has thus often been ignored. A hymn cannot be poetic, the aesthetic argument goes, because it is banal. Tennyson regretfully felt this division between poetry and hymnody: near the end of his life he wrote, "A good hymn is the most difficult thing in the world to write. In a good hymn you have to be commonplace and poetical. The moment you cease to be commonplace and put in any expression at all out of the common, it ceases to be a hymn."[19]

In the history of English hymns only two great poets, William Cowper and Robert Bridges, have written extensively in both fields. The clergy traditionally wrote most hymns, but men in all walks of life wrote hymns during the nineteenth century. Prominent among such lay hymnists were men in public life, such as the members of parliament Philip Pusey, Sir John Bowring, and Sir Robert Grant, as well as a Prime Minister, William Ewart Gladstone. The list includes scholars, teachers, architects, doctors, and scientists. Hymn-writing was considered one of the acceptable fields for women's endeavors and their output was prodigious, particularly of hymns of personal devotion and hymns for children. The lack of literary training of many hymn writers helps to explain some of the valid criticism of hymns on aesthetic grounds: their poor poetic quality and their limited vision. And since hymns were frequently used as a didactic device, they often commented on wholly mundane matters; they could be preachy, melodramatic, or banal. As one scholar summarizes the case,

> There are certainly many people . . . who see in hymns a symbol of everything that was ineffective, pompous and Pecksniffian in the church of the nineteenth century. They are the folk song not of the army advancing with the royal banners but of a gang of hypocrites and time-servers. They are the smeary carols of that dreadful superiority and spiritual snobbery which has distinguished some of the frequenters of parish churches and working class Gospel halls. . . . Those who hate the superiority of the religious hate hymns as its expression; those who identify the church with the political party at variance with their own hear hymns as the 'express' of political reaction, or of cynical and pious oppressiveness.[20]

Whatever the merits of the debate about the literary or philosophical quality of hymns, aesthetic value per se seems an irrelevant criterion in a study of the "inward thoughts of a generation." The social historian must examine the impelling vision of the hymn writers, Pecksniffian or otherwise, if he hopes to investigate fully Victorian ideas and values, for hymns embody some of the most cherished thoughts of Victorian society.

The unsettling events of the late eighteenth and the nineteenth centuries—the thrust toward democracy, the industrial revolution with its consequent urbanization and disruption of traditional class structure and rural life patterns, revolutionary philosophies created by the new scientific and historical scholarship—made deep impressions on Victorian society. Victorian society, as stable as it seems on the surface, was a society in transition and the changes that occurred in social thinking were reflected in Victorian literature.

Because they were an expression of ideals, hymns reflect changes in social thinking over a period of time. In 1871 the Congregational Church Committee on publications recognized that hymns change; understanding that hymns must fit the contemporary needs of society, they decided that a supplement to the twelve-year-old *Hymn Book* must be prepared. The Committee's justification for the added expense illustrates the influence of changing cultural ideas on the church: "A great change of opinion and feeling has taken place in the churches with regard to the forms which the Service of Praise should assume."[21]

Changing attitudes often appeared first in the hymns which were published privately, but by the end of the century these changes were evident even in the denominational hymnals. We need only to look at the hymns on the subject of social welfare for an example. At the beginning of the century most hymns which mention the poor view them as God's chosen people. The only alleviation of the lot of the poor suggested in the early hymnbooks is charity, and even the hymns of charity are few. The social quiescence of the early Victorian churches is best summed up in Mrs. Cecil Frances Alexander's popular hymn *All things bright and beautiful*:

The rich man in his castle,
  The poor man at his gate,
God made them, high or lowly,
  And ordered their estate.

By the third and fourth decades of the century, however, paralleling the growth of social and industrial unrest in England, hymns began to appear in newspapers and privately published hymnbooks vigorously demanding social justice. Perhaps the most well-known of these is Ebenezer Elliott's *When wilt thou save the people*? which was first published in a Sheffield newspaper in 1832. By the turn of the century popular opinion about the problem of social welfare had shifted sufficiently to impel even the editors of the conservative *Hymns Ancient and Modern* to adopt an apologetic stance for the dearth of hymns concerning social and economic conditions in the 1904 edition; they were subjects which, by the editors' own admission, "appeal so largely to our time."

In hymns we find evidence of changing attitudes about many of the subjects which concerned the Victorians; the following chapters will trace some of these changes. By following these changes in popularly published hymns, we can identify the extent to which England's transformed economic and social conditions were appreciated and assimilated by society in general. By tracing these changes in the denominational hymnals, we can identify the shift in social thinking in one of society's most conservative institutions, the church.

This is not to say that hymns reflect only the changes in Victorian popular culture. The majority of the hymns, in fact, show evidence of a profound inertia in social thinking. All institutions, by their very nature, tend to be conservative. One of the chief functions of Christian churches is to preach the doctrine of redemption and salvation. This promise has offered generations of worshipers comfort and assurance in a world full of uncertainty and it is this security and comfort that has traditionally attracted the majority of Christians to the church. The desire for security is a conservative tendency and to a conservative the disruption of established patterns and rituals is often viewed as a threat to that security. Change within the church has been, therefore, particularly threatening to most of its adherents. Changes in hymnbooks are particularly resented by most congregations; anyone who has tried to introduce new hymns or to eliminate old favorites from the congregational repertoire, knows the resentment reserved for those who tamper with the canon of hymns. This institutional conservatism created an attitude reminiscent of the Presbyterian church treasurer who, on his death bed assigned his job to his brother, saying, "I am going the way of all the earth; but you will be a member of the Session in my stead. Let me give you one rule for your guidance; oppose all impruvements."[22]

This foot-dragging tendency is evident in all of the nineteenth-century churches, and the conservative bent is reflected in the denominational hymnals—hymns of social comment that did not agree with the traditional social ethos were accepted with great reluctance. Once again, the problem of social justice is a case in point. By the end of the nineteenth century, English society in general seems to have accepted the idea that laissez faire theories were inadequate in dealing with many of the problems of social amelioration. The state, in answer to this change of social ethos, had begun to create a system of social welfare. Within the church, however, the argument was still strongly voiced that secular humanitarianism was not a concern of the church, and consequently, that social justice was not a proper theme for hymns. Well into the twentieth century some hymnologists would argue that only those songs that were specifically religious could be called hymns.[23] Other hymn writers argued for a more liberal application of the name and urged the inclusion of hymns of brotherhood and social welfare in the hymnbooks. It is precisely in these areas of conflict between the thrust toward change and the conservative tendency to seek security in the familiar past that we find those dichotomies that most disturbed the Victorians.

A methodological question had to be asked early in this study: how do we measure change or inertia within a medium of popular culture such as hymns? The most obvious answer seemed to be to limit the hymns to those of one denomination. Certainly that approach would allow a more exact study: by taking only the hymns contained in the hymnbooks sanctioned by one denomination, the student could analyze the contents quantitatively. B. F. Crawford has done just that for

American Methodist hymnals in his *Religious Trends in a Century of Hymns*.[24] He has been able to document theological and liturgical trends during the century under study such as, among others, the decline of interest in the doctrines of salvation and sin and of death and judgment and the increase of interest in social concerns. This type of study could be done for English Methodist hymnals. It could also be done for Congregational hymnals, for after the formation of the Congregational Union in 1831, that central body took on the task of publishing and periodically supplementing or revising an authorized denominational hymnal. For these two denominations, then, a quantitative method of study might prove feasible.

For the other denominations, however, the evidence is not so neatly packaged. As the next chapter illustrates, many denominational churches strongly resisted congregational hymn-singing for much of the century. Consequently, most of them did not produce a denominational hymnal until late in the century. The Anglican Church is a prime example: *Hymns Ancient and Modern* was not published until 1861 and, even then, the hymns were collected and edited by an independent Board of Governors without official sanction of Convocation or Parliament. *Hymns Ancient and Modern* was a conservative collection; it emphasized the church's liturgical functions and was not well received by the evangelical wing, which had, for the most part, already adopted other hymnals. Before the publication of *Hymns Ancient and Modern* the choice of hymnbooks depended upon the individual congregation or vicar; in 1855 in Nottingham, for instance, the five central churches each used a different hymnbook.[25] But even after 1861 the disunity continued; it was only at the end of the century that the three best-known Anglican hymnbooks (*Hymns Ancient and Modern*, *The Hymnal Companion to the Book of Common Prayer* edited by E. H. Bickersteth, and *Church Hymns*, published by the Society for the Propagation of Christian Knowledge) predominated in Anglican churches.[26] The Presbyterians were also late in sanctioning a denominational hymnal. The General Baptist Annual Association appointed a committee which sanctioned John Deason's *General Baptist Hymn book* in 1830; in 1851 the committee substituted *The New Hymn Book* compiled by J. B. Pike and J. Carey Pike; and in 1879 the committee sanctioned the *Baptist Hymnal* edited by W. R. Stevenson. Throughout most of the nineteenth century, however, the Particular Baptists had their own hymnbooks. For these denominations, then, it will be a much more difficult task to attempt to quantify the denominational hymns.

There is a further reason why I did not attempt a study of denominational hymnals. That is, that too much interesting material would be left out. In the nineteenth century, books of hymns were published by the hundreds, possibly by the thousands. In format, hymnbooks varied greatly: the most impressive are the hard-covered, indexed, denomination-sponsored collections of several hundred hymns, variously arranged according to the order of the service, or according to subjects, or simply alphabetically ordered. At the other end of the scale are the paper-covered collections of perhaps a dozen hymns which sold for as little as a halfpenny. Of the latter type, we can only guess at the number and variety: they were fragile and inconsequential and their survival has been fortuitous. Many hymnbooks were privately published or published for the use of one congregation. Single hymns appeared in newspapers, magazines, or tracts, never to be republished. I have decided, therefore, to survey as many of the hymns as possible, from as wide a range of sources as possible, to see what common themes appear.

But, the social scientist will argue, that is a very unscientific method of approach; there must be some quantification of evidence. To this objection, I can only present the difficulties of quantifying hymns. Certainly, a very popular hymn should carry greater weight as evidence than, for instance, a hymn published privately in a volume for invalids. But the problems of determining the popularity of a hymn are many. Publication in a denominational hymnal would seem, at first glance, evidence of its popularity. Louis Benson and James King used this method in determining the best hymns from, respectively, all Protestant churches and the Anglican Church.[27] They counted the number of times a hymn was published in denominational hymnals. This method, however, tends to insure the inclusion largely of those hymns which were theologically middle-of-the-road and of the older hymns which were familiar to congregations. From this writer's own experience, there are many hymns in sanctioned hymnbooks that are never sung. If we try to determine popularity by actual usage, we run into greater problems. Little evidence has survived on the subject of what hymn was sung on any given occasion—the incidents where observers have noted the hymn are infrequent and scattered.

Even in cases where there is evidence of a hymn's popularity, it is difficult to determine whether the popularity was due to the words of the hymn or the coincidence of a stirring tune to which it was set. The relationship of hymn to music and of music to individual consciousness and, thus, to attitudes and behavior is a fascinating subject but, as yet, a largely unexplored area of cultural studies. I suspect that the music may be more effective than the words in creating the emotional response or association with the past discussed above. Most people, even those who attend church and sing hymns regularly, have difficulty remembering the words of a hymn without musical accompaniment. My students in a Popular Consciousness of Religion course have conducted interviews with older persons who have consistently attended church. Even those respondents who indicate that hymns were an important part of their religious experience often have difficulty recalling the lyrics, particularly when they get beyond the first verse. This does not necessarily mean that the words are unimportant. First, as an individual artistic and pious statement of the hymn writer, the meaning of the lyrics must be accorded the same serious consideration as any other literary artifact. Further, although we cannot at the present time quantitatively evaluate the effect of the lyrics on the person who sings or reads or hears the hymn, we must assume that each time the hymn was repeated, the meaning was reinforced in his consciousness. The cumulative effect of a large number of hymns which present the same point of view almost certainly will be influential on the singer's concept of social reality. Finally, in the English tradition of hymns the lyrics were emphasized more than they have been in the American tradition. Most English hymnbooks were printed without tunes; in most churches only the hymnbooks used by the choir contain music and lyrics. They were intended to be used as devotional books as well as singing books and, therefore, the hymns were experienced as poetry as well as song. For all of these reasons, then, the feasibility of setting up an accurate system for quantitatively evaluating the popularity or effect of individual hymns seems at the present time, unlikely.

Analysis of the whole body of Victorian hymns was further complicated by the great diversity of authors—of their social and religious backgrounds and their intentions in writing hymns. In terms of class origins, hymn writers run the gamut from the landed gentry to the working class. On the one hand we have Mrs. Cecil Frances Alexander, wife of the Bishop of Derry and Raphoe, who lived in the romantic, medieval, Irish countryside and who gave God's sanction to the social and economic chasm between "the rich man in his castle" and "the poor man at his gate." On the other hand, we have Ebenezer Elliott, commonly known as the "Corn Law Rhymer," an ironworker in Sheffield, who wrote wrathful hymns about social injustice. Ministers and bishops wrote hymns from within their chapels and cathedrals; Robert Owen published a volume of radical democratic hymns from outside the church. Although some of the hymn writers wrote them simply as an immediate pious expression of their religious experience or for a specific church ceremony, others wrote them for commercial reasons. The sales of hymnbooks were so large that some individuals like Mrs. Alexander, the Taylor sisters, James Montgomery, Horatius Bonar and some groups, like the committee which compiled *Hymns Ancient and Modern*, made considerable revenues from these sales. Needless to say, most hymnology books prefer to perpetuate stories of the pious type and, consequently, little has been written about the commercial enterprise of hymn-writing.

One final problem has nagged at the present writer during this study—that is the problem of time—the lag between the occurrence of an idea or a problem in the mind of the hymn writer, the voicing of that theme in hymns, and the publication of the hymn. This institutional time lag presents a unique problem for this study. Novels, poetry, and paintings have frequently been used by social historians as sources. All of these are usually presented to the public soon after they are created. Hymnbooks, on the other hand, are collections of hymns and many of the hymns contained therein were written long before the hymnbook was published. James King estimated that it often takes twenty to fifty years for a good hymn to achieve great popularity.[28] Denominational hymnals are notoriously slow to include new material; newspapers and journals, on the other hand, frequently published the newest hymns, written in the heat of debate. To minimize this chronological discrepancy, this writer has attempted to identify the author and the date of composition for all hymns used in this study. This was not always possible, however; therefore, the hymnal edition or other source in which I found the hymn will be given also.[29] I have included in this study a number of hymns which were written before the nineteenth century as indicative of nineteenth-century attitudes; only those hymns which can be found in nineteenth-century hymnbooks are included here. A number of American hymns have also been included, but these may also be found in English nineteenth-century hymnbooks, particularly those published after the middle of the century, when there was a great influx of American hymns, reversing the trend of the previous century.

This study does not pretend to be a definitive exposition of nineteenth-century hymns. They are many hymns which have been ignored, particularly the liturgical, theological, and devotional hymns which largely defy sociological analysis. It is, instead, a survey of a vast untapped reservoir of evidence about the social history of Victorian England. I hope that by exploring the most prominent themes from a multitude of hymns, I will be able to reveal some of the most vital social concerns of Victorian Christians.

CHAPTER I

HISTORY OF HYMNS

HYMN-SINGING is today an integral part of most congregational Christian worship. For many it is the most vital and affective part. But this has not always been true: as a part of congregational worship, hymn-singing is a relatively modern development. As recently as a century and a half ago, many English churches did not accept hymns as a legitimate expression of man's praise to God. To understand the place of hymns in nineteenth-century England, we must briefly trace the history of hymns.

We know from scriptural evidence that the early Christian Church recognized congregational singing. Jesus and his disciples sang a hymn after their meal, before leaving for Gethsemane.[1] St. Paul urged the primitive Christians to "speak to one another in psalms and hymns and spiritual songs."[2] Modern scholars, however, cannot say with assurance how these hymns were sung nor what their content was beyond the traditional psalms of the Hebrew King David.[3]

Although hymns were sung by the early Christians, in the following centuries a prejudice against hymns grew up, probably because of the growing authority of the Bible. This objection to hymns as unscriptural would be a recurring theme in the centuries-long battle for their acceptance. It is a legitimate objection: hymns are poetic expressions and poetry often takes license with theology. People enjoy singing songs primarily because of their poetic and musical qualities, not because of the orthodoxy of their lyrics. It is interesting, therefore, that scholars speculate that these early hymns may have been used as antidotes to heretical poetry.

Ephraim of Syria, Ambrose of Milan, Gregory of Nyssa, and Hilary of Poitiers are generally credited with gaining acceptance for the use of metrical hymnody in the Christian Church. The Latin hymns of Ambrose were so popular among Christians that "his critics accused him of having bewitched the people."[4] As long as Latin remained the common language of western Christians the Ambrosian-type of hymns retained the popularity of folksongs. Church councils varied in their attitude toward hymns: the Council of Laodicea forbade the use of "private psalms"; by the seventh century, however, the Council of Toledo threatened with excommunication the churchmen in Spain and France who resisted the use of hymns in divine worship.[5] The church's policy toward hymns varied from time to time and from place to place, but during the Middle Ages the Latin and vernacular hymns which were available were not used in the mass. They were intended for private devotions or extramural church functions such as the gatherings of the Dominican preachers.

Until the sixteenth-century reformation public worship services, except for the sermon, were in Latin. Therefore, as Latin died out as the common tongue, and in northern Europe where it was spoken only by the educated minority, the singing inside of the church was confined to the priests and the choir. The Reformation changed this. The Protestant reformers insisted that public worship be conducted in the vernacular "to the end that the congregation may be thereby edified."[6]

The reformers were not, however, a unified body. In theology they split into three or four broad camps, differing bitterly especially over the interpretation of the sacraments. The reformers' differences were not limited to theology, however; they also divided on liturgical questions. One of these points of dispute was the composition of the songs of praise to be used in divine service.

The Lutheran view was the more universalist, humane, and emotional: hymns of contemporary human composition were considered an acceptable form of praise. The great outpouring of hymns from Luther's pen, including the now universally popular *Ein feste Burg* (a paraphrase of Psalm 46), were set to popular secular tunes and to the familiar chant and hymn tunes, thus insuring the spread of Luther's ideas. Other Lutheran poets paraphrased the traditional liturgy and texts, setting them to sacred and secular tunes. So great was the success of these hymns that a contemporary Romanist complained that "the whole country is singing itself into this Lutheran doctrine."[7] The Lutheran hymns, however, did not greatly affect England until the nineteenth century, when a burst of enthusiasm for hymn-singing and the romantic movement's interest in the antique sent translators on a worldwide quest for new material. During the middle years of the nineteenth century many of the German hymns were translated and included in English denominational hymnals.

The major influence on the later English reformation, in the area of hymnody as well as theology, was not Luther but the French-Swiss reformer Calvin. What was being sung in the Calvinist churches were the psalms, but the psalms in such a new and lively form that they became popular among both Roman Catholics and Calvinists. These were the vernacular, metrical psalms of Clement Marot, a former French court poet of Francis I.[8] The new form of psalmody received Calvin's blessing for use inside the churches. Outside of the church, in their private devotions, the French Protestants continued to sing their spiritual "chansons," or hymns. The English exiles to the continent brought back to England the Calvinist insistence on the absolute authority of the Bible; only those hymns warranted by scriptural usage were acceptable for singing in the church services. This meant that the English Protestant churches would use psalms and some few scriptural paraphrases in the church services, while continuing the use of more freely composed "hymns" in private devotions and in the less important services such as morning and evening prayer.

The meter of the French tunes made them difficult to adapt to English; therefore, the English metrical Psalter was homegrown. Thomas Sternhold, a Groom of the Robes to Henry VIII, published a collection of his own psalms in familiar meter; this collection was enlarged after Sternhold's death by John Hopkins, and the book was printed several times during Edward's reign. During the period of the Marian exiles and during the early years of Elizabeth's reign, psalms were added and subtracted until 1562, when the English Psalter was produced in its final form, bearing the title *The Whole Book of Psalmes Collected into Englysh Metre, by T. Starnhold, I. Hopkins and others.* The "Old Version," as it was later to be called, was never officially authorized by either Convocation or Parliament but it became sanctioned by tradition and, although a number of rival metrical translations were issued during the succeeding century and a half, none could challenge its supremacy. Loyalty to Sternhold and Hopkins was certainly not due to its poetic quality. An often quoted nineteenth-century judgment of these psalms was that

> their piety was better than their poetry; they had drank more of Jordan than of Helicon. . . . Sometimes they make the Maker of the tongue speak little better than barbarism, and have in many verses such poor rhyme that two hammers on a Smith's anvil would make better music.[9]

A modern commentator agrees: "The metrical psalms of Sternhold and Hopkins did not break the laws of God, but they played ducks and drakes with the laws of metre."[10]

By the end of the seventeenth century some of the public was ready to accept a new translation of the psalms. In 1696 Nahum Tate and Dr. Nicholas Brady published a "New Version." William III accepted the dedication and, although Tate and Brady's psalter was "allowed" by order of the King in Council, it was never officially authorized. Some Anglicans considered the "New Version" an improvement on the Old; others remained faithful to Sternhold and Hopkins. The two rival versions continued to contend for adherents for the following two centuries. To modern tastes there is little to choose between the two. A story is told of Bishop Wilberforce who, when driving through the streets of London with a friend, passed a drysalter's shop. "What is a drysalter?" the friend asked. The bishop replied, "Tate and Brady."[11]

The dullness of eighteenth-century congregational praise was not due solely to the unpoetic quality of the psalms. The method of psalm singing was partly at fault. In an age when many congregations could not read and most churches could not and would not afford multiple copies of the Psalter, a clerk read each line to the congregation, after which the worshipers sang the line; this practice was known as "lining out." The practice of lining out did not disappear from some provincial English churches until near the end of the nineteenth century. Sung pieces at a time, each line interrupted by a clerk who often could neither read accurately nor speak distinctly, it is not surprising that psalm-singing called forth comments like Lord Rochester's:

> *Sternhold* and *Hopkins* had great Qualms,
> When they translated *David's Psalms*,
> To make the Heart full glad:
> But had it been poor *David's* Fate
> To hear thee Sing and them Translate
> By G_ 'twould have made him Mad.[12]

One example of a Tate and Brady psalm was sung:

O turn my pi. . .
O turn my pi. . .
O turn my pious soul to thee.

In England vernacular hymns of "human composure" were written as far back as Anglo-Saxon times, but there is no evidence that they were sung in the churches. For almost two hundred years after the Reformation we have few hymns other than metrical psalms. A few poems by Elizabethan and Stuart poets have been adapted in more modern times to be sung in church, but, for the most part, the monopoly of the metrical psalms was unquestioned. In 1623 George Wither published what has been described as "the earliest attempt at an English hymn-book,"[13] but although the king ordered it to be bound up with the Old Version, the Stationers' Company, which had a monopoly on the Old Version, was able to force its withdrawal. The hold of the Old Version was loosened somewhat during the last half of the seventeenth century by the acceptance of psalm paraphrases, a halfway house on the road to the development of hymnody. Hymns for private devotions were also well accepted by the public, among which the most long-lasting are the Morning and Evening hymns of Bishop Ken.

When church congregations finally began to accept hymn-singing, it was in the nonconformist churches that the movement was initiated. Benjamin Keach, a Baptist pastor in Southwark, London, introduced the practice of singing a hymn at the close of the Lord's Supper; it was done, he claimed, in imitation of the apostles. Keach composed the hymns himself, and while he published some appended to his theological writings in the 1670s, his complete collection of three hundred hymns was not published until 1691. This innovation was not unanimously accepted by the denomination, however. In 1689 the General Baptists declared the hymn-singing was "so strangely foreign to the evangelical worship that it was not conceived always safe to admit such carnal formalities."[14] In fact Keach's own congregation was divided on the issue of hymn-singing and in 1693 the dissidents formed their own church. The quality of Keach's hymns is questionable; none has survived in common use today.

It was not long, however, before a poet of some merit tried his hand where Keach had failed. Isaac Watts was an independent (Congregationalist) minister. During his lifetime he wrote some 600 hymns, the quality of which varies, but a surprising number of them—approximately 400—are found in hymnals today.[15] Watts has been given the title "father of English hymnody" not only because of his hymns but also because of the frontal assault he launched on the system of psalmody. Many of the psalms, he claimed, voiced concepts which were not Christian; the Old Version included verses urging primitive, blood-thirsty sentiments such as the wish "that thy foot may be dipped in the blood of thine enemies: and that the tongue of thy dogs may be red through the same." Watts wrote:

> Some of them are almost opposite to the spirit of the Gospel: Many of them are foreign to the State of the New Testament, and widely different from the present circumstances of Christians. . . . Thus by keeping too close to David in the House of God, the Veil of Moses is thrown over our hearts.[16]

He formulated a new set of criteria for the Christian hymn:

> FIRST, it should be evangelical; not in the sense that New Testament songs be allowed to supplement Old Testament Psalms, but so that the whole body of Church Song be brought within the light of the Gospel.
>
> SECOND, it should be *freely composed*, as against the Reformation standard of strict adherence to the letter of Scripture, or the later paraphrasing of Scripture.
>
> THIRD, *it should express the thought and feeling of the singer*, and not merely recall the circumstances or record the sentiment of David or Asaph or another.[17]

Following his own rules, Watts wrote and published four books of hymns: *Hymns and Spiritual Songs* (1707); *Horae Lyricae*, containing poetry as well as hymns (1706-9); *Divine and Moral Songs, attempted in easy Language for the Use of Children* (1715); and *Psalms of David Imitated in the Language of the New Testament* (1719). The popularity of these hymns in Watts' own time and for succeeding generations is attested by the many editions of the books; of the *Divine and Moral Songs* alone, "between 1715 and 1880 there were over 68 separate editions of this work, not counting reprints, of which there were many."[18] The list of Watts' hymns included in nineteenth-century hymnals is too long to include here; suffice it to say that two of Watts' hymns, *Our God, our help in ages past* and *When I survey the wondrous Cross*, were repeatedly listed as favorite hymns. Benjamin Jowett is reputed to have asked a group of Oxford dons to list their favorite hymns. Each don returned only one: *Our God, our help in ages past*, saying that it fulfilled all requirements for a perfect hymn.[19] Watts' rank as a poet and hymn writer is, nevertheless, still hotly debated today. Even Watts' greatest admirers admit that the quality of his work is uneven, that his subjectivity and sentimentality at times are obnoxious, and that his starkly Calvinistic theology is, particularly in his children's hymns, foreign to modern ears. The continued use of Watts' hymns in hymnbooks, however, speaks for itself: they appealed to his own and future generations.

Later in the eighteenth century other nonconformists followed in the path marked by Watts, but only a few names will be mentioned here. Dr. Philip Doddridge, another Congregational minister, wrote more than 350 hymns which were published in 1749, after his death. These hymns are noteworthy because of their concern for human affairs and especially their attempt to relate Christ's ministry to social justice. Although we cannot dwell on them at any length here because they are outside the chronological scope of this study, some mention of them must be made because they antedate, by a hundred years and in almost total isolation, the nineteenth-century hymnic campaign for social justice. In his hymn about the good Samaritan Doddridge writes,

Father of mercies, send thy grace
All-powerful from above
To form in our obedient soul
The image of thy love.

When the most helpless Sons of Grief
In low distress are laid,
Soft be our hearts their Pains to feel,
And swift our hands to aid.[20]

Again:

Thy face with reverence and with love
I in thy poor would see;
O let me rather beg my bread
Than hold it back from thee![21]

By our own standards these hymns would be classified as an appeal for charity rather than social justice. But when we realize that Doddridge stood alone as a hymn writer in such vehement demands for charity, we can begin to comprehend the enormous change between eighteenth-century and twentieth-century conceptions of social justice.

During the eighteenth century, hymn-singing developed largely among the dissenting congregations, although not all of the dissenters participated in this practice. Dissenters generally emphasized the importance of the individual in his relationship to God rather than the corporate identity of the church. This emphasis on the layman's experience naturally led to congregational participation in the service. Furthermore, eighteenth-century philosophical tendencies towards deism infiltrated nonconformist thought. The deists believed in the goodness and rationalism of man. In their worship services they stressed the participation of the congregation. This led to a new emphasis on hymns.

The hymns which were sung by the dissenting congregations were largely evangelical in nature. They stressed the individual's relationship to God. Horton Davies has noted the prominence of first-person pronouns in eighteenth-century hymns.[22] The subjectivity of the hymns of Watts and Doddridge and others allowed these congregations to express their emotions and led to an "enthusiasm" which marked many dissenting congregations by the end of the century.

For an eighteenth-century English Churchman, "enthusiasm" was one of the most damaging charges that could be made, and hymns were often considered a sign of enthusiasm. Louis Benson relates a story about Samuel Johnson which illustrates the Church's stand:

> "I gave her privately a crown," wrote Dr. Johnson of a girl who came to the sacrament in a bed-gown, "though I saw Hart's hymns in her hand." What seemed memorable to that kind heart was not his act of charity, but his having surmounted on the occasion a churchman's rooted prejudice against hymns.[23]

When Thomas Tregenna Biddulph became Vicar of St. James' in Bristol in 1799, he was violently attacked in a pamphlet which claimed he was a dissenter in disguise. The evidence for this conclusion was Biddulph's use of hymns in the service.[24]

Enthusiasm was not the only charge which the Church lodged against the use of hymns. Such hymns of human composure were also thought by many Anglicans to be illegal. "The rubrics provided for canticles, psalms, and anthems, but not for hymns in the services of public worship appointed in the Book of Common Prayer."[25] A letter written to the editor of the liberal *Gentleman's Magazine* in 1852 exemplifies the conservative attitude:

> Mr. Urban,
> What evil genius hath possessed you and your correspondents to make you so angry with our *excellent*, *most valuable*, and *perfect* public liturgy? . . . Our liturgy, Sir (that perfect model of gospel worship) was originally composed by the special aids of the Holy Ghost, and is so *perfectly* free from errors that the wit of men and angels cannot mend it. . . . therefore, neither king, parliament, nor convocation, can have any power to make the least alteration in that unchangeable book, till they can first prove that they have a new revelation from heaven.[26]

Although Churchmen and conservative laymen might inveigh against them, the popularity of hymns could not be denied. William Vincent calculated at the end of the century that "for one who has been drawn away from the Established Church by preaching, ten have been induced by music."[27]

This popularity of hymn-singing during the eighteenth century must be ascribed in large part to two individuals who came from within the Established Church: John and Charles Wesley. The story of the brothers' upbringing, of their efforts during Oxford years to create a group of "methodic" Christian disciples, of their missionary efforts in Georgia where they were influenced by the pietistic Moravian Brethren, and of their dramatic and evangelistic inner awakening and conversion have been told many times. We are concerned here with their hymns, and although all 6000 of them[28] cannot be reviewed, we must digress somewhat in a survey of these hymns because of the prominent role they played in nineteenth-century religious life.

Wesley's first hymnal was published in Georgia and was intended for the use of his congregation there. The hymns were not well received. When John left Georgia, after several conflicts with the colonists, a list of grievances was presented against him to the Grand Jury for Savannah. Among those grievances were the charges that

> the said Rev. person . . . deviates from the principles and regulations of the Established Church, in many particulars inconsistant with the happiness and prosperity of this Colony, as—
>
> Prima, by inverting the order and method of the liturgy.
>
> 2. By changing or altering such passages as he thinks proper in the version of the Psalms publicly authorized to be sung in the church.
>
> 3. By introducing into the church and service at the Alter compositions of psalms and hymns not inspected or authorized by any proper judicature.[29]

On his return to England in 1738 John Wesley again sought out the Moravians, and it was at this time that he underwent an experience of conversion. The experience seems to have been much like Luther's; it took place, in fact, during a reading of Luther's preface to the Epistle to the Romans:

> About a quarter before nine, while he [Luther] was describing the change which GOD works in the heart through faith in Christ, I felt my heart strangely warmed. I felt I did trust in Christ, Christ alone for salvation; and an assurance was given me that He had taken away my sins, even mine, and saved me from the law of sin and death.[30]

Soon after this John began "field-preaching"; barred from preaching in the Churches, he carried the news of God's love to all who would listen. The enthusiasm with which the gospel was proclaimed frightened many contemporary churchmen and as a result of this fear the Wesleys were ostracized from the Anglican churches, and from many of the more conservative nonconformist chapels.

> The Wesleys worked behind the hedges separating them from both Church and dissent. In so far as either had any real knowledge of the Wesleys and their work, they were regarded by churchmen as schismatics and ranters, and by socially respectable dissent as sentimentalists and sensationalists. They sought to reach the masses neglected by Church and dissent alike, and by methods disapproved of by both. They forsook the conventional order, aroused intellectual contempt, awakened intense theological bitterness and incurred social ostracism, and even personal violence. It is difficult now to reproduce, even to the imagination, "the Reproach of Methodism," and to appreciate the isolation of the Methodist Movement from contemporary religious activity or stagnation.[31]

In the Wesleyan services hymns played an important part. They proclaimed the theology of a church a-borning; hymns were to the Methodists what creeds were to the Established Church. After a close study of Methodist hymns, Louis Benson declares that the hymns were probably the most important propaganda device of the new theology: "the hymns prefigured the constitution of the new Church and formed the manual of its spiritual discipline."[32]

Congregational singing allowed Methodist worshipers to voice the feelings which were incited by the sermon—spiritual experience of God's love and Christ's sacrifice. S. G. Dimond, in *The Psychology of the Methodist Revival*, suggests that the hymns had an important psychological effect on worshipers:

Their power of suggestion, their educational value, and the effect of the music with which they were associated contributed in a marked degree to the creation of the desired emotional experience, and to the permanent influence of the religious ideas and impulses which were the psychological centre and soul of the movement.[33]

Hymn-singing was a powerful emotional experience and needed careful direction. Therefore, Wesley soon published his seven rules for singing Methodists:

1. Learn the tune.
2. Sing them as they are printed.
3. Sing all. "If it is a cross to you, take it up and you will find a blessing."
4. Sing lustily and with a good courage.
5. Sing modestly. Do not bawl.
6. Sing in time. Do not run before or stay behind.
7. Above all, sing spiritually. Have an eye to God in every word you sing. Aim at pleasing him more than yourself, or any other Creature. In order to do this, attend strictly to the sense of what you sing, and see that your heart is not carried away with the sound, but offered to God continually.[34]

The hymns that the Wesleyans sang were intensely evangelistic; they were concerned almost entirely with man's salvation through the intercession of Christ.

Wesley is obsessed with one theme: God and the Soul: for the stage in space and time on which that drama is set he has little concern. He is always at Calvary; no other place in the universe matters, and for him the course of historic time is lost in the eternal NOW.[35]

The hymns ignore almost completely the mundane setting of the worshipers, lifting their aspirations from this world to the next. Because the Wesleys made their appeal largely to the middle and lower classes, this otherworldly focus would greatly influence the social ideals of those classes. Elie Halévy has argued that the Methodist disdain for things of this world would be an important factor in stemming revolution in England in the early years of the nineteenth century.[36] The antirevolutionary tendencies of evangelical theory in general, and the Methodists in particular, will be investigated more fully later in this study.

One other criticism of Wesleyan hymnody must be mentioned here because it has made such an impression on the minds of students of the Victorian period. The blood imagery and sexuality of many Wesleyan hymns has long been noticed. Southey called attention to it early, attributing these images to the Moravian influence on Wesley.[37] Most church scholars have ignored the subject or kept their references on "this unpleasant subject" to footnotes.[38] But in 1958 Gordon Rattray Taylor applied a Freudian interpretation to some of the Wesleyan hymns.[39] Six years later E. P. Thompson delved at some length into the subject, essentially reiterating Taylor's interpretation of the Wesleyan hymns: he found "perverted eroticism," "the association of feminine—or more frequently, ambivalent—sexual imagery with Christ," Christ as "maternal, Oedipal, sexual and sado-masochistic," and a "cult of death."[40] Thompson felt that

> since joy was associated with sin and guilt, and pain (Christ's wounds) with goodness and love, so every impulse became twisted into the reverse, and it became natural to suppose that man or child only found grace in God's eyes when performing painful, laborious or self-denying tasks. To labour and to sorrow was to find pleasure and masochism was "Love."[41]

He added that "Death was the only goal which might be desired without guilt, the reward of peace after a lifetime of suffering and labour."[42] Taylor's and Thompson's findings about work, pain, sorrow and death will be investigated below.

The success of the Wesleys in drawing adherents from outside the Established Church[43] caused evangelicals within the Church to follow their example. During the last three decades of the eighteenth century a spate of evangelical hymns appeared, differing from the Wesleys' in their Calvinist emphasis on man's sinful nature and the consequent narrowness of election.[44] Among the most well known of the Calvinist hymns from this period was Augustus Toplady's *Rock of ages, cleft for me* (1776), which was such a favorite of Gladstone's that it was sung at his funeral. Perhaps the most influential of these hymnals was the *Olney Hymns*, published in 1782 by William Cowper and John Newton. In its emphasis on the individual experience and its introspection, it set the standard for much of nineteenth-century evangelical hymnody. A few examples from this volume that have retained their popularity for more than a hundred years are *God moves in a mysterious way* (1773), *O for a closer walk with God* (1772), and *There is a fountain filled with blood* (1771).

Although many hymns were being written and sung in both chapel and church by the beginning of the nineteenth century, the attitude toward hymn-singing was still ambivalent. Dr. Julian lists forty-two books of hymns published for use in Anglican churches between 1801 and 1820, and many parish priests adopted eighteenth-century evangelical hymnals for congregational use.[45] On the other hand, some bishops forbade the use of hymns in their dioceses on the grounds that the Book of Common Prayer made no provision for them in the liturgy. In a charge of 1820 the Bishop of Peterborough condemned the use of hymns as lawbreaking.[46] In 1819 Thomas Cotterill, Vicar of St. Paul's, Sheffield, imposed a new edition of a hymnbook upon his congregation. Some of his parishioners objected and brought suit against him in the York Consistory Court. Archbishop Vernon Harcourt mediated a compromise: in 1820 Cotterill issued a smaller edition, dedicated to and approved by the Archbishop.[47] After 1820, legal action against Anglican hymn-singing stopped.

Although legal action stopped after 1820, for the remainder of the century opposition to hymn-singing ran high among conservative churchmen. Reginald Heber compiled a book, *Hymns Written and Adapted for the Weekly Church Service of the Year*, in 1820 and submitted it to the Archbishop of Canterbury for his authorization. But approval was withheld and the book was not published until 1827, a year after Heber's death. When John Keble published his book of hymns, *The Christian Year*, in 1827, he intended it "not for the congregation but for the soul at his bedside" because of the opposition of high churchmen.[48] A review of the Church press by W. K. L. Clarke reveals the temper of the conservatives at mid-century:

> The *British Critic* (1840) criticises the "hymns and tunes which, rising and spreading from the conventicle, have at length found admission into some of our churches;" it condemns their "passionate fervour and self-confidence," so different from the Book of Common Prayer; "the temper and spirit of both cannot be right." The same paper in 1842 writes: "There cannot be a more miserable bondage than to be compelled to join in the so-called hymns that now infest our churches" and stigmatises the "passionate and exaggerated descriptions of spiritual experience to which the worshipper may be an entire stranger." . . . The *Christian Remembrancer* in 1851 condemns the new Roman Catholic fashion of singing "methodistical hymns" (the same number says that Browning's women are forward and immodest). No wonder the *Ecclesiastic* in 1850 says: "A stiff and sullen Anglicanism proscribed all metrical hymns as savoring of the conventicle."[49]

The main criticism of hymns voiced by high churchmen seems to have been the association of hymns with dissenting churches. Anthony Trollope's outspoken Low Churchman, Mr. Slope, however, opposed music in the church for the opposite reason: he thought it sensuous and smacking of Romanism.[50] In 1854 an Anglican bishop objected to the singing of an Easter hymn, *Jesu, meek and lowly*, because it was "contrary to the spirit of the Book of Common Prayer."[51] At the turn of the century opposition still ran strong in some quarters; for instance, Bishop Gore declared that hymns were illegal:

> none of the practices objected against High Churchmen was more illegal than the modern habit of hymn-singing. . . . The services were flooded with evangelistic and revivalistic hymns, many of which were good and even necessary at times, but all of which were alien to the spirit of the Prayer Book and to antiquity. By the use of metrical forms any kind of doctrinal innovation could be introduced.[52]

So entrenched was the feeling against hymns among the conservatives that *Hymns Ancient and Modern*, the present-day standard, although not authorized, Anglican hymnbook, was not published until 1861.

Surprisingly, the Established Church was not the only source of opposition to hymns. Among some nonconformists there remained a strong feeling against hymns of "human composure," especially among Presbyterians. The most telling point against hymns was that they were unscriptural. In 1848 the liberal plea was expressed by W. L. Alexander:

> We plead, therefore, for the use of hymns of human composition in our public Psalmody; and for this we think we have the sanction not only of common sense, but as shown in a former Lecture, of the church of the apostles and early christians.[53]

But thirty years later the conservatives were arguing as vehemently as ever against the use of any material but Psalms as praise:

> III. God is certainly the best judge as to what shall constitute the matter of his praise. . . .
>
> IV. God has given a distinct book of praise in the Bible. It is the "Book of Psalms." This book was evidently a growth. The oldest one in the collection, probably (the 90th) was written by Moses. Through a period of a thousand years or more, additions continue to be made. By whose hands

> all were collected into one book we do not know; but we can hardly doubt that the collecting and arranging was done under divine guidance. . . . Our Lord when on earth distinctly recognized it as the "Book of Psalms" (Luke xx. 42).
>
> V. This Book of Psalms is inspired. . . .
>
> VI. This Inspired Book of Psalms was designed to be used in singing the praises of God. . . .
>
> VII. The authority thus to use the Book of Psalms has never been withdrawn. . . .
>
> VIII. Divine authority must be shown for the introduction of any other songs to the worship of God. God is a jealous God. He has shown his jealousy specially with respect to his worship, the matter and manner of it. . . . It is unsound, unscriptural doctrine, which teaches that God may be worshipped in any way not appointed in his word. . . .
>
> IX. No authority has been given to make or sing in the praise of God other songs besides those contained in the Bible. . . .
>
> X. The psalms of the Bible are all-sufficient as the matter of God's praise.[54]

In 1882 the Presbyterian Synod inquired into the practice of praise in its churches. The results showed that out of 279 churches responding, 218 confined themselves largely to metrical psalmody.[55] Hymns were being written and sung by Presbyterians, but their use depended upon the preferences of individual congregations. It was only in 1898, with the publication of the *Church Hymnary*, that the Presbyterian churches of England, Ireland and Scotland officially authorized the use of hymns in public services.[56]

However much the conservatives inveighed against hymns, during the nineteenth century they were written by the tens of thousands and volumes were published by the hundreds. They were sung almost everywhere, forming a truly popular culture of their own. In the way of all popular cultural mediums, they performed a double-edged function of reflecting as well as forming popular ideas. In the following chapters we will examine various aspects of this common culture.

CHAPTER II

EVANGELICALISM

THE evangelicals were the dominant force in achieving the gradual acceptance of congregational hymn-singing in England. It was from evangelicals such as Watts, Cowper, Newton and the Wesleys that eighteenth-century English hymnody received its most popular and characteristic hymns. Until the third decade of the nineteenth century the evangelical hymnwriters had an almost complete monopoly of the field. Because of this strong evangelical influence during the formative period, English hymnody was dominated by the evangelical world view, an outlook which continues to a marked degree into the present century. After the 1820s nonevangelicals wrote more hymns, and their churches gradually accepted the practice of congregational hymn-singing. The Oxford Movement encouraged the writing and translating of many hymns. But it is the contention of this writer that during the whole of the nineteenth century the evangelical outlook dominated English hymnody. Evangelicals viewed hymns as an integral part of their total religious expression, while the High Churchmen in the Church of England tended to restrict hymns to specific liturgical functions. The evangelicals wrote and published more hymns and by mid-century evangelical hymns had been adopted in large numbers by the editors of nonevangelical hymnbooks. An understanding of evangelicalism is, therefore, essential to an understanding of nineteenth-century English hymnody.

The term "evangelical" has been used in a variety of ways. For a student of eighteenth-century English history the followers of Wesley are immediately called to mind. In the early nineteenth century the term was often used loosely and disparagingly to connote any religious "enthusiast." Present-day English historians often restrict the use of that title to the more fundamentalist and ascetic party within the Church of England. Evangelicalism is often confused with puritanism because many evangelicals are puritans. The problem of definition stems from the fact that evangelicalism is not restricted to one denomination or sect. The beliefs of evangelicals are common to all protestant denominations except the Unitarian. It is the emphasis which evangelicals place on certain beliefs which distinguishes them from other protestants.

The first essential tenet of evangelicalism is a belief in the absolute supremacy of Holy Scripture. As Bishop Ryle, a leading nineteenth-century Anglican evangelical wrote, "Here is the rock: all else is sand."[1] Before approximately 1850 the evangelical belief in scriptural supremacy was most often translated as a belief in the literal interpretation of the Bible and an assumption of the infallibility of the Bible on all questions. One of the consequences of these beliefs was the repression of all religious doubts and questions. Consequently, evangelicals tended to conservatism in all areas of life—the old ways were the best ways—and critical inquiry was deprecated. Although the evangelical movement produced many scholars, most of them were anti-intellectual. By the end of the nineteenth century, however, Biblical literalism was battered by science and higher criticism and some evangelicals felt compelled to modify their belief in the literal interpretation of scripture. An early twentieth-century evangelical Anglican bishop, for instance, chided the literalists because they made the Bible an absolute authority. This position, he thought, was too close to the Roman Catholic idea of infallibility: "The Bible has occupied a supreme position in the estimation of the Evangelical movement, and quite rightly, but in the minds of some of its votaries the Infallibility of the Bible has taken the place which the Infallibility of the Church has held in Roman minds."[2] Even though the bishop might question the exact interpretation of scripture, as an evangelical he still assigned it the primary, if not an infallible, position of authority.

The second major feature of evangelicalism is the paramount importance it attaches to the crucifixion. Speaking of Dwight Moody's evangelical revival in the 1870s and 1880s, an observer wrote, "Practically, the one burthen of the evangelists was Christ crucified for us, and calling us, by the Holy Spirit, into a life of regenerate peace and power in union with Himself."[3] Evangelicals emphasized the essentially sinful nature of man and his inability to achieve salvation by his own efforts; this was particularly true of those evangelicals who lived before the middle of the nineteenth century. Whether they followed the Calvinist view of salvation limited to the elect few or the Wesleyan view of unlimited grace, the evangelicals all believed that, because of his sinful nature, man could not be saved by his own puny efforts. To quote Bishop Ryle again, "No external patching, mending, whitewashing, gilding, polishing and varnishing will meet the case."[4] Sinful man's only chance for redemption lay in his acceptance of Christ's sacrifice. "The Cross of Christ brought man and God together. This great fact has always been the central theme of the Evangelical message."[5]

The third feature of evangelicalism is the extreme emphasis it places on the individual experience of conversion. Christ made a full and complete sacrifice for man's redemption; no further intermediary is needed between sinful man and God. Man need only accept Christ's atonement with simple and child-like faith—in the words of a popular Victorian hymn metaphor, man need only open the door of his heart to Christ's knocking. Because of its emphasis on the individual conversion experience, evangelical religion tended to be subjective and introspective in nature. During the periods of evangelical revival, in fact, this subjective emotionalism became especially noticeable, encouraging a pietism which rejected worldly concerns and focused instead on man's inner spiritual life and on his afterlife.

The evangelical outlook, with its emphasis on the supremacy of Biblical authority, on the centrality of Christ's atonement, and on the individual experience of conversion and salvation, is not peculiar to nineteenth-century England nor to any other time or place. Evangelicalism is common to many western Christian renewal and reform movements. Martin Luther's rebellion against the Roman church is a prominent example. He contradicted the Church's doctrine of ecclesiastical authority, proclaiming instead the supremacy of scripture. At the Diet of Worms he declared that his ultimate authority was scripture and his individual conscience: "Unless I am convicted by Scripture and plain reason—I do not accept the authority of popes and councils, for they have contradicted each other—my conscience is captive to the Word of God."[6] According to Luther's own testimony, it was his contemplation of the Cross that brought about his realization of God's love and, hence, his conversion in the years prior to 1519.[7] And in his proclamation of the "Priesthood of all believers," Luther declared the importance of the individual's relationship to God. In this evangelical emphasis Luther was followed by most of the other sixteenth-century religious revolutionaries.

In the years immediately after their creation, the protestant churches exhibited an evangelical enthusiasm that is common to revival movements. But, as time passed and where these churches became established, they tended gradually to lose their enthusiasm and evangelicalism. The supremacy of scripture was eroded or replaced by ecclesiastical authority, the centrality of the crucifixion was displaced by disputes concerning other theological problems, and the importance of the individual experience of salvation was diminished by an increased emphasis on corporate worship and liturgy. Historically, this movement toward corporate emphasis has called forth further revival movements in a seemingly endless cycle.

By the eighteenth century in England a low point in this cycle had been reached. The Church of England had become notoriously complacent. The fox-hunting, two-bottle, pluralist, nonresident, ill-educated parson typifies in the popular mind the established church in the eighteenth century. Even the nonconformist churches had reached a low point in terms of evangelical missionary imperative: they had lost the enthusiasm of the previous century, they had become more institutionalized, and they were attracting fewer worshipers. The Wesleyan revival, which spread across England in the second half of the eighteenth century, revived evangelicalism. From the Methodist Connexion evangelicalism spread, to some extent, to all other churches: to the denominations of Old Dissent, Presbyterians, Independents, Baptists, and even to the Quakers; to the New Dissent of the Countess of Huntingdon's Connexion, the General Baptists, and the Methodist break-away denominations of the nineteenth century; and even to the Church of England, within which an Evangelical Party or School formed. According to a contemporary church historian, these evangelicals "constituted by far the most prominent and spiritually active party during the greater part of the period."[8]

The pervasiveness of the evangelical revival did nothing to insure its acceptance, however. Within many of the older churches and even chapels, in fact, the enthusiasm (a word generally repugnant to the establishment) of the evangelicals caused their ostracism and abuse. A tract written in the eighteenth century described the Methodists as "furious disciples of Antichrist, reverend scavengers, filthy pests and plagues of mankind." Another says "their doctrines coincide with the rankest heresies that ever defiled the church, particularly those of the Simonians, Gnostics, Montanists, and Antinomians."[9] John Wesley and George Whitefield endured physical as well as verbal abuses on their rounds of field preaching and were many times in danger for their lives. Although the physical dangers decreased as the nineteenth century wore on, evangelical enthusiasm continued to arouse enmity. H. C. G. Moule repeats the story of Charles Simeon, the evangelical vicar of Trinity Church, Cambridge in the early years of the nineteenth century, who "could not walk from King's College gate to St. Mary's Church without the risk of a pelting with dirty missiles on the way."[10] This antipathy toward enthusiasm was directed particularly at the revivalist evangelicalism during the later years of the nineteenth century. The Young Men's Christian Association which was organized in the 1840s, the Moody and Sankey campaigns of the 1870s, the Salvation Army movement which began in 1878, and the Torrey, Chapman and Alexander revivals of the turn of the century, all encountered opposition from the organized churches of all types because of their enthusiasm.

Each of these evangelical revival movements was accompanied by an outburst of song and the hymns of these movements were particularly disdained by the establishment. During the revivals of the late nineteenth century, Ira Sankey introduced into Great Britain the American type of gospel hymn, which used repetitious refrains, rousing choruses, and often adopted popular tunes from the music halls and streets. After mid-century evangelical missionary services were most often characterized by loud and enthusiastic congregational singing of favorites such as "There Were Ninety and Nine," "Almost Persuaded," or "Will You Let the Saviour In?" William Booth and most other evangelists considered the gospel hymns a very effective device for drawing the unchurched back into the Christian fold.[11] These innovations in style were enormously popular,[12] but their very popularity created a renewal among the institutional churches of the age-old disdain for enthusiasm. "I cannot think," wrote Henry Venn Elliott about the revival hymns, "that souls get to heaven by exciting or marching music."[13] In defense of the new type of hymn, William Booth argued in a rather pragmatic manner:

> Objections may be felt by some friends to the occasional consecration of tunes hitherto called secular; but I have only to reply that I have sought to print just that music which has been sung amidst the most overpowering scenes of salvation in this country and America during the last thirty years, and those who appreciate such music can be expected to favour my design.[14]

The argument against the new hymns employed by the evangelical missions was often couched in stylistic or aesthetic terms: they were criticized for their "jingling" tunes, the banality of their language, and their emotionalism. Underlying these aesthetic arguments, however, we can see the age-old conflict of two opposing concepts of religion: the corporate, hierarchical, rational aspects of religion emphasized by the institutional church and the individualistic, subjective, emotional relationship between God and man which was emphasized by the evangelicals. During the nineteenth century the subject of hymnody provided one more battlefield on which the larger question of man's relationship to God could be fought. Characteristic of these arguments is David Breed's contention at the beginning of the twentieth century that the gospel song could not be classified as a hymn:

> A hymn is one thing; a sacred song is another thing. Each has its distinct character and uses. Sometimes they overlap, but they never lose their distinct character and their appropriate purpose. A true hymn is worship; a sacred song is not. The ultimate objective point contemplated in a hymn is God himself; in a sacred song it is the hearer. A hymn co-ordinates with prayer. A sacred song co-ordinates with exhortation.[15]

While the style of the nineteenth-century gospel hymns was new, their content was not. They contained the essential elements of all evangelical thinking. Central to the evangelical hymns is their reverence for scripture. It is their authority and their inspiration.

> O wonderful words of the gospel!
> O wonderful message they bring,
> Proclaiming a blessed redemption
> Thro' Jesus our Saviour and King.[16]

Filled with the inspiration of the gospel message, the evangelicals felt an imperative to evangelize—to carry the message to others, abroad as well as at home.

> Preach the gospel, sound it forth,
> Tell of free and full salvation;
> Spread the tidings o'er the earth,
> Go to ev-ry tribe and nation.[17]

Under the evangelical imperative to mission, the scriptural message would conquer the world:

March we forth in the strength of God,
With the banner of Christ unfurled,
That the light of the glorious gospel of truth
May shine throughout the world.
Fight we the fight with sorrow and sin
To set their captives free,
That the Earth may be filled with the glory of God,
As the waters cover the sea.[18]

This imperative to mission will be discussed more fully later. Suffice it here to say that the evangelical churches and chapels would be in the vanguard of the missionary enthusiasm of the nineteenth century.

The core of the gospel message for the evangelical was the promise of salvation brought by Christ. The Cross was, therefore, an image of overwhelming importance in evangelical hymns. Evangelical hymnbooks are filled with hymns describing the crucifixion or adoring the crucified Christ. Because of the emotional intensity of his hymns concerning the crucifixion and their almost amatory physiological details, Isaac Watts has been accused of "fondling Christ."[19] For example,

Alas! the cruel spear
Went deep into his side,
And the rich flood of purple gore
Their murderous weapons dyed.[20]

William Cowper continued this tradition:

There is a fountain filled with blood,
Drawn from Immanuel's veins,
And sinners, plunged beneath that flood,
Lose all their guilty stains.

The dying thief rejoiced to see
That fountain in his day;
And there would I, though vile as he,
Wash all my sins away.[21]

Some critics of the evangelical treatment of the Passion have criticized its cloying sweetness or its "morbid concentration on physical details bordering on the sadistic and repulsive."[22] Horton Davies has characterized this tendency as the "introspection of lyrical spiders forever examining their own insides."[23] Gordon Rattray Taylor interprets these hymns in Freudian terms,[24] finding an example of anal regression in Watts' lines,

His heart is made of tenderness,
His bowels melt with love.

He finds an example of womb-regression in Toplady's *Rock of Ages*:

O precious Side-hole's cavity
I want to spend my life in thee . . .
There in one Side-hole's joy divine,
I'll spend all future Days of mine.
Yes, yes, I will for ever sit
There, where thy Side was split.

Finally, Taylor finds oral regression in David Culy's hymn on the eucharist:

Now we afresh has eat Christ's flesh
Not raw, but throughly boil'd,
Not sod [i.e. stewed], nor unapprov'd to God,
In whom he's reconciled.
God tasted first of that Lamb roast
The Priest has offered,
He likes the Smell and Savour well,
This is our Father's Bread.

However repressed or repulsive these hymns may seem to some modern tastes, they were certainly very popular in the eighteenth century and although fewer of these hymns were written in the nineteenth century, the older hymns of this type continued to be published and sung. Numerous examples of the types cited above appear in almost every evangelical hymnbook reviewed by this writer. In addition, some nineteenth-century hymn writers continued to write hymns in the same vein. Ira Sankey wrote:

Behold a Fountain deep and wide,
Behold its onward flow:
'Twas opened in the Saviour's side,
And cleanseth 'white as snow.'

From Calvary's cross, where Jesus died
In sorrow, pain, and woe
Burst forth the wondrous crimson tide
That cleanseth 'white as snow.'[25]

Toplady's *Rock of Ages* continued to be one of the most popular hymns throughout the century.

Christ is the focus of the evangelical's thoughts, but it is not enough simply to contemplate Christ hanging from the Cross. By an act of faith the Christian can physically experience conversion; and the experience is often expressed in intimate physical terms:

And if with lively faith we view
  His dying toil and smart,
And hear Him say, "It was for you!"
  This breaks the stony heart.

A heavenly joy His words convey;
  The bowels strangely move;
We blush, and melt, and faint away,
  O'erwhelmed with His love.

In such sweet posture let me lie,
  And wet Thy feet with tears,
Till, joined with saints above the sky,
  I tune my harp with theirs.[26]

Through this conversion experience the evangelical seeks to create a personal relationship between himself and his Saviour. Jesus is the refuge of the weary and worn; he holds, he soothes, he comforts with an intimacy that most Victorians reserved for their hymns.

I heard the voice of Jesus say,
  Come unto Me and rest;
Lay down, thou weary one, lay down,
  Thy head upon My breast.

I came to Jesus as I was,
  Weary, and worn, and sad,
I found in Him a resting-place,
  And He hath made me glad.[27]

He is the comforter of the guilty:

With my burden I begin,
Lord, remove this load of sin!
Let thy blood for sinners spilt
Set my conscience free from guilt.

Lord! I come to Thee for rest,
Take possession of my breast;
There thy blood-bought right maintain,
And without a rival reign.[28]

In the sentimental terms of the evangelical, Jesus becomes a friend and a brother:

One there is, above all others,
  Well deserves the name of Friend;
His love beyond a brother's,
  Costly, free, and knows no end;
  They who once His kindness prove
  Find it everlasting love.

. . . .

Could we bear from one another
  What He daily bears from us?
Yet this glorious Friend and Brother
  Loves us, though we treat Him thus;
  Though for good we render ill,
  He accounts us brethren still.[29]

Harry Escott attributes the creation of the subjective hymn to Isaac Watts,[30] but it was Charles Wesley who developed this "cross clinging" tendency fully. Bernard Manning wrote: "He is always at Calvary; no other place in the universe matters, and for him the course of historic time is lost in the eternal NOW."[31] Manning continues, "Take one rough, and not exhaustive, test. Of the 769 hymns in one edition not fewer than 84 have as their first word the Name: Jesus, Christ, or Saviour. One in every nine *opens* so."[32] For the Wesleys Jesus was the comforter in whom the seeker of salvation could hide.

Jesus, lover of my soul,
  Let me to thy bosom fly,
While the billows near me roll;
  While the tempest still is high;
Hide me, O my Saviour, hide me,
  Till the storm of life is past;
Safe into the haven guide,
  Oh, receive my soul at last.

Other refuge have I none,
  Hangs my helpless soul on Thee;
Leave, oh, leave me not alone,
  Still support and comfort me;
Thou, O Christ, art all I want,
  Boundless love in Thee I find;
Raise the fallen, cheer the faint,
  Heal the sick, and lead the blind.[33]

One of the most popular hymns of the Evangelical Anglicans, *Rock of Ages*, said in one stanza,

Nothing in my hands I bring,
Simply to Thy Cross I cling;
Naked, come to Thee for dress;
Helpless, look to Thee for grace. . . .[34]

The popularity of the subjective hymn continued into the nineteenth century. After a study of the hymns which were used during the revivals of the 1860s and 1870s, J. E. Orr concluded that the most popular were the hymns of experience—those which were introspective, personal in nature, and on the subject of salvation and sanctification.[35]

This emphasis by the evangelicals on the fullness of Christ's sacrifice underscored the protestant creed that man was saved by faith alone. Man's own efforts toward salvation were futile.

Though I have labored again and again,
All my self-cleansing is utterly vain;
Jesus, Redeemer from sorrow and woe,
Wash me and I shall be whiter than snow.[36]

There is, for the evangelical, nothing that he can do on this earth to achieve his own salvation but submit himself to God's will.

Since man's own efforts toward salvation were considered useless, the evangelical often became otherworldly. He withdrew from the pleasures and problems of this world and focused his attention instead on the next world. This world-rejecting asceticism is not peculiar to protestant evangelicals. It is a thread which runs through the entire history of Christianity, surfacing periodically, often in a fit of reforming zeal which has been as often as not labeled heresy by the discomfited church hierarchy. The English evangelicals often exhibited an almost gnostic rejection of the world in their hymns.

This life's a dream, an empty show,
But the bright world, to which I go,
Has joys substantial and sincere;
When shall I wake and find me there?[37]

* * *

Emptied of earth I fain would be,
The world, myself, and all but Thee,
Only reserved for Christ that dies,
Surrender'd to the Crucified.[38]

* * *

Far from the World, O Lord, I flee,
  From strife and tumult far;
From scenes where Satan wages still
  His most successful war.[39]

* * *

O leave we all for Jesus—
  The world that fades away,
The flesh with its wild passions,
  And Satan's tyrant sway;
We leave it all for Jesus,
  Nor will we count it loss;
For who, the fine gold gaining,
  Will grudge to lose the dross?

We leave it all for Jesus!
  Earth's voices filled the air,
Fain had she lured with pleasure,

Or pressed us back with care;
But "Hear My Voice, O daughter,"
The Heavenly Bridegroom cried;
"Leave also thine own country,
And come and be My Bride."[40]

This world is pictured as "the valley of the shadow," as a "desert," as "darksome and dangerous," and as "hostile." In their hymns the evangelicals yearn for heaven as a relief from the woes of this world.

I'm but a stranger here,
Earth is a desert drear,
Heaven is my home;
Danger and sorrow stand
Round me on every hand;
Heaven is my fatherland,
Heaven is my home.[41]

Heaven is pictured as a haven of rest:

Jerusalem! my happy home!
Name ever dear to me!
When shall my labours have an end,
In joy and peace, and thee?[42]

It is particularly from the hymns of the late nineteenth-century revivals, and especially from American hymns, that the commercial images of heaven as a land with "golden streets" and "golden gates" come. Interestingly enough, the images of heaven's delights are extremely mundane—the most common images are those of nature and riches.

Beautiful land! so bright so fair,
Untold glories linger there;
Crystal rivers and shining strand:
Home of the Christian, beautiful land![43]

Since heaven is a land of beauty to be sought after, for the evangelical, dying becomes a joyful act.

"Onward, upward, homeward!"
Joyfully I flee
From this world of sorrow,

With my Lord to be;
Onward to the glory,
Upward to the prize,
Homeward to the mansions,
Far above the skies.[44]

E. P. Thompson has noted the frequency of this yearning for death in other evangelical literature of the nineteenth century:

> Those who could read were deluged, throughout the early nineteenth century, with the tracts which celebrated "Holy Dying." No Methodist or evangelical magazine, for the mature or for children, was complete without its death-bed scene in which (as Leigh Hunt also noted) death was often anticipated in the language of bride or bride-groom impatient for the wedding-night. Death was the goal which might be desired without guilt, the reward of peace after a lifetime of suffering and labour.[45]

By their otherworldly focus, evangelicals rejected the life of this world. Whatever smacked of pleasure or beauty was considered a temptation of the devil. "Love not this world," said the Methodist Conference of 1855. It had "observed, with sincere regret, the existence, in some quarters, of a disposition to indulge in and encourage amusements which it cannot regard as harmless or allowable."[46] Erik Routley has charged that "The *Congregational Hymn Book* of 1836 could almost be accused of subscribing to the gnostical heresy of the damnation of matter, so frightened was it of any hymn about God's creation."[47] This sentiment was frequently voiced in hymns.

Well I know each subtle snare—
Worldly pleasure, worldly care,
Pomp, and vanity, and pride—
All to draw thee from My Side.

Passing fair the world may seem,
Yet 'tis all a fading dream;
And its glory and its light,
Ending in the endless night.[48]

Among the subtle snares that the evangelicals shunned, surprisingly enough, were the beauties of nature. The English have maintained a reputation among themselves and foreigners as essentially a rural people. They retained their love of the countryside and a class system based on land ownership long after they had become a predominantly urban society. Nevertheless, if hymns are a reliable barometer of feelings, we must conclude that during most of the nineteenth century the evangelicals denied the aesthetic worth of natural beauty. This disparity in attitudes toward nature can, perhaps, be explained by the fact that the evangelical movement was centered in the cities and the industrial and mining towns and not in the countryside. It is one more indication of the class conflict between the rurally-oriented upper class and the urban middle class; the conflict here is geographical and not economic. When nature images are employed in the evangelical hymns they usually remind the singer that beauty is ephemeral.

The morning flowers display their sweets,
And gay their silken leaves unfold,
As careless of the noon-tide heats,
As fearless of the evening colds.

Nipt by the wind's unkindly blast,
Parched by the sun's directer ray,
The momentary glories waste,
The short-lived beauties die away.[49]

The few hymns that do praise nature are most often addressed to children, such as this one from the Salvation Army hymnbook, which points out the thorns among the flowers and the temporality of natural beauty:

Let us gather up the sunbeams,
Lying all around our path;
Let us keep the wheat and roses
Casting out the thorns and chaff;
Let us find our sweetest comfort
In the blessings of today,
With a patient hand removing
All the briars from the way.

Strange we never prize the music
Till the sweet-voiced bird has flown!
Strange that we should slight the violets,
Till the lovely flowers are gone!
Strange that summer skies and sunshine
Never seem one-half so fair,

As when winter's snowy pinions
Shake the white down in the air.[50]

As the nineteenth century progressed children's hymns increasingly used cheerful images of nature—blue skies, sunshine, gentle animals (sheep were a favorite), and flowers. But for the most part the hymn writers who used nature images were not evangelicals.

How deeply engraved on the evangelical conscience these antithetical feelings about nature were, can be seen by the *Rivulet* controversy of 1856, which Erik Routley has called "the battle of flowers."[51] Hymns had caused controversy before; they had even caused lawsuits. But, for the first time in English history, for approximately eighteen months, a book of hymns was thrown into the national limelight. In November 1855, Thomas Toke Lynch, pastor of a small Congregational church on Grafton Street, London,[52] published a little book of hymns entitled *Hymns for Heart and Voice: The Rivulet.* In a chapter of his history of the Congregational Union entitled "Almost Wrecked," Albert Peel reviews in detail the bitter fighting within the Congregational Union over that hymn book.[53] The battle was waged so virulently in religious journals that, as the title indicates, the denomination was almost wrecked.

The charge against Lynch was that he dared to combine nature and religion, a most undoctrinal combination for an evangelical minister. James Grant, the editor of the *Morning Advertiser*, fired the first shot: the book, he claimed, "might have been written by a Deist, and a very large portion might be sung by a congregation of Freethinkers"—it had "not one particle of vital religion or evangelical piety." Dr. John Cambell, editor of the Congregational Union's magazines, soon came to the forefront to lead the opposition to Lynch. Cambell condemned the *Rivulet* as "incomparably the most unspiritual publication of the kind in the English tongue." The *Glasgow Examiner* recommended that all right-thinking people should read a Baptist tract which examined "the Pernicious Errors of Mr. Lynch's Rivulet": "Every friend of vital religion, be he Independent, Baptist, Presbyterian, or Episcopalian, should further the circulation of this pamphlet." Charles Haddon Spurgeon, the popular Baptist preacher, joined the fray, complaining from the pulpit of the "the non-doctrinal scheme" which "carnal preachers" were advocating.[54]

Lynch fired some answering shots of his own. In another small book entitled, *The Ethics of Quotation and Songs Controversial: by Silent Long*, he poked fun at the evangelical demand that every hymn be a complete exposition of theological doctrine.

When sugar in the lump I see,
  I know that it is there,
Melt it, and then I soon suspect
  A negative affair;
Where is the sugar Sir? I say,
  Let me both touch and see;
Sweetness instead of sugar, Sir,
  You'll not palm off on me.

Don't tell me that the sugar lumps,
  When dropt in water clear,
That they may make the water sweet,
  Themselves must disappear;
For Common sense, Sir, such as mine
  The lumps themselves must see;
Sweetness instead of sugar, Sir,
  You'll not palm off on me.

For instance, Sir, in every hymn
  Sound doctrine you should state
As clearly as a dead man's name
  Is on his coffin plate;
Religion, Sir, is only fudge,
  Let's have theology;
Sweetness, instead of sugar, Sir,
  You'll not palm off on me.[55]

The Congregational Union finally settled its internal disputes, which had grown far beyond the question of the use of nature in hymns, in May 1857. The nature controversy was ultimately, although unofficially, decided in Lynch's favor. By 1884, when Garrett Horder published his *Congregational Hymns*, a special section entitled "Nature" included twenty-two hymns.

Nature was only one of the "carnal" temptations that the evangelicals feared in their contact with the world. Since their vision was focused on salvation in the next world, their lives were restricted to the strait and narrow path; any indulgence in worldly pleasure, however innocent it might seem to nonevangelical eyes, could be considered irreligious. The Clapham Sect, an early nineteenth-century circle of well-to-do Anglican evangelicals, were frequently and severely criticized by their contemporaries for their prosperity. But G. R. Balleine writes of them: "Little did critics guess the almost monastic self-discipline by which these well-to-do Christians ordered each day of their lives . . . every temptation of self-indulgence was rigidly held in check."[56] They could sing with feeling,

Father, whate'er of earthly bliss,
Thy sovereign will denies,
Accepted at thy throne of grace,
Let this petition rise.
Give me a calm, a thankful heart
From every murmur free;
The blessings of thy grace impart,
And make me live to Thee.[57]

In their effort to avoid earthly pleasures the evangelicals seem at times to have advocated pain and suffering as a more appropriate means of attaining salvation. The *Invalid's Hymnbook* proclaimed the benefits of suffering:

Sickness is a school severe,
Where the soul, (in childhood here,)
Wayward 'neath a milder sway,
Learns to think, and learns to pray.
Blest and wise its discipline,
There the teacher is divine.

Wert thou thoughtless, led away
By each folly of the day?
Cleaving to the things of earth,
Mindless of thy heavenly birth?
Bless the hour which broke their spell,
Made thee sick to make thee well.

Wert thou selfish, thinking not
On the starving sufferer's lot?
Fed with dainties, gaily dress'd,
Wert thou by the poor unbless'd?
Now for sufferers thou wilt feel,
God has wounded but to heal.

. . . .

Wert thou proud, exalted high
By affluence, station, ancestry?
Oft with supercilious ken
Glancing at thy fellow-men?
God now strips thee, lays thee low,
All thy nothingness to show.

. . . .

Is the one thing needed most
That which thee no pains has cost?
Hast thou earthly science prized,
But the themes of heaven despised?
God now warns thee; thus He saith,
"Soul awake! Thy sleep is death!"[58]

Purification by suffering was not limited to the invalid, however. Trials were used by God to test all men.

I asked the Lord, that I might grow
In faith, and love, and every grace;
Might more of his salvation know,
And seek more earnestly his face.

I hoped that in some favoured hour
At once he'd answer my request
And by his love's constraining power,
Subdue my sins, and give me rest.

Instead of this he made me feel
The hidden evils of my heart;
And let the angry powers of hell
Assault my soul in every part.

"Lord, why is this?" I trembling cried;
Wilt thou pursue a worm to death?
"Tis in this way," the Lord replied,
"I answer prayer for grace and faith."

"These inward trials I employ,
From self and pride to set thee free;
And break thy schemes of earthly joy,
That thou mayst seek thy all in me."[59]

E. P. Thompson, when reviewing the Methodist influence on the working class, criticized this outlook severely, saying that it was unspontaneous, unnatural, and masochistic:

It is difficult to conceive of a more essential disorganization of human life, a pollution of the sources of spontaneity bound to reflect itself in every aspect of personality. Since joy was associated with sin and guilt, and pain (Christ's wounds) with goodness and love, so every impulse became twisted into the reverse, and it became natural to suppose that man or

> child only found grace in God's eyes when performing painful, laborious or self-denying tasks. To labour and to sorrow was to find pleasure, and masochism was "love." It is inconceivable that men could actually *live* like this; but many Methodists did their best.[60]

Speaking from his own experience of a Methodist upbringing in the first years of the twentieth century, Peter Fletcher confirms this bleak view of the evangelical life:

> It was the inescapable evidence that despite the complete sincerity of their faith, their unflagging devotion to their Church and their earnestness in prayer, the abundance and joy of life escaped my parents; it was this that troubled my spirit and increasingly disturbed my mind during my formative years. No doubt God works in a mysterious way; but can it be a vision of His truth that resigns people to a way of living that is slow dying, believing that it is good?[61]

Certainly, in terms of twentieth-century psychology this evangelical discipline "warps" the personality. But we must remember that we are looking at an age different from our own and beware of tendencies to write a psychological Whig history. Instead of criticizing the evangelical outlook, as Thompson does, a more fruitful inquiry would seem to be that of Gordon Rattray Taylor, who attempts to discover why so many Victorians (whom Taylor labels puritans, patrists, and anal-moralists, but who were strikingly evangelical in their religious thought) held the world view that they did. Whether we agree with Taylor or not that the desire for the evangelical discipline was a result of the experience of denial during early childhood, we must agree that the evangelical discipline answered some profound social need of the time. The evangelical revival movements of the whole of the nineteenth century drew enormous crowds. One historian estimated that "probably half a million people heard the Gospel preached" during the Moody-Sankey campaign of 1873-1875.[62] When Charles Haddon Spurgeon, a fundamentalist Baptist preacher, preached in London, the crowds overflowed the Surrey Gardens Music Hall. The lessening of otherworldly emphasis toward the end of the nineteenth century, as many nonconformist churches relaxed their decrees against pleasure and secular goals, may in fact have made those churches less attractive to many Victorians. Kenneth Young claims that the end of the century emphasis on Christian social service led "to a line of Nonconformist 'political' ministers . . . . Significantly, as they have increased so have congregations declined."[63] K. S. Inglis has pointed out that "the corrosion of spirituality by participation in worldly pleasures was a special danger to the sects which in every generation have kindled their communal life from the flame of the puritan tradition."[64] We must conclude, therefore, that however unattractive the otherworldly evangelical outlook may be to Christians who emphasize the humanist tradition (a tradition which found an increasing number of adherents by the end of the nineteenth century), it attracted great numbers of Victorians.

Before we conclude this isolated study of evangelicalism we must look briefly at one last aspect of the evangelical outlook: their attitude toward social service. Victorian attitudes, both evangelical and nonevangelical, toward social service will be discussed at greater length later. A number of writers have argued that the evangelical revival fostered a demand for social justice—in the words of J. Wesley Bready, it "illumined the central postulates of the New Testament ethic, which made real the Fatherhood of God and the Brotherhood of men, which pointed the priority of personality over property, and which directed heart, soul and mind, toward the establishment of the Kingdom of Righteousness on earth."[65] There is a strong element of truth in the argument. As these same scholars have often noted the most outstanding political leaders of the nineteenth-century movement for social justice, men like Wilberforce and Shaftesbury, Richard Oastler, Michael Sadler, and John Fielden, to mention only a few, were strongly influenced by evangelical religion. In the field of voluntary charity, likewise, the leaders came predominantly from evangelical churches: for instance, Robert Raikes, David Nasmith, George Williams, William Booth, and Thomas John Barnardo. A number of writers have taken the contrary view, however, that evangelicalism, because of its otherworldly focus, ignored social problems. "The essence of Chapel lay in the saving of souls . . . and not in the amelioration of temporal conditions or the righting of social wrongs."[66] In practice the evangelicals seem to have been ambivalent in their attitude toward social welfare: as individuals they were among the leaders in charity, but in their church hymns they largely ignored the problem.

Earthly conditions were unimportant to the followers of Jesus:

Happy they who trust in Jesus,
    Sweet their portion is and sure:
When the foe on others seizes,
    He will keep His own secure;
        Happy people!
    Happy, though despised and poor.[67]

The evangelical hymns tell the singer that all of the deficiencies of life would be compensated for in heaven:

Sitting by the gateway of a palace fair,
Once a child of God was left to die:
By the world neglected, wealth would nothing share;
See the change awaiting there on high.

What shall be the ending of this life of care?
Oft the question cometh to us all;
Here upon the pathway hard the burdens bear,
And the burning tears of sorrow fall.

Follower of Jesus, scanty tho' thy store,
Treasures, precious treasures wait on high;
Count the trials joyful, soon they'll all be o'er;
O the change that's coming bye and bye.

Upward, then, and onward! onward for the Lord;
Time and talent all in His employ;
Small may seem the service, sure the great reward;
Here the cross, but there the crown of joy.[68]

Man's attempts to right the wrongs on earth were misdirected; God would punish wrongdoers eventually.

Fear not, O little flock, the foe
Who madly seeks your overthrow,
    Nor dread his rage and power;
What though your courage sometimes faints,
His seeming triumph o'er God's saints
    Lasts but a little hour.

Be of good cheer; your cause belongs
To Him who can avenge your wrongs;
    Then leave it to your Lord;
Though hidden yet from all our eyes,
He sees the Gideon who shall rise
    To save us by His word.[69]

* * *

Faint not, Christian! though the world
Has its hostile flag unfurled;
Hold the Cross of Jesus fast.
Thou shalt overcome at last.[70]

The poor and heavy laden were urged to bear their earthly load meekly and "murmur not" at earthly injustice.

O troubled heart, there is a home,
Beyond the reach of toil and care;
A home where changes never come;
Who would not fain be resting there?

Yet when bow'd down beneath the load
By heav'n allow'd thine earthly lot;
Look up! thoul't reach the blest abode,
Wait, meekly wait, and murmur not.[71]

Elie Halévy has written of the spread of the evangelical outlook from Methodism to the whole of English society; we "witness Methodism bring under its influence, first the Dissenting sects, then the Establishment, finally secular opinion."[72] The quietist outlook of the evangelicals, their acceptance of suffering and injustice in imitation of Christ because of their assurance of a better world to come, was very influential to nineteenth-century social attitudes, especially during the first three-quarters of the century. And it was in part through hymns that these attitudes were taught.

CHAPTER III

THE DIDACTIC CHURCH

WRITING in 1848 in *Politics for the People*, Charles Kingsley complained, "We have used the Bible as if it were a mere constable's handbook—an opium-dose for keeping beasts of burden patient while they were being overloaded—a mere book to keep the poor in order." Kingsley was outraged that religion should be used for the utilitarian purpose of keeping the lower classes in their place. And yet, in most societies religion has traditionally served the very practical purpose of supporting the established social order. To this end the Christian church—and in this regard it is no different from any other institutionalized religion—has preached a social ethic of obedience and submission to the government in power and to the established social order. The church does this by sanctioning a given code of behavior: those people who conform to the prescribed behavioral norm will achieve salvation, while those who fail to conform are ostracized from the religious community and, presumably, are damned. In sociological terms, the code of behavior approved by a given society is most often determined by that society's most influential groups, always with a view (not always conscious or deliberate) of maintaining the group's dominance.[1] From the point of view of the least influential classes, this didactic function of the church may be seen as an effort at social control, at internal colonialism—in Kingsley's words, an effort simply to keep the "beasts of burden . . . , the poor in order." In terms of biblical imagery the church's didactic function is to separate the sheep from the goats, that is, to set a standard of "respectable" behavior to be followed by the compliant sheep, with probable eternal damnation and temporal punishment for the recalcitrant goats.[2]

The English protestant churches of the nineteenth-century were certainly no exception to this rule. In fact, they set a standard of social morality which, in its concern for probity and conduct, was unequaled except perhaps during the seventeenth-century rule of Cromwell's Major-Generals. The Victorians were particularly concerned with enforcing a social ethic because in traditional Christian fashion they held a pessimistic view of the innate morality of mankind. Many Victorians feared that men would revert to a bestial state if a social ethic of submission and humility was not imposed upon society. The French revolution had greatly increased the Englishman's fear of an outburst of violence, particularly an outburst from the lower classes. One of the most potent arguments made against democracy was that the lower classes needed the moral guidance of their betters. Hippolyte Taine, a nineteenth-century French traveler and observer, accurately reflected the elite's view of the English masses:

> The appetites, in this race, are violent and dangerous: see them for example, as depicted in Fielding's and Smollett's novels; and their scandalous eruption during the carnival of the Restoration. To bridle them, public opinion, religion and conscience are not excessive forces. For they have need of all their strength to keep this Caliban in check: he is far more savage and far uglier than the merry, jovial satyr in France or Italy. So that they are right to push severity to the point of prudishness: the more damaging the flood is apt to be, the more necessary it becomes to watch and strengthen the dykes.[3]

Taine's belief that "religion" was an appropriate instrument of social control is instructive and Taine, in fact, likens the English clergy to the French magistracy.[4]

Repression of man's aggressive instincts may come from many social institutions but in the Victorian world the church bore the main burden for teaching morality. Without religion, most Victorians thought, society would become depraved and uncontrollable; man would return to a Hobbesian state of nature. Not for them, Pierre Bayle's sanguine view of a moral society composed of atheists or David Hume's sceptical view that utility and sentiment not religion, were the basis of morality. It was the church's function to teach all men, but particularly the weaker elements of society—the young and the poor—how they should act. Winston Churchill, in describing his early experiences as an imperial army subaltern, attributed this attitude to his superiors. They were concerned with the church primarily as a didactic institution.

> Some of the senior officers also dwelt upon the value of the Christian religion to women ("It helps to keep them straight"); and also generally to the lower orders ("Nothing can give them a good time here, but it makes them more contented to think they will get one hereafter"). Christianity, it appeared, had also a disciplinary value, especially when presented through the Church of England. It made people want to be respectable, to keep up appearances and so saved lots of scandals.[5]

For transmitting the social ethic, hymns were one of the church's most effective devices. That it was a legitimate function of hymns to encourage subordination among the lower classes, was openly conceded by the editor of *Simple Hymns for Infants' Schools*, who wrote in his preface,

> Should it be said that this [vulgarity of most hymns for poor children] is of no consequence, as it respects the lower classes, it is replied, that although any system of instruction which raises them above the lot assigned by Providence, is wholly undesirable, yet refinement of taste, engrafted upon religion, is a most likely method to produce that subordination so necessary to cultivate in the present state of society.[6]

This is not to say that all nineteenth-century hymns had a didactic purpose. To the contrary, there were other types of hymns: hymns which are timeless and defy sociological analysis, devotional and doctrinal hymns, and liturgical hymns. But a great number of Victorian hymns were didactic, for the nineteenth-century churches felt that one of their primary functions was to prescribe and proscribe behavior, and hymns helped the churches define acceptable Christian behavior.

The hymns also defined the rewards and the punishments of the sheep and the goats. The promise of heaven was prominently displayed in the evangelical hymnbooks; it was to be the reward for good behavior. It is depicted as a "bright world," "my happy home," "Beautiful land! so bright so fair," as "mansions,/ Far above the skies." With the use of the "gospel" hymns in the revival services at the end of the century, the images of heaven became more commercial—"golden streets" and "golden gates." The hymns left no doubt that heaven was the reward of God's sheep.

On the other hand, for those who did not behave, there was the threat of hell. In many churches, particularly those with Calvinist learnings, fear was an acceptable means of attaining conformity:

Fear is a grace which ever dwells
With its fair partner, love;
Blending their beauties, both proclaim
Their source is from above.

Let terrors fright th' unwilling slave.
The child with joy appears;
Cheerful he does his Father's will,
And loves as much as fears.

Let fear and love, most holy God,
Possess this soul of mine;
Then shall I worship Thee aright,
And taste Thy joys divine.[7]

Fear of hell and the punishment associated with damnation was used frequently and effectively, particularly by missionary preachers. The depiction of hell fire and brimstone was a stock-in-trade of both sermons and hymns in the revival services. One example from the Salvation Army hymnbook should suffice.

Stop, poor sinner, stop and think,
Before you farther go—
Can you sport upon the brink
Of everlasting woe?
Hell beneath is gaping wide,
Vengeance waits the dread command,
Soon to stop your sport and pride,
Once again I charge you, stop;
For, unless you warning take,
Ere you are aware, you'll drop
Into the burning lake.

Ghastly death will quickly come,
And drag you to the bar;
Then to hear your awful doom,
Will fill you with despair,
All your sins will round you crowd,
Sins of blood and crimson dye;
Each of vengeance crying loud,
And what will you reply?[8]

The didactic impulse of the church was particularly evident in the missionary hymns. Missionary efforts were predominantly evangelical and evangelicalism was firmly rooted in the older, Christian gnostic tradition of rejection of the mundane. Evangelical hymns give ample evidence of this attitude: "This life's a dream, an empty show," "Emptied of earth I fain would be," "Far from the world, O Lord, I flee,"

O leave we all for Jesus—
    The world that fades away,
The flesh with its wild passions,
    And Satan's tyrant sway; . . .[9]

This evangelical rejection of the mundane and emphasis upon the next world manifested itself in attitudes of social, economic, and political quietism in many evangelical churches and in the missionary efforts which they pursued. But this complacency was not limited to the evangelicals. The Victorian churches, by and large, accepted the established social and economic order. The Church of England, of course, had a particularly favored place in that traditional order and, therefore, as a body, opposed social change. During the early decades of the century there was a movement, supported by many nonconformist churches, to disestablish the Church of England, but after the church reforms of the 1820s and 1830s, the political movement dissipated into ineffectiveness. One reason for this complacency among most English churches, nonconformist as well as established, was the belief that the basic order of society was divinely ordained. As the second verse of the hymn *All things bright and beautiful* stated,

The rich man in his castle,
    The poor man at his gate
God made them, high and lowly,
    And ordered their estate.[10]

Even those who envisioned a new and better world at the second coming of Christ, urged men to patiently accept their trials in this world:

Fight the fight, and run the race,
Work in our appointed place;
Waiting for the glad new birth
Of Thy perfect heaven and earth.[11]

Not everyone, of course, was won over by these hymns of social complacence. Hymns had bitter associations for some, who recognized the church's teachings as an attempt to bolster the established social hierarchy. For the radical young miner Ned, in W. E. Tirebuck's novel *Miss Grace of All Souls*, the singing of a hymn recalls the class differences between mine owners and miners, differences which he thinks the church helps to perpetuate. When the Ockleshaw family sings *Rock of Ages cleft for me*, Ned says that the title should be changed to "Rock o' Ages, cleff for mesters," because "that's what aw seem to hide in it for."[12] To men like Ned, hymns represented the worst of the church, the hypocrisy of the dominant group which encouraged its social and economic inferiors to meekly accept the *status quo*.

Let us now turn to the hymns in Victorian hymbooks to see what behavioral norms they prescribe. Perhaps the most prominent social ideal was that of the vigorous and honest workman. In his analysis of the Victorian mind, Walter Houghton has written, "Except for 'God,' the most popular word in the Victorian vocabulary must have been 'work.' It was, of course, the means by which some of the central ambitions of a commercial society could be realized: money, respectability, and success. But it also became an end in itself, a virtue in its own right."[13] Nineteenth-century hymnbooks bear out this judgment. Work for God is, of course, highly praised, but work of any sort is also lauded. John Ellerton's *Behold us, Lord, a little space* (1870) tells the singer that God's blessing is won not only by going to a church service but also by work, if we work honestly and patiently:

Thine is the loom, the forge, the mart,
    The wealth of land and sea,
The worlds of science and of art,
    Revealed and ruled by Thee.

. . . .

Work shall be prayer, if all be wrought
    As Thou wouldst have it done,
And prayer, by Thee inspired and taught,
    Itself with work be one.[14]

By the honesty of our work, it says, we can capture the world for God. The theme appears repeatedly in the hymnbooks—work is an act of piety, pleasing to God.

Their earthly task who fail to do,
Neglect their heavenly business too;
Nor know what faith and duty mean,
Who use religion as a screen;
Asunder put what God hath joined,
A diligent and pious mind.

Full well the labour of our hands
With fervency of spirit stands;
For God, who all our days hath given,
From toil excepts but one in seven:
And labouring while we time redeem,
We please the Lord, and work for Him.

Happy we live, when God doth fill
Our hands with work, our hearts with zeal;
For every toil, if He enjoin,
Becomes a sacrifice divine,
And like the blessed spirits above,
The more we serve, the more we love.[15]

If work is lauded, rest on earth is frowned upon. The good Christian is urged to intense activity.

To breathe and wake and sleep.
    To smile, to sigh, to grieve,
To move in idleness through earth,—
    This, this is not to live,

. . . .

Up, then, with speed, and work;
    Fling ease and self away;
Thou hast no time to lose in sloth,—
    Up, watch, and work and pray![16]

The hymns tell men that rest in the form of death will come soon enough for all men. The nearness of death, then, becomes a goad to work harder.

Work, for the night is coming:
    Work, through the sunny noon;
Fill brightest hours with labour,
    Rest comes sure and soon.

Give every flying minute
    Something to keep in store:
Work, for the night is coming,
    When man works no more.[17]

As the factory system demanded that men work on more rigidly defined schedules, the Victorians became acutely aware of time, particularly of wasted time. This increased temporal consciousness is reflected in hymns:

A minute, how soon it is flown!
And yet how important it is!
God calls every moment his own,
For all our existence is his;
And tho' we may waste them in folly and play,
He notices each that we squander away.[18]

The Victorian glorification of work derived in part from the ascetic protestant economic ethic, so ably analyzed by Max Weber in *The Protestant Ethic and the Spirit of Capitalism.* The laborer's work, however mundane it was, was a glorification of God; the reward for such work would be received in the next world. Laziness and idleness were sinful because they were nonproductive. Labor became, to the Protestant churches, particularly the Calvinist churches, what ascetic monasticism was to the Catholic church—the surest road to heaven. The habit of industry, which would suppress the temptation to idleness, luxury, and frivolity, should therefore be inculcated in all Christians in order to save their souls. A hymn which appears frequently in late Victorian hymnbooks, perfectly exemplifies the Victorian effort to teach the habit of industry. The words of the hymn were originally written in the late seventeenth century by Bishop Ken for the boys at Winchester School, but by the nineteenth century the hymn had become generally popular. It had been set to a tune and appeared in many general hymnbooks.

Awake, my soul, and with the sun
Thy daily gage of duty run;
Shake off dull sloth and joyful rise
To pay thy morning sacrifice.

Redeem thy mis-spent time that's past,
And live this day as if thy last;

Improve thy talent with due care;
For the great day thyself prepare.

Let all thy converse be sincere,
Thy conscience as the noon-day clear;
Think how all-seeing God thy ways,
And all thy secret thoughts surveys.[19]

These habits of industry were called "earnestness" by the Victorians. Signs of a Victorian Christian's earnestness were found in a man's willingness to work and to fight the forces of evil. This theme of struggle and striving is common to Christian thought at any time, but it became particularly prominent in the Victorian period. In the Manichaean struggle between the forces of good and evil, the Christian individual became the deciding factor. Hymns urge him, therefore, to active participation in the struggle:

Fight the good fight with all thy might!
Christ is thy strength, and Christ thy right;
Lay hold on life, and it shall be
Thy joy and crown eternally.

Run the straight race through God's good grace,
Lift up thine eyes, and seek his face;
Life with its way before us lies.
Christ is the path, and Christ the prize.[20]

The images are active: fighting and running. The language is, in fact, the language of the public-school boy: competition, fighting, racing, and winning prizes. It is interesting that Thomas Hughes, in his best-selling book *Tom Brown's School-Days*, used the themes of struggle and fighting to describe Tom's coming to manhood. As young Tom listens to his headmaster, Thomas Arnold, preaching,

> . . . little by little, but surely and steadily on the whole, was brought home to the young boy, for the first time, the meaning of his life: that it was no fool's or sluggard's paradise into which he had wandered by chance, but a battle-field ordained from of old, where there are no spectators, but the youngest must take his side, and the stakes are life and death. And he who roused his consciousness in them showed them at the same time, by every word he spoke in the pulpit, and by his whole life, how that battle was to be fought; and stood there before them their fellow-soldier and the captain of their band.[21]

The chapter in which Tom begins to experience his adolescent epiphany is entitled, "How the Tide Turned." Hughes began each chapter with a poetic quotation. For this chapter the quotation was from the American civil war poem by James Russell Lowell, *The Present Crisis*, a poem which the Englishman Garret Horder later adapted as a hymn. In that hymn Christian sheep are separated from the goats according to their willingness to participate in the struggle:

Once to every man and nation
Comes the moment to decide,
In the strife of truth with falsehood,
For the good or evil side;
Some great cause, God's new Messiah,
Offering each the bloom or blight,
And the choice goes by forever
'Twixt that darkness and that light.[22]

There was a rigidity about Victorian religion, especially among the nonconformists, that saw man's nature and his behavior in absolute terms—he was good or evil, saved or damned, sheep or goat, once and for all time. It was this rigid Old Testament morality which Matthew Arnold labeled Hebraism. It is in hymns like *Once to every man and nation* that the uncompromising nature of Victorian moral attitudes can best be seen.

Hymns urged all men to join the struggle against evil. This fight, and the suffering which accompanied it, would build character and would refine man's religious impulses. In this struggle, the Victorian social ethic put the responsibility for a man's destiny on the individual. "We make or mar ourselves," claimed a conservative clergyman at the end of the century, "we are the masters of our real fate or fortune."[23] Self-discipline and self-reliance—what Samuel Smiles called "Self-Help"—became the catchwords of the century. It was each man's responsibility to struggle against temptation:

Yield not to temptation,
For yielding is sin,
Each vict'ry will help you
Some other to win;
Fight manfully onward,
Dark passions subdue,
Look ever to Jesus,
He'll carry you through.

Shun evil companions,
Bad language disdain.
God's name hold in rev-rence
Nor take it in vain;
Be thoughtful and earnest,
Kind-hearted and true,
Look ever to Jesus,
He'll carry you through.[24]

This strenuousness became by the end of the century almost an end in itself. As religious doubts increased because the old religion was questioned by the new criticism and science, this active stoicism seems for some to have taken the place of religious certainty. In his preface to his translations of Manlius (1903), Housman wrote, "How the world is managed and why it was created, I cannot tell; but it is no featherbed for the repose of sluggards."[25] The hymns clearly put the responsibility for socially acceptable behavior squarely on the individual. His own actions determined whether he was good or evil, sheep or goat.

Work, earnestness, struggle, self-help—these were the active virtues, the positive behaviors, that hymns encouraged Victorian Christians to cultivate. But hymns were not always positive; the greater number of didactic hymns stressed the negative. They proscribed certain behaviors. It was, perhaps, in these negative hymns that the church was most blatantly didactic. One small nondenominational hymnbook entitled simply *Hymns and Poems*, for instance, addresses each of its hymns to persons in the various occupations and social strata.[26] Each is told to accept his or her station in life meekly and cheerfully and to make the best of the available opportunities to please God by working hard. Particularly interesting are those hymns which are addressed to the lower classes and to the young. In these hymns the didactic purpose is especially pronounced: the social ethic which is propounded is one of hard work, honesty, self-help, and at the same time, social quiescence. The terms in which this ethic is stated, however, are almost entirely negative. The sempstress is told, for instance, that she must wait patiently for her reward in the next world, where Christ will wipe away her tears and she will have everlasting rest. The "Ragged Boy's Hymn" consists simply of a list of behaviors which are forbidden by God under the threat of being barred from heaven. (Poor boys must have been feared by the hymn writer primarily as potential thieves, for the hymn asks the young pauper to forswear his desire for the rich man's hoard.)

I would not take what is not mine,
for hoards of wealth untold,—
Far better grasp the red-hot steel,
than touch another's gold;
The love of money, God hath said,
of evil is the root,
And if dishonesty thence spring,
destruction is the fruit.

I would not take what is not mine,
though none were near to see,
Conscience would my accuser stand,
and God my judge would be;
The covetous desire, the wicked
thought I would control,—
What shall it profit man to gain
the world, and lose his soul?

I would not take another's goods,—
the loser might repine,
His loss might heavy seem to him,
but small compared to *mine*;
For oh! more precious far than all
the wealth of nobles given,
An honest name, a quiet conscience,
and the hope of heaven![27]

Poor girls, on the other hand, must have been viewed not as potential thieves but as so hardworking that they had to be warned against plying their trade on the Sabbath: "My basket now untouched must lie,/This day I neither buy nor sell."

One of the more obvious and blatant efforts of the Victorian churches to proscribe improper behavior was the "temperance" movement (more accurately called the "teetotal" movement). As early as 1743, John Wesley had urged his followers to abstain from producing, trading, or consuming spiritous liquors, but the "gospel temperance" movement only permeated English churches in the second half of the nineteenth century and was largely a result of American influence. Except for the Primitive Methodists and the Bible Christians, the English churches in the first half of the century generally took a stand for moderation rather than total abstinence. In 1841 the Methodist Conference closed their chapels to teetotal meetings and the following year a group of 600 Methodists broke away from the Conference and organized as the Teetotal Wesleyan Methodists as a protest against the Conference's stand on moderation. The attitudes of the nonconformist churches toward drinking during the first half of the century were not standardized, but they were generally much more relaxed in this respect than they would be in the last half of the century. The following story by Peter Fletcher indicated what the attitude was in most Methodist churches at about mid-century:

> My grandmother used to tell me with great pride that when she was a girl, it was the duty of the Chairman of the Quarterly Meeting—at which the elders of the church organized its affairs and audited its accounts—to provide a barrel of beer for the refreshment of the members, and the event was not regarded as a success unless most of the company finished the day under the table.[28]

But after mid-century the teetotalers gained more adherents and more power. In 1862 the Church of England Total Abstinence Society was founded. By the 1870s the "temperance" movement was strong enough in the Nonconformist chapels to become a force in Liberal politics and for the next three decades the temperance movement produced a series of legislative proposals to curb the drink traffic.

The church temperance movement of the latter half of the century based the rightness of the cause on biblical injunctions.

> Who the sacred page perusing,
> Precepts, promises, and laws,
> Can be guiltless in refusing
> To promote the temp'rance cause?
>
> There we hear the Holy Spirit,
> By the servant Paul, declare,
> Drunkards never can inherit
> Heav'nly mansions, bright and fair.[29]

The teetotalers appealed particularly to the young on the theory that drunkenness was best prevented if children were enlisted before they had acquired a taste for a drink. In 1909, when the Church of England Temperance Society numbered 639,233 members, 486,888 of the members were juveniles.[30] We must, of course, question the strength of conviction of many of these young teetotalers. In *The Long Sunday*, Peter Fletcher recalls the circumstances which occasioned many of these pledges:

> No boy or girl over the age of ten had the slightest objection to signing Pledge Cards. Every temperance lecturer brought a supply with him and we wrote our full names in block letters on the dotted line whenever we were asked to do so. We were not interested in strong drink, one way or the other, but the earnestness of the gentlemen who addressed us on this topic made it clear to us that they would be very disheartened if their efforts were not rewarded by our co-operation, so we signed. My own opinion—derived from a surreptitious sampling of the Empire Burgundy father occasionally took 'for medicinal purposes' as he was careful to explain, was that nobody in his senses would drink the stuff for pleasure anyway.[31]

Children were exhorted to temperance because it was God's law; teachers were urged to adopt the cause to save youths' souls. Hymns written for this cause were numerous.

Propitious guides of youth,
   Employed in Sabbath schools,
Who, from the page of truth,
   Teach heaven's sacred rules,
Assist the Saviour's work t'advance,
By inculcating *temperance.*

A cause both great and good,
   Worthy of your esteem;
Then treat it as He would,
   Who died man to redeem.
And on the youthful mind impress
The sad effects of drunkeness.

Your labours are made vain
   To lead them to the skies,
For while *strong drinks* are used,
   They fall a sacrifice;
And often leave religion's sway,
To perish in the drunkard's way.

. . . .

Great God, stretch forth thy hand,
   Our wandering youth to save,
O! banish from our land,
   What digs the drunkard's grave;
Urge teachers to enforce thy laws,
By pushing on the temperance cause.[32]

By the last decades of the century the church temperance movement had taken on the aura of a crusade and it absorbed much of the missionary spirit of the times. Sure that they were fighting God's battle, the temperance crusaders meant to save the intemperate from damnation.

Preserver of the human race,
  Our guardian and our guide;
Grant to us wisdom, power, and grace,
  And over us preside.

Increase our zeal—disperse our fear,
  And make us strong and bold
To stem the drunkard's mad career,
  And bring him to Thy fold.

Help us to rescue and preserve
  Thy young and rising race;
Secure the sober ere they swerve,
  And sink into disgrace.

Our foes forgive—our cause defend,
  Our members multiply;
And keep us faithful to the end,
  Till we triumphant die.[33]

Although special hymnbooks were printed for temperance meetings, it was the rare hymnbook of any denomination that did not include at least one temperance hymn by the end of the century.

There were many temperance songs which were entirely secular but which were passed off as hymns. Kenneth Young quotes two such songs from a collection "by someone called Hoyle . . . the lowest—and the most popular—of all the hymn-books." The first is about the exemplary behavior of Merry Dick:

Merry Dick you soon would know
If you lived in Jackson's Row;
Each day with a smiling face
He is ready at his place,
Should you ever with him meet
In the shop or in the street,
You will find him blithe and gay,
Singing out this merry lay:

My drink is water bright, water bright, water bright;
My drink is water bright
From the crystal spring.

The second is the familiar melodramatic story of the small child sent to fetch his father from the public house:

Father, dear father, come home with me now,
The clock in the steeple strikes one;
You promised, dear father, that you would come home
As soon as your day's work was done.
Our fire has gone out, the house is so dark,
And mother's been watching since tea,
With poor brother Benny so sick in her arms
And no one to help her but me.
Come ho-o-me, come ho-o-me,
O father, dear father, come home.[34]

By the time the clock in the steeple strikes three, Bennie has died; his last words were, "I want to kiss Papa goodnight."

The temperance movement soon spread into peripheral areas, such as the attempt to ban tobacco, in an effort to proscribe other aspects of social behavior. Many of these temperance "hymns" were purely secular, as was this delightful selection from the *National Temperance Hymnal*:

What gives the breath an awful smell,
And hinders one from feeling well?
A single word the tale will tell—
Tobacco.

Refrain: Tobacco's a curse in the land
I pledge you, my friend,
I'll never defend
That villainous weed, Tobacco.[35]

It was largely such didactic efforts as the temperance movement which have created the currently popular image of "Victorianism" as Pecksniffian prudery.

It was not simply prudery, however, that made the Victorians look to the church for moral leadership—it was the fear that if the church lost its traditional place as an ethical leader, the result would be decadence and chaos. If we understand this secular social role of religion in the nineteenth century, we can better understand the agony of the establishment in the last half of the century when traditional beliefs were called into question by new discoveries and theories in geology, biology and biblical criticism. The ramifications of this doubt went far beyond theology; for many, it called into question the maintenance of the established social order.

Religious men in all periods have had their doubts about religious questions and the Victorians were no exception. Although many historians note that certitude was one of the outstanding traits of the Victorians, in religion and philosophy the doubts were always there. What distinguishes the first half of the century from the second was that in the earlier period most men kept their uncertainties to themselves, whereas in the later period these doubts were not only expressed, but frequently published. In 1859 Darwin published *Origin of Species*; this was followed by a spate of publications which called traditional church pronouncements into question, most notably, *Essays and Reviews* (1860), and Bishop Colenso's *Commentary on Romans* (1861).

The doubts which were recognized after 1860 are reflected in the hymns of the last half of the century.

> Awake, O lord, as in the time of old!
>   Come, Holy Spirit, in Thy power and might;
> For lack of Thee our hearts are strangely cold,
>   Our minds but blindly groping tow'rds the light.
>
> Doubts are abroad: make Thou these doubts to cease;
>   Fears are within: set Thou these fears at rest!
> Strife is among us: melt that strife to peace!
>   Change marches onward: may all change be blest![36]

For many thinking men the resolution of these doubts was an agonizing struggle of faith and reason, and many, like Tennyson, came to the conclusion that the conflict between religion and science could only be resolved by faith:

> We have but faith; we cannot know;
> For knowledge is of things we see;
> And yet we trust it comes from Thee,
> A beam in darkness: let it grow.

Let knowledge flow from more to more,
But more of reverence in us dwell,
That mind and soul, according well,
May make one music as before.[37]

But for many in the establishment this quiet resolution was not an adequate answer. They determined to fight the "seducing errors" with scripture and tradition.

Church of the living God,
Pillar and ground of truth,
Keep the old paths the fathers trod
In thy illumined youth.

Lo, in thy bosom lies
The touchstone for the age;
Seducing error shrinks and dies
At light from yonder page.

. . . .

Fear not, though doubts abound
And scoffing tongues deride;
Love of God's word finds surer ground
When to the utmost tried.

. . . .

Move, Holy Ghost, with might
Amongst us as of old;
Dispel the falsehood, and unite
In true faith the true fold.[38]

While the Church fought Colenso's Biblical criticism and his attack on the sacramental system in the court, a clergyman, Samuel J. Stone, fought them in the hymnbooks. His most famous, *The Church's one foundation*, is evidence of the heat of battle:

The Church shall never perish!
 Her dear Lord to defend,
To guide, sustain and cherish,
 Is with her to the end;
Though there be those who hate her,
 And false sons in her pale,

Against or foe or traitor
She ever shall prevail.

Though with a scornful wonder
Men see her sore oppressed,
By schisms rent asunder,
By heresies distressed,
Yet saints their watch are keeping,
Their cry goes up, "How long?"
And soon the night of weeping
Shall be the morning of song.[39]

But the battle was doomed to be lost by the traditionalists. During the nineteenth century the face of England had changed too much. The old social ethic was based on an organic view of society, hierarchically organized and allowing g eat inequalities in rank and property but theoretically providing for the welfare of all of its members by a belief in voluntary charity. Such an ethic was no longer adequate for an industrial, individualistic, utilitarian, materialistic society. By the end of the century parliament was recognizing its communal responsibility for the social welfare of the nation, although the realization was often made reluctantly. Romantic dreamers such as the adherents of Young England, who wanted social improvement through a return to the golden age of individual responsibility, were discredited by the end of the century. A professional bureaucracy of state officials responsible for the commonweal was being created by the last half of the century.

The irreversibility and profundity of the change was not obvious on the surface; it would not become obvious until after the Great War. The traditional class structure was seemingly maintained throughout the century: the landed aristocracy retained a large part of its social and political influence until the last decades of the century, when agricultural depression and then death duties began to erode its economic well-being. The creed of individualism seemed dominant in politics: the Liberal Party under Gladstone still espoused a belief in laissez-faire and Free Trade, while passing legislation like Working Men's Housing.

And, so, the churches fought on, believing that the questioning of the old religion and the social ethics which it taught would bring about moral anarchy. As Mrs. Humphry Ward wrote, "My dear friend, the problem of the world at this moment is—how to find a religion?—some great conception which shall be once more capable, as the old were capable, of welding societies, and keeping man's brutish elements in check."[40]

The didactic function of a social institution becomes particularly important in a period of change, such as the nineteenth century. Change causes intense anxiety among the privileged classes because it brings with it changes in life patterns, a new perspective on social organization, and changes in social behavior. The response of the dominant class will be to use social institutions to inculcate traditional morals and genteel behavior. Thus, during the nineteenth century hymns were used as much to propagate acceptable modes of behavior as to teach theology and to accompany ritual. By the second half of the century the threats to traditional social structure were compounded by questioning of scripture and theology. Consequently, during the second half of the century, the number of hymns attempting to regulate social behavior increased and became much more strident and mundane in their demands for conformity.

CHAPTER IV

HYMNS FOR CHILDREN

THE Victorian age was characterized by, among other things, a greater interest in and concern for children: early nineteenth-century legislative and philanthropic reform movements were aimed primarily at protecting children; family life, and particularly the role of motherhood, became the focus of a sentimentalized ideal of English life; childhood was romanticized in art and literature; and the education of children became a national concern.[1]

Traditionally the education of English youth had been the responsibility of the church. Nineteenth-century Englishmen clung so tenaciously to this tradition that Anglicans and Nonconformists alike resisted creating a system of public education until late in the century. Few Englishmen in the early years of the century advocated that formal education be given to all children, but most would have agreed that the churches were responsible for propagating Christian and ethical precepts to the young, particularly for the purpose of insuring social order. For instance, Adam Smith, who believed that the state should not provide public education believed, nevertheless, that some kind of instruction should be provided to make the people more orderly. In *Wealth of Nations* he wrote,

> The more they are instructed, the less liable they are to the delusions of enthusiasm and superstition, which among ignorant nations, frequently occasion the most dreadful disorders. An instructed and intelligent peo-

ple besides, are always more decent and orderly than an ignorant and stupid one.[2]

To further this didactic purpose, the Sunday School movement was begun in the last years of the eighteenth century and by 1888 it is estimated that three out of every four children in England and Wales attended a Sunday School.[3] Although the effectiveness of the Sunday Schools is often debated, many individuals who attended them felt that the ethical precepts which the schools preached had a formative effect on their lives.[4] The purpose of the Sunday Schools was expressed in typically idealistic terms by a verse from a Baptist sermon announcement in 1814:

> Delightful task! to rear the tender thought
> To teach the young idea how to shoot,
> To pour the fresh instruction on the Mind
> To breathe the enlivening Spirit, and to fix
> The generous Purpose to the glowing breast.[5]

Many of the churches and Sunday Schools used hymns to teach lessons. W. L. Alexander recognized this practice, and when he published a plea in 1848 urging the Scottish churches to allow the singing of hymns of "human composition" in addition to the psalms which they already sang, he cited the effectiveness of hymns in inculcating lessons:

> And first among these [incidental benefits] I would place the opportunity afforded by the psalmody of the church for instilling, in an attractive and memorable manner, religious truth into the minds of the people. In every proper hymn or psalm, there is an embodiment of some great principle or idea of a devotional kind; this is set forth in a poetical or at least rhythmical form, and the words thus put together, being sung to an attractive tune, the idea not only comes to be familiar to the mind, but what is of more importance, it comes to be surrounded with agreeable associations, which tend to make us love it, and cling to it. . . . In regard to the younger and less instructed part of our congregations, especially, may this beneficial result be expected to display itself.[6]

Nineteenth-century hymn writers, publishers, and parents certainly must have agreed with Alexander about the didactic effectiveness of hymns, for the hymnbooks for children published during the century outnumber the hymnbooks of any other single category, and the more popular children's hymnbooks were reprinted frequently. Cecil Frances Alexander's *Hymns For Little Children*, for instance, ran into one hundred editions.

The forewords of a number of the hymnbooks suggested that the child should be encouraged not only to sing the hymns, but to memorize them on a regular schedule. That this was not an uncommon practice can be seen in Charlotte Brontë's novel, *Villette*. When young Polly wished to win the approval of Graham, her sixteen-year-old friend and substitute father, she memorized hymns:

> "Have you learned any hymns this week, Polly?"
> "I have learned a very pretty one, four verses long. Shall I say it?"
> "Speak nicely, then: don't be in a hurry."
> The hymn being rehearsed, or rather half-chanted, in a little singing voice, Graham would take exception at the manner, and proceed to give a lesson in recitation.[7]

The child learned hymns because they were approved of by the adult world. Like Polly, he was probably praised and, as W. L. Alexander had noted, the ideas contained in the hymns were thus associated with pleasantness. A Mr. Mark Whitwell sent to W. T. Stead a list of twenty-three hymns which he had memorized before he was four years old. Whitwell wrote, "I really enjoyed learning them; it was a real pleasure to me, partly because it gave my father so much pleasure to hear me repeat them."[8] Edmund Gosse recalled that one of the "games" of a social afternoon among evangelical families was for the children to recite hymns, "some rather long."[9] The children of Mrs. Sherwood's *Fairchild Family* sang hymns for entertainment and to punctuate theological discussions; young Henry Fairchild regularly memorized hymns as part of his lessons. The process of memorizing hymns in the family circle and in the schoolrooms created a shared culture among children, at least middle-class children and those children of the lower classes who were educated by middle-class principles. (In the evangelical tracts and books published for pious children, one of the commonest directives to little children is that they could educate the children of the poor by teaching them hymns.) How widely and deeply embedded this shared culture was among Victorian adults and children is indicated in Lewis Carroll's *Alice in Wonderland*: two of Watts' hymns for children were parodied as "How doth the little crocodile" and " 'Twas the voice of the lobster." The spoof was successful because the original hymns were thoroughly familiar to Carroll's audience.

The effect of this memorization process could be profound. For many Victorians the hymns learned in childhood made a deep and lasting impression. In adulthood they could remember the lyrics automatically and, even more important, that recall often included a recapitulation of the emotional climate surrounding the original learning process. Edmund Gosse, for instance, records that he and his mother read hymns together, a practice which left indelible memories:

> Both of us extremely admired the piece of Toplady which begins:-
>
> What though my frail eyelids refuse
> Continual watchings to keep,
> And, punctual as midnight renews,
> Demand the refreshment of sleep.
>
> To this day I cannot repeat this hymn without a sense of poignant emotion, nor can I pretend to decide how much of this is due to its merit and how much to the peculiar nature of the memories it recalls. But it might be as rude as I genuinely think it to be skillful, and I should continue to regard it as a sacred poem.[10]

In Gosse's case the hymns recalled profoundly ambivalent feelings: his deep attachment to and his love for his mother recalled a sense of dependence and security, but her untimely death evoked a profound sense of loss. For Gosse, and probably for many other Victorian children, hymns worked as a trigger mechanism to release unconscious or semiconscious memories of their childhood state. This ability to create feelings of transcendence of time and place, and thus to create that state of expanded consciousness which William James would call "religious experience," made hymns a powerful psychic force. We can see this force in operation in Edwin Diller Starbuck's collected data about individual conversion experiences: in a number of instances Starbuck's respondents mention that their transcendent experience was preceded by the singing of a hymn.[11]

The effect of the hymns was undoubtedly different for each individual child, depending upon the circumstances of the childhood experience. Unlike Gosse, Herbert Spencer recalled the exercise of memorizing hymns with distaste. When W. T. Stead asked Spencer to name the hymns which had helped him throughout his life, Spencer replied that none had helped him, that his feelings about hymns were entirely negative:

> If parents had more sense than is commonly found among them they would never dream of setting their children to learn hymns as tasks. With

> me the effect was not to generate any liking for this or that hymn, but to generate a dislike for hymns at large. The process of learning was a penalty and the feeling associated with that penalty became a feeling associated with hymns in general.[12]

Starbuck recounts the similarly distasteful memory of another young man:

> In addition to the torture of church and Sunday School, we were obliged to commit to memory whole psalms, chapters of the Bible, hymns, and the thing I worst of all detested was the reading of so-called 'religious books.'[13]

And then, of course, there were some rebellious youthful spirits who more or less openly resisted these attempts to indoctrinate. Kenneth Young records the "naughty" work of transposing achieved by a group of nonconformist boys:

> Here we suffer grief and pain—
> Over the road they're doing the same,
> Next door they're suffering more
> Oh, won't it be joyful when we part to meet no more.[14]

Whether the early experience of memorizing and singing hymns was pleasant or unpleasant, whether it was compliantly accepted or openly or secretly rejected, it was an experience shared by many Victorian children and one loaded with emotional associations. We must examine, then, the content of these hymns that were impressed so forcefully on the Victorian child's mind.

The impression was not always a pleasant one, for the English tradition of children's hymns was a pessimistic one. Calvinism dominated the churches' concept of childhood as it did so many other aspects of seventeenth- and eighteenth-century English religion. In the *Institutes*, Calvin wrote of children,

> Infants themselves bring their own damnation with them from their mother's wombe. Who, although they have not yet brought forth the fruits of their iniquitie, yet have the seed thereof enclosed within them. Yea, their whole nature is a certaine seed of sinne, therefore it cannot but bee hateful and abominable to God.[15]

Isaac Watts, the eighteenth-century hymn writer who wrote the first English hymnbook for children, *Divine and Moral Songs, attempted in easy Language for the Use of Children* (1715), apparently accepted Calvin's view of children. "What ferments of spite and envy," Watts wrote about children, "what native wrath and rage sometimes are found in the little hearts of infants and sufficiently discovered by their little hands and their eyes and their wrathful countenances even before they have learned to speak or to know good and evil."[16] Although Watts' theology in his hymns for adults was often liberal and humane, in his hymns for children he was, at his most characteristic, harshly Calvinistic. Children were warned of a wrathful God:

What if the Lord grow wroth, and swear,
While I refuse to read and pray,
That He'll refuse to lend an ear
To all my groans another day?
What if His dreadful anger burn
While I refuse His offered grace
And all his love to anger turn,
And strike me dead upon the place?
'Tis dangerous to provoke a God!
His power and vengeance none can tell:
One stroke of His almighty rod
Shall send young sinners quick to hell.[17]

The punishments of hell were graphically and terrifyingly described. In her memoirs, Mrs. Treffry recalled that at the age of six she was convinced of her own sinfulness when she heard the lines of another of Watt's hymns for children:

There is a dreadful hell
    And everlasting pains,
Where sinners must with devils dwell
    In darkness, fire and chains.[18]

Despite this harsh view of the world, or perhaps because of it, Watts' hymns for children continued to be republished throughout the nineteenth century.[19] Some nineteenth-century hymn writers continued this pessimistic, threatening tone. Sir Rowland Hill, for instance, viewed children as utterly depraved. In one hymn Hill says of children's quarrels,

But oh, what a horrible sight,
    When children, with anger and rage,

Like lions, will quarrel and fight,
    While none can their anger assuage.

Old Satan is then very nigh.
    Delighted that thus they have shown
A murdering spirit; and why?
    Because 'tis akin to his own.[20]

It would be wrong to attribute these threatening attitudes only to the church, however, for much of the secular popular culture for children during the Victorian era was equally as frightening in its depiction of retributive justice. Edmund Gosse remembers the Punch and Judy show as terrifying:

> The momentous close, when a figure of shapeless horror appears on the stage, and quells the hitherto undaunted Mr. Punch, was to me the bouquet of the entire performance. When Mr. Punch, losing his nerve, points to this shape and says in an awestruck, squeaking whisper, "Who's that? Is it the butcher?" and the stern answer comes, "No, Mr. Punch!" And then, "Is it the baker?" "No, Mr. Punch!" "Who is it then?" (this in a squeak trembling with emotion and terror); and then the full, loud reply, booming like a judgment-bell, "It is the Devil come to take you down to Hell," and the form of Punch, with kicking legs, sunken in epilepsy on the floor,—all this was solemn and exquisite to me beyond words. I was not amused—I was deeply moved and exhilarated, "purged," as the old phrase hath it, "with pity and terror."[21]

Nevertheless, the association between church and fear was made by many Victorians; it was often an impression formed during childhood. In his *Reminiscences*, Ernest Bax recalls that the didactic narratives available in his own Methodist household of the 1860s, were of a threatening nature. This, he wrote, "was a much commended means in the Evangelical world for converting the sinner from the error of his ways. Thus, to discourage the gratification of the taste for the drama, a moral, inculcating the retribution which the Evangelical God sometimes inflicted on frequenters of 'play-houses,' was drawn from the history of fires that had taken place in theatres."[22]

This belief that justice was dispensed by an omniscient God was reinforced by a prominent image in nineteenth-century children's literature: the all-seeing eye of God. One story titled, "The Eye That Can See, and the Hand That Can Reach," tells that,

> A boy of the name of Beardsworth, in the parish of Stoke Suffolk, went out to steal wood; he climbed a tree with his axe, and cut as much as would make a fagot, taking his measures so well, that no eye saw him save that eye which sees all. He threw down his axe, and prepared to descend. Then the hand which can reach all caught him. His frock hung upon one of the short stumps which he had left; his round dress slipped over his head, or rather he slipped through it; his arms were imprisoned in the sleeves; the collar, with its strong button, embraced his neck, stopped his breath, and he died there. . . . Children, do you ever think that no one can see you? So thought John Beardsworth. Men, do you ever think that no one can catch you? So thought John Beardsworth. These are lies of the devil, told to entrap your souls. Believe them not, but believe Him who says, 'Be sure your sin will find you out.'[23]

How threatening this image must have been can be imagined. When little Emily of *The Fairchild Family* steals a plum, she dreams later "that a dreadful Eye was looking upon her from above. Wherever she went, she thought this Eye followed her with angry looks, and she could not hide herself from it."[24] The moral is reinforced for the readers of the *Fairchild Family* by a hymn:

Almighty God, thy piercing eye
    Shines through the shades of night;
And our most secret actions lie
    All open to thy sight.[25]

The same image of the all-seeing eye of God was continued in children's hymnbooks throughout the century. These two examples, for instance, are from a Methodist Sunday School hymnbook of 1879:

There is an eye that never sleeps
    Beneath the wing of night;
There is an ear that never shuts
    When sink the beams of light.

* * *

Theft will not be always hidden!
    Though we fancy none can spy,
When we take a thing forbidden,
    God beholds it with His eye.[26]

Hymns played a considerable part in reinforcing this fearful attitude toward God and the vision of God as a dispenser of worldly justice for social transgressions. For many Victorians in later life, hymns were consequently associated with threatening situations. For instance, when Janet Courtney recalled her late Victorian childhood in a Lincolnshire market-town vicarage, she began by describing the autumn winds, which symbolized for her the fears of her childhood: "To [the winds'] roar and reverberation, as Advent came round again, the child would listen trembling at night, fearing every moment to hear the sound of the Last Trump which, as she had just sung in church, was to wake the quick and dead—those dead who slept in the churchyard outside the nursery windows, and who might be looking in at the big window on the stair case if one did not run past very quickly with eyes tight shut."[27] The association of hymns with fear and death is most interesting. It was an association which was perpetuated by the pessimistic, Calvinist hymns which continued to be published for children well into the twentieth century.

During the nineteenth century, however, the complexion of children's hymns as a whole underwent a change. They did not become any less didactic, but they did become less blatant and threatening in their didacticism. For the most part the newer Victorian hymns for children supressed the overt motive of fear. Instead, they stressed a blander didacticism, more subtle psychologically, but probably just as terrifying for the child and just as effective in winning the child's compliance. One of the most popular nineteenth-century children's hymnbooks was *Hymns for Infant Minds*, written by Anne and Jane Taylor. The advertisement for this book states that it surpasses Watts because the subjects are "treated of in a manner more adapted to children, and calculated in every instance to win to what is good by love rather than deter from what is evil by terror."[28] Watts' graphic descriptions of the terrors of hell were replaced by vaguer and more generalized threats:

'Tis sin that grieves his holy mind,
　　And makes his anger rise;
And sinners old or young shall find
　　No favour in his eyes.[29]

Instead of fear of eternal punishment, the Taylors' hymns used guilt. The following hymn, entitled, "A Child's Lamentation for the Death of a Dear Mother," is an example.

And now I recollect with pain
　　The many times I grieved her sore:

Oh! if she would but come again,
I think I'd vex her so no more.

How I would watch her gentle eye!
'Twould be my play to do her will!
And she should never have to sigh
Again, for my behaving ill!

But since she's gone so far away,
And cannot profit by my pains,
Let me this childlike duty pay
To that dear parent who remains.

Let me console his broken heart,
And be his comfort by my care;
That when at last we come to part,
I may not have such grief to bear.[30]

Here the child's misbehavior has been punished by the mother's death. The youthful reader is warned, by implication, that his failure to be dutiful may result in the death of a parent. This theme of the death of a parent (particularly of the mother) after the misconduct of the child, was a common one in late Victorian hymns.

Although Victorian hymns for children spoke less of hell's tortures, they spoke a great deal of death. The presence of death in children's hymns is particularly prominent in the hymns of the evangelical hymn writers. In a public school hymnal death is described vividly and dramatically: "The feeble pulse, the gasping breath,/The clenched teeth, the glazed eye, . . ."[31] Although the hymns repeatedly call the child's attention to death, they reassure him that he has nothing to fear from death if he has been good: "Safe in our Saviour we fear not the blow." One method of insuring a heavenly reward, the evangelical hymns say, is to reject worldly pleasures, which are called "a gaudy dream/ Of pride and pomp and luxury," "the pride of sinful flesh," "these trifling pleasures here below." The child is told, in the almost gnostic tradition of the evangelical, that this life is one of "grief and pain." The temptations of this world can only lead to "burning boundless agony." He is, in fact, encouraged to anticipate death which, for the good child will be "joyful." The transience of life is reiterated again and again in children's hymns. Death is clearly the final goal which Victorian children are taught to anticipate.

The fate of the dead, the hymns say, will be determined by their earthly actions. Like adults, Victorian children bear the full responsibility for their lives:

There's not a child so small and weak
But has his little cross to take
His little work of love and praise
That he may do for Jesus's sake.[32]

Even the smallest individual is responsible for his own salvation. In hymns the concept of "self-help" is applied to religion.

The child is shown very clearly the virtues which he must cultivate to gain the heavenly reward. Chief among these virtues are submissiveness and obedience:

We must meek and gentle be,
Little pain and childish trial
Ever bearing patiently.[33]

He must imitate Jesus, who as a child was "mild, obedient, good." The child is particularly told to be obedient to his parents, to listen to his father's teaching and to obey his mother. He must suppress his temper and deny his thoughts of self. Quick temper and vanity, in fact, seem to be the most frequent specific transgressions of the naughty child.

Forgive my temper, Lord, I pray,
    My passion and my pride:
The wicked words I dared to say,
    And wicked thoughts beside.

. . . .

And who am I, a sinful child,
    Such angry words to say?
Make me as mild as He was mild,
    And take my pride away.[34]

The child is also warned against the temptation of frivolity—he must strive for earnestness. In fact, the image of a perfect Christian child presented by children's hymns is that of a monastic; he is disciplined, he contemplates God continually, he rejects worldly pleasures, and he mortifies himself for any transgression:

Lord, hear a sinful child complain,
Whose little heart is very vain,
And folly dwells within.
What it is—for thine eye can see—
That is so very dear to me,
That steals my thoughts away from thee,
And leads me into sin?

Whatever give me most delight,
If 'tis offensive in thy sight,
I would no more pursue:
Since nothing can be good for me,
However pleasant it may be,
That is displeasing, Lord, to thee,
May I dislike it too!

When I attempt to read or pray,
I'm often thinking of my play,
Or some such idle thing.
How happy are the saints in bliss,
Who love no sinful world like this:
But all their joy and glory is
To praise their heavenly King!

These trifling pleasures here below—
I wonder why I love them so:
They cannot make me blest.
Oh that to love my God might be
The greatest happiness to me!
And may he give me grace to see
That this is not my rest![35]

In addition to cultivating these passive virtues of obedience, submissiveness, humility, and earnestness, the child is expected actively to resist wrongdoing. He is warned of the temptations of sin, but other than generalizations about anger, pride, vanity, and sloth, the nature of sin is unspecified. Darker sins than children's sins often are hinted at, but not dwelt upon. In one hymn the child repeats, "Though but children, knowing little/ Of the sin we learn to flee," and then proceeds to explain how he can avoid this nameless sin by seeking Jesus.[36] The world depicted in many children's hymns is pervaded by evil spirits, by devils waiting to snatch the child's attention. The child is repeatedly warned to be on guard against this evil eminence which tempts him to sin:

There's a wicked spirit
  Watching round you still
And he tries to tempt you
  To all harm and ill.[37]

These dark and pessimistic warnings contrast strangely with another prominent category of children's hymns, a type which became more familiar as the century progressed—the sweet and gentle hymns which abounded in nature imagery and which promised children that Jesus loved them and would guard and protect them. The world of these hymns was a far cry from the threatening world of "fire and chains."

White clouds sailing in the air,
Little flowers so fresh and fair,
Greenest fields and rippling streams,
Glitter in the morning beams.[38]

* * *

Little lambs lie quiet
  All the summer night,
With their old ewe mothers
  Warm, and soft, and white.

. . . .

Lambs are not so happy,
  'Mid the meadow flowers;
They have play and pleasure,
  But not love like ours.[39]

* * *

Like as a faithful Shepherd
  Cares for His helpless sheep,
So I will guard and lead you,
  So I will safely keep;

Evil shall never harm you,
  Danger shall ne'er affright,
For I will ever have you
  Closely beneath My sight.[40]

Hymns of both types are found side by side in Victorian hymnbooks. There is an obvious ambivalence of attitudes here. Children were told on one hand that the world was a beautiful place in which to live, one filled with lambs and birds, flowers and sunshine, a benevolent world in which Jesus personally watched over good children. But children's hymns also presented a picture of a dark and ugly world, one filled with sin and evil. The dichotomy between these two world views is often expressed in Manichaean terms as a struggle by the forces of good and evil for children's souls.

Children were expected to participate actively in this struggle. Boys, of course, were particularly urged to activity in the name of Jesus.[41] In the multitude of hymns which employ military imagery, boys were warned of their "weary war to wage with sin." They were exhorted to "fight the good fight with all your might" and to "stand by your colours and battle with sin." A brief sampling of first lines of children's hymns reveals a prominent set of images which were used to urge active participation, those of labor: "Come labour on," "Work for the night is coming," "O boys, be strong in Jesus,/To toil for him is gain."

All children were particularly urged to do missionary work of some kind. For those who could not make the ultimate sacrifice of spreading the gospel in foreign lands, there was other missionary work at home to do.

If you cannot cross the ocean,
And the heathen lands explore,
You can find the heathen nearer,
You can help them at your door.
If you cannot give your thousands,
You can give the widow's mite,
And the least you give for Jesus
Will be precious in His sight.

If you cannot speak like angels,
If you cannot preach like Paul,
You can tell the love of Jesus,
You can say He welcomes all.
If you cannot rouse the wicked
With the judgment's dread alarms,
You can lead the little children
To the Saviour's waiting arms.[42]

Whatever one's Christian mission in life was, it was often visualized in terms of struggle for earnestness and truth.

Soul of the Christian, be earnest and true,
God has a mission, a life-work for you;

Kind words to utter, and good deeds to do,
Souls from their error and darkness to woo.[43]

The purpose of this struggle was to build character in children so that when they were grown they would be strong, patriotic, and Christian Englishmen. Their strength of character would enable them to resist temptation and live clean lives, to seek truth, and to aid the weak. Rudyard Kipling summed up these ideals at the end of the century in his "Father in heaven, who lovest all," a hymn originally published in a children's book, *Puck of Pook's Hill*:

Land of our birth, we pledge to thee
Our love and toil in the years to be,
When we are grown and take our place
As men and women with our race.

Father in heaven, who lovest all,
O help thy children when they call,
That they may build from age to age
An undefiled heritage.

Teach us to bear the yoke in youth,
With steadfastness and careful truth,
That, in our time, thy grace may give
The truth whereby the nations live.

Teach us to rule ourselves always,
Controlled and cleanly night and day,
That we may bring, if need arise,
No maimed or worthless sacrifice.

Teach us to look in all our ends
On thee for Judge, and not our friends,
That we, with thee, may walk uncowed
By fear or favor of the crowd.

Teach us the strength that cannot seek,
By deed or thought, to hurt the weak,
That, under thee, we may possess
Man's strength to comfort man's distress.

Teach us delight in simple things,
And mirth that has no bitter springs,
Forgiveness free of evil done,
And love to all men 'neath the sun.

Land of our birth, our faith, our pride,
For whose dear sake our fathers died;
O Motherland, we pledge to thee
Head, heart, and hand through the years to be.[44]

In Kipling's hymn we see the Victorian ideal of the Christian child: patriotic, hardworking, steadfast, honest, controlled and clean, God-fearing, strong but helpful to the weak, and possessing the simple virtues of delight, mirth, forgiveness and love.

A society's ideals are, perhaps, nowhere more evident than in its aspirations for its children, because the younger generation represents the possibility of utopian reform of the world. Victorian children's hymns present a picture of extremely high ideals. In the hymns children were exhorted to repress their personal feelings and desires and to achieve the good of others. They were to work for the family, for society, for God, and for England. The ideal of the social ethic taught by the hymns was the pure, altruistic and unfaltering hero, who fights selflessly for right and wins, an ideal which, in its absolute definition, was impossible for achievement by most men. This discrepancy between the ideal and reality helps, perhaps, to explain one source of what critics of the Victorians have labeled their hypocrisy. The standards which they set almost inevitably doomed all but the strongest to failure, a failure which could only be covered by pretense.

In addition to these unrealistically high standards, there are, however, several ambivalences contained within these ideals. We have already pointed out the paradoxical conflict of *weltanschauungen* in the hymns, the unresolved dichotomy between the world as benevolent or malevolent. In addition to this theological conflict, there is a pronounced ambivalence in the hymns' didactic message concerning the child's conduct. Children were taught to be passive—to be submissive, humble, and obedient, to deny their individual impulses. At the same time, they were taught to be vigorously active—to struggle mightily against temptation and sin and for truth and a better world; in other words, to strengthen their individuality and character. This conflict in role models, between the demands that a child be both submissive and aggressive, must have created a great deal of tension and psychological confusion for young adults. Like Lewis Carroll's Alice, many Victorian children, raised with a schizophrenic model, must have wondered, "Who in the world am I?" The answer must have been an ambivalent one; as Carroll observed about Alice, "this curious child was very fond of pretending to be two people."

CHAPTER V

THE CONDITION OF ENGLAND QUESTION

DURING the nineteenth century England was faced with what seemed to be a novel social problem: in a time of unprecedented prosperity large segments of the population were living in a deplorable state of poverty. The continued expansion in the growth rate of population and the cluster of innovations we call the Industrial Revolution created a greatly expanded population which was increasingly concentrated in urban areas. Conditions of squalor could not go unnoticed for long, concentrated as they were around the new industrial sources of English wealth. In the last years of the eighteenth century individuals became increasingly aware of the social problems which were engulfing the lower part of English society. The traditional solutions for dealing with social distress were ineffective, but more than a century would pass before adequate solutions could be found and accepted by the society as a whole for what became known as the Condition of England Question.[1]

In 1800 there were very few examples of state intervention in private and local affairs to ensure social welfare. Yet by 1900 the English central government was regulating many segments of life for the welfare of the majority of society. During the century a change took place in popular attitudes toward the problem of social welfare, but it did not take place without a struggle. This change in English social philosophy was evident in all nineteenth-century English institutions, and in no institution did the debate rage more fiercely than in the churches.

The role of the Victorian churches in solving the Condition of England Question has received careful scrutiny in the past few decades. Several modern historians, viewing the nineteenth century from the modern vantage point of the welfare state, have condemned the Victorian churches for their failure to adopt a social philosophy that could realistically cope with the social problems of an urban industrial society.[2] Why, they ask in angry voices, did it take so long for the church to fulfill the role which Christ had set out so clearly in the social gospel he preached? In attempting to answer these questions, historians tend to separate the church from other social institutions, to expect the churches to uphold a social vision different from that of other institutions. But churches, like other institutions, tend to reflect popular contemporary social values. Once again, hymns are a barometer of those values.

The eighteenth century left little in the way of effective traditions and solutions for ameliorating the lot of the poor. The Poor Laws, based on Elizabethan statutes, made the parishes responsible for the poor, but by the end of the eighteenth century the system of parish relief had proved unworkable. The eighteenth century also left but a small legacy of hymns of social comment. The vast majority of eighteenth-century hymns were pietistic: they focused inward on man's spiritual condition or heavenward. Phillip Doddridge was a rare exception to the rule; he contributed a group of hymns which were reprinted occasionally in nineteenth-century hymnals. One such from the 1872 edition of *The Hymnary*, an Anglican High-Church hymnal, reads:

O Fount of good, to own Thy love
  Our thankful hearts incline:
What can we render, LORD to Thee,
  When all the worlds are Thine?

But Thou hast needy brethren here,
  Partakers of Thy grace.
Whose names Thou wilt Thyself confess
  Before the FATHER'S face.

In each sad accent of distress
  Thy pleading voice is heard;
In them Thou may'st be clothed and fed,
  And visited, and cheered.

Help us then, LORD, Thy yoke to wear,
To joy to do Thy will;
Each other's burdens gladly bear,
And love's sweet law fulfil.

Thy Face with reverence and with love
We in Thy poor would see;
And while we minister to them,
Would do it as to Thee.

Do Thou, O LORD, our alms accept,
And with Thy blessing speed;
Bless us in giving; greatly bless
Our gifts to them that need.[3]

Even Doddridge failed to address the question of social justice—that is, the question of whether the social and economic system as it then existed was good and just. Rather, Doddridge wrote about traditional Christian charity, assuming that "the poor are always with us." .Other than Doddridge there were few eighteenth-century hymn writers who considered social conditions a proper subject for hymns. One reason was that the evangelicals were writing most of the hymns and most evangelicals did not consider life on this earth a primary concern of Christians. Their concern was for heaven and not for earth:

We've no abiding city here:
This may distress the worldling's mind,
But should not cost the saint a tear,
Who hopes a better rest to find.

We've no abiding city here;
Sad truth, were this to be our home;
But let the thought our spirits cheer,
We seek a city yet to come.

. . . .

But hush, my soul, nor dare repine;
The time my GOD appoints is best;
While here, to do His will be mine,
And HIS, to fix my time of rest.[4]

The evangelical attitude of rejection of this world was a dominant theme of nineteenth-century hymns.

Teach us to aim at heaven's high prize,
And for its glory to despise
  The world and all below;
Cleanse us from sin; direct us right;
Illuminate us with Thy light;
  Thy peace on us bestow.[5]

This rejection of earthly things led many hymn writers to look upon the poor as a group especially favored by God. In an age when heaven was viewed as a compensation for earthly deficiencies, the poor and the distressed, who were denied earthly favors, were considered to be well on their way to heaven.

What poor despised company
Of travellers are these,
That walk in yonder narrow way,
Along that narrow maze?

Refrain: I'd rather be the least of them
  That are the Lord's alone,
  Than wear a royal diadem
  And sit upon a throne,
  Than wear a royal diadem,
  And sit upon a throne.

Ah, these are of royal line,
All children of a King;
Heirs of immortal crowns Divine;
And lo for joy they sing.

But some of them seem poor, distrest,
And lacking daily bread;
Ah! They're of boundless wealth possest,
With heavenly manna fed.[6]

In one hymn children were taught to voice gratitude for what they did receive from God's bounty:

Poor and needy though I be,
God Almighty cares for me;
Gives me clothing, shelter, food,
Gives me all I have of good.

. . . .

Though I labour here awhile,
He will bless me with his smile;
And when this short life is past,
I shall rest with him at last.[7]

In another hymn they were told that they should be grateful that they were not rich because riches harden the heart and make salvation more difficult:

In this our low and poor estate,
Thy mercy, Lord, is clearly shown;
For hadst thou made us rich and great,
How hard might then our hearts have grown![8]

As we have tried to show in the chapter on evangelicalism before, the main theme in evangelical hymnody was one of quietism. God's creation was beyond man's understanding; acceptance of one's earthly lot became a Christian duty.

Though lowly here our lot may be,
High work have we to do;
In faith and trust to follow Him
Whose lot was lowly too.

. . . .

Thus may we make the lowliest lot
With rays of glory bright;
Thus may we turn a crown of thorns
Into a crown of light.[9]

In what has become one of the best-known comments of nineteenth-century social quietism, Mrs. Cecil Frances Alexander wrote this verse:

The rich man in his castle
The poor man at his gate,
God made them, high or lowly
And ordered their estate.[10]

Christians were urged to accept their earthly lot without complaint, in imitation of Christ.

If he the scorn of wicked men
 With patience did sustain,
Becomes it those for whom He died
 To murmur or complain?[11]

Religion was supposed to satisfy the needs of the afflicted. Wilberforce wrote of the "more lowly path" of the poor: "It is their part faithfully to discharge its duties and contentedly to bear its burdens. . . . The peace of mind which Religion affords indiscriminately to all ranks affords more true satisfaction than all the expensive pleasures that are beyond the poor man's reach."[12] Church attendance on the Sabbath made amends for the shortcomings of this life, said one hymn:

How welcome to the saints when pressed
With six days' noise, and care, and toil,
Is the returning day of rest,
Which hides them from the world awhile!

Though pinched with poverty at home,
With sharp afflictions daily fed,
It makes amends if they can come
To God's own house for heavenly bread.[13]

The poor and hungry could be fed with religion, their needs fulfilled with the gospel:

Come, Thou soul-transforming Spirit,
 Bless the sower and the seed!
Let each heart Thy grace inherit:
 Raise the weak, the hungry feed!
  From the gospel,
 Now supply Thy people's need![14]

Evangelicalism is essentially a personal religion which places the Gospel at the center of its teaching. For the evangelical, the salvation of the individual soul is the ultimate goal of religion; everything else is secondary. Consequently, the evangelical churches purposefully ignored social action. The Methodist policy of noninvolvement has long been noted. In his seminal work on the influence of Methodism,[15] Elie Halévy contends that the politically quietistic religious revival of the eighteenth century was instrumental in averting political revolution in England:

> The church they established was at once the most conservative in the political opinions of its members, and the most hierarchical in its internal organization, of all the Protestant sects.
>
> This is how Methodism bent the popular impulses of 1739 to the form which most favored the respect for and maintenance of existing institutions. . . . A force capable of expending itself in displays of violence or popular upheavals assumes, under the influence of a century and a half of Methodism, the form least capable of unsettling a social order founded upon inequality of rank and wealth.[16]

Probably no remark has been more widely quoted than Jabez Bunting's that "Wesleyanism is as much opposed to Democracy as it is to Sin." In 1801 three Methodists were arrested for "disaffection." Consequently, they were, according to a modern critic, "expelled from the Wesleyan Connexion solely for their democratic sentiments."[17] G. M. Young attributes the defeat of Chartism in the late 1840s and the pacification of the 1850s in large part to "the resolute opposition which Wesleyans offered to subversion in society or state."[18]

The history of the Congregational Church in the first half of the nineteenth century shows a similar detachment from social questions. Albert Peel, after a careful scrutiny of the Congregational Union's *Proceedings* during the early part of the century declares:

> . . . the only trace of a social conscience to be observed in the Union's proceedings is in reference to slavery. First, the preaching of the Gospel, second, the securing of religious freedom—on these the aims of the Independents were concentrated, and they had not yet felt the call to the struggle for the remedying of social ills.[19]

R. T. Jones, another Congregationalist historian, concurs:

> . . . during the first quarter of the century [they] took a thoroughly Evangelical attitude towards social distress. . . . Their social attitude was governed by their conviction of the supreme importance of personal salvation. . . . The idea of improving man's economic and social condition as an end in itself they would have found quite incomprehensible.[20]

Among the evangelical enthusiasts this attitude continued throughout the Victorian era. The revivals which took place during the second half of the nineteenth century often took the traditional attitude of noninvolvement in earthly concerns. The Salvation Army was formed by William Booth in 1879 to evangelize the urban poor, but in its early days, its main impetus was toward spreading the gospel message. Salvation was the Army's concern, Booth frequently repeated, not the creation of heaven on earth. Even after 1886, when Booth became convinced that poverty must be cured because it was an impediment to salvation, the main thrust of the Army was to help the poverty-stricken individual to become a productive member of society, not to change the social system which produced poverty. Many traditional evangelicals agreed with the popular Baptist preacher Charles Spurgeon that the battle of the church was "the truth of God *versus* the invention of men."[21] Throughout the century this attitude of non-involvement in earthly concerns would mark evangelical social philosophies.[22] This is not to say that complaisance was limited to the evangelicals. In 1830 John Keble, a leader of the Tractarians, wrote in a sermon:

> Differences of rank, power and riches between man and man is no doubt God's appointment, as much as differences of health and strength. And when we speak or think unkindly of our neighbor, for being nobler or richer or of more consequence than ourselves, we do in fact grumble against our Maker, and set up ourselves as better judges than He of what is really good for us. And if we die in such a Temper as that, our end can be no other than everlasting destruction. On the other hand, a cheerful submission to authority, a desire to find one's superiors in the right, and such a respect for them and ourselves . . . are real parts of sound Christian wisdom.[23]

Echoing this sentiment in a novel, the Tractarian Rev. William Gresley wrote in *Colton Green* (1846) that

> God has placed men in their respective stations in order to make trial of their spirits, until the number of his elect be accomplished: the poor, in the patient endurance of their allotted toil, in soberness, obedience and faith—the rich and the influential, in the charitable provision which they afford their poor dependent brethren for knowing and doing the will of Him Who made them.[24]

Nor was this conflict of heaven and earth a problem limited to nineteenth-century churches; it is a problem as old as the church itself. Christianity presents the adherent with a constant dilemma: on the one hand, it demands a submission of the will of man to the omnipotent will of God; on the other hand, Christianity demands acts of love and brotherhood which entail human decision, will, and action.

The tension resulting from this paradox is most easily resolved by embracing one commandment and ignoring, as much as possible, the other. The evangelical solution has traditionally been to submit themselves to God's will. Historically, the evangelical solution has proved unsatisfactory because of the tendency of organized churches to equate God's will with the existing social, economic, and political organization. The evangelical argument thus tends to become, in its institutional form, a self-serving, hypocritical justification of the *status quo*. The hypocrisy becomes evident in the need to justify, at the same time, both the value of being a poor Christian and value of being a rich Christian. If hymns for the "poor of the flock" encouraged them to view their condition of poverty as a positive benefit in their quest for eternal salvation, the question of the justification of wealth naturally arises. The response was the encouragement of charity.

One of the reasons why the established social order, with its discrepancies of wealth, was considered acceptable was that most Victorians understood that God's gifts to the fortunate entailed a personal obligation to help the unfortunate. Consequently, all of the churches, evangelical and nonevangelical alike, joined in the movement for voluntary charity. The lame, the halt, the blind, the widow, the orphan, the prostitute, the alcoholic, all of the individuals who for some reason found it impossible to support themselves in an industrial society, were helped haphazardly by the churches. Voluntarism was considered beneficial not only to the recipient of the charity but also to the donor because it instilled in the latter self-discipline and responsibility on a local level. In the secular literature throughout the century, from Carlyle to Disraeli to William Morris, the theme of social improvement through individual responsibility to the local community is a strong and continuing thread.

Nineteenth-century hymns repeatedly urged fortunate Christians to help their less fortunate fellow men:

Teach us, O Lord, with cheerful hearts,
As Thou hast bless'd our various store,
From our abundance to impart
A liberal portion to the poor.

To Thee our all devoted be,
In whom we breathe, and move, and live:
Freely we have received from Thee;
Freely may we rejoice to give.

And while we thus obey thy word,
And every call of want relieve;
Oh! may we find it, gracious Lord!
More bless'd to give than to receive.[25]

A hymn written for "The Child of Affluence" clearly makes the point that charity is an obligation of wealth:

How many poor indigent children I see,
Who want all the comforts bestowed upon me.
But though I'm preserved from such want and distress,
I am quite as unworthy of all I possess.

While I am partaking a plentiful meal,
How many the cravings of appetite feel!
Poor creatures as young and as helpless as I,
Who yet have no money their wants to supply.

If I were so destitute, friendless, and poor,
How could I such hardship and suffering endure?
Then let me be thankful, and humbly adore
My God, who has graciously given me more.

And since I with so many comforts am blessed,
May it be my delight to relieve the distressed;
For God has declared, and his promise is sure,
That blessed are they who consider the poor.[26]

Hymns urging voluntary charity are found in almost every nineteenth-century hymnal, although even these are surprisingly few in number in the denominational hymnals, and they are usually placed, in those hymnals arranged by subject, in a special section titled "Almsgiving." They urge charity especially to those who cannot help themselves.

We give Thee but Thine own,
Whate'er the gift may be:
All that we have is Thine alone,
A trust, O Lord, from Thee.

. . . .

To comfort and to bless,
To find a balm for woe,

To tend the lone and fatherless
Is angels' work below.[27]

Charity is most often linked with mission work. The giver of charity is directed to feed the recipient's soul as well as his stomach.

What shall we render, bounteous Lord!
For all the grace we see?
Alas! the goodness worms can yield
Extendeth not to Thee.

To tents of woe, to bed of pain,
We cheerfully repair;
And, with the gift thy hand bestows,
Relieve the mourners' care.

The widow's heart shall sing for joy,
The orphan shall be glad;
And hungering souls we'll gladly point
To Christ, the Living Bread.[28]

The motive for almsgiving is clearly stated. Those who are generous are more assured of gaining God's grace and heaven.

Yes; the sorrow and the suffering,
Which on every hand we see,
Channels are for tithes and offerings
Due by solemn right to Thee;

Right of which we may not rob Thee,
Debt we may not choose but pay,
Lest that face of love and pity
Turn from us another day.[29]

The title of this hymn, incidentally, is *Lord of Glory who hast bought us.* The primitive motive of barter with God seems predominant. The obligation to give charity is often expressed in the commercial language of debt and repayment.

We lose what on ourselves we spend;
We have as treasure without end
Whatever, Lord, to Thee we lend,
Who givest all.

Whatever, Lord, we lend to Thee,
Repaid a thousand fold will be;
Most gladly will we give to Thee,
Who givest all;

To Thee, from whom we all derive,
Our life, our gifts, our power to give;
Oh, may we ever with Thee live.
Who givest all![30]

The commercial language of this hymn particularly offended W. R. Inge, a late nineteenth-century churchman, who wrote in *Outspoken Essays*, "If I desire a future life because I have made certain investments in good works, on which I hope to make a handsome profit, . . . that has no more to do with religion than if I invested my money on the faith of one of the very similarly worded prospectuses which I find on my breakfast table."[31] A poem for children echoed Inge's complaint that charity given with expectations of reward was not charity:

The Bible bid us give, and then
Not hope for any thing again:
'Tis good the poor to clothe and feed,
But such a motive spoils the deed;
And God, who understands your thought,
Sets all your goodness down for nought.[32]

However, the attitude urged most frequently in hymns was one of barter:

Yes, there are joys that cannot die,
With God laid up in store;
Treasure beyond the changing sky;
Brighter than golden ore.

The seeds which piety and love
Have scatter'd here below,
In the fair fertile fields above
To ample harvest grow.

The mite my willing hands can give
At Jesu's feet I lay;
Grace shall the humble gift receive,
Abounding grace repay.[33]

As the moral of a children's story expressed it, "He that giveth to the poor, lendeth to the Lord; and that which he hath given will He pay him again."[34]

Children's hymn books and the children's sections of denominational hymnals are a particularly fertile source for hymns of charity.

Oh, what can little hands do
  To please the King of heaven?
The little hands some work may try
To help the poor in misery:
  Such grace to mine be given!

O, what can little lips do
  To please the King of Heaven?
The little lips can praise and pray,
And gentle words of kindness say:
  Such grace to mine be given.[35]

Works of charity abounded among nineteenth-century Christians. One is hard pressed to find a novel of the period without a character who goes on regular rounds of ministering to the sick or orphaned. But charity, as many modern commentators have observed, is an ambulance service. It cannot cure the social ills of an industrialized society; it can only pick up the mangled bodies resulting from the disaster. And yet, until the end of the century the denominational hymnals, almost without exception, were content with a small number of hymns urging charity in their "Almsgiving" section, hymns such as these quoted.

This is not to say that there were no hymns urging a broader or more radical conception of social justice in the first half of the nineteenth century. There were a few, but they were not found in the denominational hymnals. Most were privately printed or printed in newspapers or appeared in hymnals such as the *National Chartist Hymn Book*, which was collected by the "moral right" Chartists who opposed O'Conner's tactics of violence.

During the 1830s and the 1840s working men were organizing and agitating for the Charter and Factory Acts. The anti-Corn Law agitation voiced further discontent with the social situation. Many of the participants in these movements were religious men, or at least came from religious backgrounds, and it was only natural that they should sing hymns. For instance, although Robert Owen rejected organized religions, in 1840 he published a book called *Social Hymns*. To those accustomed to church liturgy, the processionals of the church came readily to mind when marching music was needed.

> When in 1832 there was a gathering of 12,000 workers in Yorkshire to support Michael Sadler's Ten Hours Bill, the marchers . . . on their return from York, where they had listened to hours of speech-making by their leaders, Sadler, Richard Oastler, and Bull, . . . sang "Praise God from Whom All Blessings Flow" as they marched into Leeds in the pouring rain.[36]

Not all Chartists, however, were so conservative in their choice of hymns. A Chartist camp meeting near Rochdale in 1834 used the same tune—"Old Hundred"—for a different purpose; they sang

> They call the earth and land their own,
> And all they give us back's a stone.[37]

Hymns were a natural vehicle of protest to those men who were churchgoers. Some few wrote in the wrathful tradition of the Old Testament prophets, crying out against social wrong. One of these was Ebenezer Elliott, a Unitarian known as the "Corn Law Rhymer" for his anti-Corn Law poetry. In 1832 he published the following hymn in a Sheffield newspaper:

> When wilt thou save the people?
> O God of mercy, when?
> Not kings and lords, but nations,
> Not thrones and crowns, but men.
> Flowers of thy heart, O God, are they;
> Let them not pass, like weeds, away;
> Their heritage a sunless day;
> God save the people!
>
> Shall crime bring crime forever,
> Strength aiding still the strong?
> Is it thy will, O Father,
> That man shall toil for wrong?
> "No," say thy mountains; "No," thy skies;
> Man's clouded sun shall brightly rise,
> And songs ascend instead of sighs:
> God save the people!
>
> When wilt thou save the people?
> O God of mercy, when?

The people, Lord, the people,
Not crowns and thrones, but men.
God save thy people; thine they are,
Thy children, as thy angels fair;
From vice, oppression and despair:
God save thy people![38]

Interestingly, this hymn of Elliott's was one of the few radical hymns which would gain admission into some denominational hymnals in the next half century.

George Loveless, one of the Tolpuddle martyrs, wrote his "Hymn of Freedom" from prison:

God is our Guide! from field, from wave,
From plough, from anvil, and from loom,
We come, our country's rights to save,
And speak the tyrant faction's doom:
We raise the watchword "Liberty."
We will, we will, we will be free!

God is our Guide! No swords we draw,
We kindle not war's battle fires,
By reason, union, justice, law,
We claim the birthright of our sires;
We raise the watchword, "Liberty,"
We will, we will, we will be free![39]

In 1836 Edward Osler rewrote an earlier hymn of Isaac Watts' and published it in a collection of Anglican hymns:

Come, let us search our hearts, and try
  If all our ways be right:
Is God's great rule of equity
  Our practice and delight?

Have we to others truly done,
  As we would have them do?
Envious, unkind, and false to none;
  But always just and true?

In vain we speak of Jesus' blood,
  And place in Him our trust,
If, while we boast our love to God,
  We prove to men unjust.

Thou, before whom we stand in awe,
  And tremble, and obey,
Write in our hearts thy perfect law,
  And keep us in thy way.[40]

The best known early nineteenth-century hymn writer who considered social problems in his hymns was James Montgomery, the editor of the *Sheffield Iris*, who was jailed three times because of his revolutionary publications. Most of Montgomery's hymns tend toward evangelical introspection, but at times he spoke out against oppression:

Hail to the Lord's Anointed,
  Great David's greater Son!
Hail, in the time appointed,
  His reign on earth begun!
He comes to break oppression,
  To set the captive free,
To take away transgression,
  And rule in equity.

He comes with succour speedy
  To those who suffer wrong
To help the poor and needy,
  And bid the weak be strong;
To give them songs for sighing,
  Their darkness turn to light,
Whose souls, condemned and dying,
  Were precious in His sight.

By such shall He be feared
  While sun and moon endure,
Beloved, obeyed, revered;
  For he shall judge the poor,
Through changing generations,
  With justice, mercy, truth.
While stars maintain their stations,
  Or moons renew their youth.[41]

Some hymns accused the priests of the churches of oppression:

O Thou who didst create us all,
  With wonder-working skill—

Say, do the priests who on us call,
  Obey thy sovereign will?

While telling how the Saviour heal'd
  The deaf, the dumb, the blind—
They strive to keep for ever seal'd
  Our free-born powers of mind!

While telling how the Saviour toil'd
  Among the humble poor—
They scorn the widow and her child,
  And drive them from their door!

While telling how the Saviour fed
  The multitudes of old—
They rob us of our daily bread,
  And starve our babes for gold![42]

* * *

Our streets are filled with woe;
  Starvation and distress;
And widow's tears are seen to flow
  For children, fatherless.

And yet the priests declare,
  We must contented be!
But, by our country's wrongs, we swear,
  Our country shall be free![43]

Other hymns accused the wealthy of sanctimoniously using the church to hide their theft:

Thou shalt not steal! 'tis God that speaks
  With voice of dreadful majesty:
The thunder rolls, the mountain quakes,
  And trembling owns the Deity.

Thou shalt not steal! then why defraud
  The toil-worn labourer of his hire?
Why not deal out a just reward
  For work performed, which you require?

Thou shalt not steal? the poor must toil—
  Yes, from their cradles to their graves,—

For men whose hearts are full of guile,
Who steal their rights, and make them slaves!

Thou shalt not steal! ye men of wealth,
How came you by your heaps of ore?
O was it not by fraud and stealth,—
By deeds unchristian, and impure?

Thou shalt not steal! ye Pharisees,
Who pray with sanctimonious look,—
Remember, God your actions sees!—
You steal,—and he *shall* you rebuke![44]

There were some hymn writers who wrote in more directly mundane political terms, urging political organization under the People's Charter:

See the brave, ye spirit-broken,
Who uphold your righteous cause:
Who against them hath not spoken?
They are, just as Jesus was,
Persecuted
By bad men and wicked laws.

Rouse them from their silken slumbers,
Trouble them amidst their pride;
Swell your ranks, augment your numbers,
Spread the Charter far and wide:
Truth is with us,
God himself is on our side.[45]

As Louis James has pointed out, some of the radicals who came from religious backgrounds borrowed "the meter, style, and even the imagery of Christian hymnology" to express their anger:

Crucified! crucified every morn,
Beaten, and scourged and crowned with thorn!
Scorned, and spat on, and drenched with gall:
Brothers, how shall we bear that thrall?
Chorus:—Mary and Magdalen! Peter and John!
Answer the question, and bear it on.[46]

The title "hymn" was used by some political writers to express thoughts that were wholly secular. The following lyric was sold and sung as a hymn at a Chartist meeting near Sheffield in 1839:

Sad oppression now compels,
Working men to join themselves;
Ye suffers don't no more delay,
Work with might while it is day.

Refrain: I a Chartist now will be
And contend for liberty.

The Charter springs from Zion's hill,
Though opposed, go on it will;
Will you serve its sacred cause,
And receive its equal laws?

Union is our Captain's name,
By just laws he'll rule the main
Before his face he'll make to flee,
All bad laws of tyranny.

Brothers and sisters now unite,
And contend for your just rights;
Then soon the poor will happy be,
Glorious times we all shall see.

And the Chartists' song will be,
My country and sweet liberty.[47]

By mid-century English churches and churchmen were at least aware of if not more receptive to, the idea of Christian responsibility for social conditions. The majority of the clergy in the Anglican church were still being raised in a society that was oriented toward rural and aristocratic traditions, but if they read at all they were aware of the depressed conditions of the lower classes in the cities. Mid-century novels on the subject were numerous. Blue books of parliamentary commissions investigating conditions in mines and factories were available. English churchmen were shocked by the results of the religious census of 1851, which indicated that the majority of Englishmen were not regular churchgoers. This shock caused many to look at the traditional church in a new way. Edward Miall's journal, *Nonconformist*, ran a series of letters by workingmen in 1848 which denounced, among other things, the "almost total lack of sympathy manifested by the ministers of religion of every denomination with the privations, wants, and tastes of the working classes."[48] The Arnolds and Maurice were suggesting new avenues of Christian service. But by mid-century the church had taken little formal action on the Condition of England. Late in the century Scott Holland would recall the mid-century church's attitude in these terms: "In the huge and hideous cities the awful problem of industry lay like a bad dream, but Political Economy warned us off the ground. We were assured that the free play of competitive forces was bound to discover the true equipoise."[49]

After about 1850 a few hymns urging social justice appeared in denominational hymnals; but the hymnals largely reflected the complacent attitude of the general public. Mid-century hymns of social welfare were not an abundant domestic product; many of those that began to appear in England after mid-century were imported from America. According to Eric Routley, American religion has been characterized, except during the Revivals, by a liberal and social Gospel.[50] When Thomas Hughes wanted a hymn to symbolize Tom Brown's conversion to the Arnoldian ideal of social service, he chose James Russell Lowell's *Once to every man and nation* (1844):

Then to side with truth is noble,
When we share her wretched crust,
'Ere her cause bring fame and profit,
And 'tis properous to be just;
Then it is the brave man chooses,
While the coward stands aside
Till the multitude make virtue
Of the faith they had denied.

. . . .

Though the cause of evil prosper
Yet 'tis truth alone is strong;
Truth forever on the scaffold,
Wrong forever on the throne;
Yet that scaffold sways the future,
And, behind the dim unknown,
Standeth God within the shadow
Keeping watch above his own.

In a survey of nineteenth-century hymns of general social service, Percy Dearmer found that of the seven written before 1850, four were of American origin.[51]

In number the hymns of social service that came from within the denominational churches were few, although the number slowly increased. One of the reasons for the slowness of this growth was that during the second half of the century the churches' attention was focused elsewhere. With few exceptions, theologians marshaled their talents to fight the implications of Darwinism and German Biblical criticism. The Anglican church hierarchy was fighting a series of tract and courtroom battles with, among others, the authors of *Essays and Reviews* and Bishop Colenso.[52] The nonconformists were drawn into the theological controversy and spent much of their energy either defending Biblical inerrancy or developing a new theological justification for evangelicalism.[53]

Many of the churchmen who were concerned with the church's work in society were caught up in evangelical missionary work in a great revival movement that began in 1859 and, according to one historian, lasted until the years immediately preceding the First World War.[54] Because the goal of evangelical missions is conversion and salvation, their message was largely introspective and individualistic rather than extroverted and communal. When we look at the hymnbooks of the revival movement we rarely find any mention of social justice; we find, instead, a total absorption in God's love and offer of grace, Jesus' call to man, man's longing for (or rejection of) salvation, and the imperative to spread the evangel. For example, the Congregational Union's hymnbook for home missions, published in 1890, contains a section titled "Service," but the only service urged is spreading the gospel message.[55] The Pastoral Aid Society of the Anglican Church published a hymnbook for home missions in 1887 which contains not a single reference to worldly conditions.[56] Another Anglican home mission hymnal published twenty-six years later contained a selection of hymns for "Service and Mission," but these too were limited to spreading the gospel.[57] William Booth, the founder of the Salvation Army, complained, "I am sick of singing sentimental rubbish that had no connection with the soul's immediate interests. It won't do a man good to set him for ever and ever singing about the right and beautiful streets and stars and streams of Paradise."[58] And yet, the *Salvation Army Music* was almost entirely made up of hymns of the "over Jordan" and "heaven is my home" type. In one of the hymnbooks of the

Sankey and Moody campaign, there is only one hymn of secular service to man.[59]

It was not until the last decades of the nineteenth century that strong voices were heard within the Church of England urging a concerted movement for social justice, demanding that social justice be considered not only a part, but the most important part, of the Christian mission. Novels, such as Mrs. Humphry Ward's *Robert Elsmere*, proclaimed the traditional role of the Church to be a failure and demanded that new Christian action, action for social justice among the lower classes, take the major role in future church work. Tracts and books urged that reform efforts be coordinated and that the clergy be trained for social service:

> First, in order that the clergy may be equipped for dealing with social questions, our divinity students should receive thorough training in social economics—theoretical and practical. Second, in order to train Church members for effective service, classes for social study should be formed in all our congregations. Third, in order to secure unity in the sphere of social service, and prevent overlapping, the Churches should unite in a comprehensive scheme of social endeavour.[60]

The appendix to *Lux Mundi*, published in 1889, on "Some Aspects of Christian Duty," urged a transition from political to ethical economics.

The last three decades of the century were the "Age of the Social Question." In an effort to organize and coordinate individual efforts at charity, the Charity Organization Society was founded in 1869. Although the C. O. S. was successful in achieving its goals, it continued in the laissez faire tradition of opposing any extension of state or municipal action. This extension of social philosophy was left to the theoretically socialist organizations. In 1887 Stewart Headlam founded the Guild of St. Matthew, which urged the necessity of the Church's efforts to modify the social order in the light of Christian principles. The Christian Social Union was founded in 1889 under the chairmanship of Scott Holland. Its guiding principles were:

(i) To claim for the Christian Law the ultimate authority to rule social practice.

(ii) To study in common how to apply the moral truths and principles of Christianity to the social and economic difficulties of the present time.

(iii) To present Christ in practical life as the Living Master and King, the enemy of wrong and selfishness, the power of righteousness and love.[61]

During the last decades of the century, paralleling the movement of the churches into social reform there was a spurt of hymn-writing on the theme of social justice. The new hymns emphasized the brotherhood of all men:

Father of men, in whom are one
All humankind beneath thy sun,
'Stablish our work in thee begun.
Except the house be built of thee,
In vain the builder's toil must be:
O strengthen our infirmity!

Man lives not for himself alone,
In others' good he finds his own,
Life's worth in fellowship is known.
We, friends and comrades on life's way,
Gather within these walls to pray:
Bless thou our fellowship to-day.[62]

They urged the obliteration of earthly distinctions and a sharing of earthly burdens:

Bind us all as one together
In Thy Church's sacred fold,
Weak and healthy, poor and wealthy,
Sad and joyful, young and old.
Is there want, or pain, or sorrow?
Make us all the burden share.
Are there spirits crush'd and broken?
Teach us, LORD, to soothe their care.[63]

A Christian life was to be a life of service to the less fortunate, in imitation of Christ:

Teach us the lesson thou hast taught,
To feel for those thy Blood hath bought,
That every word, and deed, and thought
May work a work for thee.

For all are brethren, far and wide,
Since thou, O Lord, for all hast died:
Then teach us, whatsoe'er betide,
To love them all in thee.

In sickness, sorrow, want, or care,
Whate'er it be, 'tis ours to share;
May we, where help is needed, there
Give help as unto thee.[64]

By the end of the century the tone of some of these hymns had changed. Joining the quiet hymns of alms and service, were angry hymns of wrath, demanding social justice. Canon Henry Scott Holland made a powerful plea for reform; but Holland used the traditional metaphor of feeding the hungry with the gospel and he placed the responsibility for change on God:

Judge eternal, throned in splendour,
Lord of lords and King of kings,
With thy living fire of judgment
Purge this realm of bitter things:
Solace all its wide dominion
With the healing of thy wings.

Still the weary folk are pining
For the hour that brings release:
And the city's crowded clangour
Cries aloud for sin to cease;
And the homesteads and the woodlands
Plead in silence for their peace.

Crown, O God, thine own endeavour:
Cleve our darkness with thy sword:
Feed the faint and hungry heathen
With the richness of thy Word;
Cleanse the body of this empire
Through the glory of the Lord.[65]

Edward Carpenter placed the responsibility for righting the social, economic, and legal wrongs of the past squarely on England:

By your young children's eyes so red with weeping,
By their white faces aged with want and fear,

By the dark cities where your babes are creeping,
  Naked of you and all that makes life dear;
    From each wretched slum
    Let the loud cry come;
  Arise, O England, for the day is here!

. . . .

Over your face a web of lies is woven,
  Laws that are falsehoods pin you to the ground,
Labour is mocked, its just reward is stolen,
  On its bent back sits idleness encrowned.
    How long while you sleep,
    Your harvest shall it reap?
  Arise, O England, for the day is here![66]

G. K. Chesterton wrote with bitterness of man's selfishness and cruelty:

O God of earth and altar,
  Bow down and hear our cry,
Our earthly rulers falter,
  Our people drift and die;
The walls of gold entomb us,
  The swords of scorn divide,
Take not thy thunder from us,
  But take away our pride.

From all that terror teaches,
  From lies of tongue and pen,
From all the easy speeches
  That comfort cruel men,
From sale and profanation
  Of honour and the sword,
From sleep and from damnation,
  Deliver us, good Lord!

Tie in a living tether
  The prince and priest and thrall,
Bind all our lives together,
  Smite us and save us all;
In ire and exultation
  Aflame with faith, and free,
Lift up a living nation,
  A single sword to thee.[67]

By the end of the century the voices had become more strident in their demands for Christian social justice but the number of voices was still small. When Percy Dearmer became Secretary of the Christian Social Union in London in 1894 and tried to find suitable hymns for the mid-day sermons at the Church of St. Edmund, King and Martyr in Lombard Street, he noted the deficiency in the denominational hymnals. "We could find in the book used in the church no hymns that were concerned with man's duty to his neighbor; and we grew weary of the doleful tune and depressing words of 'Thy Kingdom come, O Lord.' We wanted hymns that expressed faith and hope."[68] Ten years later the editors of the 1904 revision of *Hymns Ancient and Modern* prefaced the new edition of that hymnal with an apology for the dearth of hymns on the subject of social conditions. This lack they attributed to the small interest on the part of hymn writers: "The defect lies largely with the composers of our hymns, and not with the compilers of the collections. . . . few hymn writers . . . apparently have been inspired by the social and national aspects of Christianity which appeal so largely to our time."[69]

By the end of the century the Church of England evidenced a strong movement toward social justice, but many members, perhaps the majority, would have agreed with R. W. Dale, who is reputed to have stated that ". . . he was convinced that the Church was in its very essence a religious institution established for religious ends; that social and political reforms, however desirable, were not the objects of its activity; and that so to regard them would be to degrade the Church into a political organization."[70] It is interesting to note that in a book written in 1910 on *The History of the English Church in the Nineteenth Century*, a chapter on "The Church and Social Problems" discusses only the subjects of divorce, remarriage, and the temperance movement.[71] In the two chapters on the subject of "Missions" only foreign missions were mentioned.

The nineteenth-century English churches have frequently been criticized for ignoring social problems. Certainly, at the end of the century there were still many people who believed that earthly problems were not the concern of the church. In the words of a contemporary observer,

> A Church to be a Church must maintain her protest that the problem which most concerns us to get solved is not outward concerns but the human heart; it is sin—and with this problem no one deals, or can deal, save Him who was crucified on Calvary for the sin of the world. . . . To

> blame the Churches for not taking sides in industrial troubles, and political struggles, is to blame them for not doing what they were not organized to do. For a Church to become a judge or a divider among men, is to depart from the fundamental idea of a Church and become something else. Get the kingdom of God within—in a man's heart—and you may trust him to seize every element which tends to the building up of the kingdom of God in the world outside him.[72]

In our own time these socially conservative feelings are still being voiced. There is always a danger that churches which emphasize humanistic and social concerns will tend to ignore the theological or specifically Christian aspects of religion. The eternal conflict between the mundane and the spiritual—the humanistic and the evangelical—aspects of the Christian message had surfaced and was openly argued at the end of the nineteenth century.

By the end of the century hymns advocating a radical, humanistic plan for social justice were being published—not by the denominational churches but by quasi-religious organizations. For example, the Labour Church, founded in 1891 in protest to the social values of the organized churches, published its first hymnbook in 1892.

> It contained some hymns found also in orthodox Christian hymnals, but none in which specifically Christian doctrine is proclaimed. Newman's "Lead Kindly Light," was sung in the Labour Churches; but there is no word in that hymn to which an agnostic could object. Jesus was named only once in this collection, in a verse by Whittier. Some mentioned God; others spoke the language of secular radicalism, good Cheer, or homely—even conservative—morality ("Be kind to thy father—for when thou wert young, Who lov'd thee more fondly than he").[73]

The Council of the Union of Ethical Societies published a hymnbook in 1905 which was entirely secular. Instead of praising God, the hymns praised "what is held to be supremely sacred; . . . Duty, Truth, Beauty, Nature and Life."[74] They placed the responsibility for social justice squarely on man. A hymn in that collection by A. C. Swinburne declares, in fact, that it was man's responsibility to act as God.

> East and west went my soul to find
> Light, and the world was bare and blind,
> And the soil herbless where she trod
> And saw men laughing scourge mankind,
> Unsmitten by the rod
> Of any God.

Then "Where is God" and where is aid?
Or what good end of these?" she said;
"Is there no God or end at all,
Nor reason with unreason weighed,
Nor force to disenthral
Weak feet that fall?

O fool, that for brute cries of wrong
Heard not the grey glad mother's song
Ring response from the hills and waves,
But heard harsh noises all day long
Of spirits that were slaves
And dwelt in graves.

With all her tongues of life and death,
With all her bloom and blood and breath,
From all years dead and all things done,
In th' ear of man the mother saith,
"There is no God, O son,
If thou be none."[75]

Another amazing little hymnbook printed for a "lyceum" in Newcastle in 1893, contains a collection of songs which combine evangelical otherworldliness with radical humanism and idealism. They envision the building of heaven on earth: "Thumb-worn creeds the truth repressing/ Will, like shadows, fade away"; "Want, from the starving poor depart!/Chains, from the captive fall!"; "Our world is waking from her dream,/ To snap her creed-forg'd chains asunder." Of the many "hymns" in this book that rail against social injustice and dream of the perfect world to come, we can quote only one here:

Sometime, when right comes uppermost
   The old wrongs all must die,
Pure love will conquer evil's host,
   And all his pow'r defy;
Then there shall be no starving poor
   Begging the rich for bread,
Peace will unlock the prison door,
   All shall be cloth'd and fed.

Sometime, when right comes uppermost
   The land must all be free,
Price then will be the same as cost—
   That good time yet shall be;

The right to home, the right to land,
The right to life and love,
The right to work with willing hand,
All men will then approve.

. . . .

Sometime, when right comes uppermost
The Angels from above
Will fill each heart, a holy host,
With wisdom, light, and love;
Then hypocrites, with former cant,
Will not pervert the word,
Nor Pharisees' self-righteous rant,
But all shall know the Lord.

Sometime, when right comes uppermost
Monopolies must fail,
Then capital no more will boast,
For labour shall prevail;
United true hearts, strong and brave,
Combined for human good,
Will then make wealth become the slave
Of one grand brotherhood.[76]

Although the critics of the churches' lack of social awareness in the late nineteenth century were a vocal group, they were a small minority. Beatrice Webb, in her diary in 1889, criticized this humanistic religion as "a pitiful attempt by poor humanity to turn its head round and worship its tail."[77] And when Mrs. Humphry Ward's novel *Robert Elsmere* was published in 1888, the public was so worried about the pagan Stoicism advocated by the novel's hero that Gladstone thought it necessary publicly to repudiate in ten thousand words the hero's new church—the "Order of Brotherhood." For most churchgoers the quiescent hymns contained in the hymnals seem to have answered the needs of the age. It is only the vanguard of late nineteenth-century society and our own generation which sees this lack as a glaring fault, which condemns the absence in the churches of a demand for social justice. This condemnation by modern historians is unhistorical. The church is a part of society; it does not, and cannot, exist in isolation. It cannot, therefore, be judged in isolation, for the values which it reflects in its cultural artifacts, such as hymns, are the values of the society of which it is a part.

The problems of social amelioration in the nineteenth century were not resolved by society in general for more than a hundred years. In an effort to cope with the problems of industrialization and urbanization and with the problems of poverty which had become much more obvious with urbanization, nineteenth-century society had begun in a pragmatic way. Englishmen avowed their humanitarianism and, faced with the facts of abuses, they declared that they must protect those members of society who could not protect themselves. Victorians passed those laws not because of their ideologies, but in spite of their ideologies.

The cumulative effect of these stopgap efforts of humanitarian Victorians to protect society's weaker members was an acceptance, by the end of the century, of the government's responsibility to ameliorate intolerable social conditions. The Victorian church was one institution of several existing in this society. The churches' attitude toward the poor, toward social welfare, was the attitude of society in general—they ignored the problem as long as they comfortably could. By the end of the century, however, they were forced to recognize the problem. Only when the attitudes and ideologies of society in general changed, did the churches' attitudes change. The hymns on the subject of social justice, or the dearth thereof, are an accurate reflection of the attitude of the churches.

CHAPTER VI

FOREIGN MISSION

THE Christian imperative to spread the evangel abroad is as old as Christianity itself. Matthew reported that Jesus told his disciples to "Go therefore and make disciples of all nations, baptising them in the name of the Father and of the Son and of the Holy Spirit, teaching them to observe all that I have commanded you." Such was the missionary fervor of the converts that within decades the Christian gospel was being preached throughout the Mediterranean world. It was by missionary effort in the third century that England was Christianized. In turn, it was from the monasteries in the British Isles, particularly in Ireland, that Christian learning was transmitted back to Europe between the sixth and eighth centuries. The history of the Christian church, as of any church militant, has been one of periodic religious aggression, which expresses itself in missionary expansion.

During the period of overseas exploration of the sixteenth and seventeenth centuries, the Catholic Church exhibited a crusading spirit in an intensive missionary effort, but for the most part, the Protestant countries showed scant enthusiasm for missionary enterprise. The English churches made little organized attempt to spread the gospel to heathen lands until the end of the eighteenth century, when the Revival imbued them with an imperative to evangelize. Missionary societies had been formed in the seventeenth and eighteenth centuries but their efforts were on a small scale. The Society for the Promotion of Christian Knowledge was founded in 1689 within the Anglican communion for the purpose of disseminating the printed gospel. The Society for the Propagation of the Gospel in Foreign Parts, another Anglican organization, was founded in 1701, but its missionary work in the eighteenth century was limited largely to the white colonists in foreign lands, although it did provide some schools for American and West Indian Negroes in the eighteenth century. In the 1760s the Methodists began their work among the West Indian Negroes. In 1784 the English Protestants had only about twenty missionary stations abroad. Of the approximately two hundred missionaries who manned these stations, more than half of them were Moravian. There were no British missionaries in Africa or Asia; nor did the Church of England have any bishops outside of Britain.[1]

It was not until the last decade of the eighteenth century that enthusiasm for mission led to the creation of the great British missionary societies. In 1792 the Baptist Missionary Society was formed and sent its first missionary, William Carey, to India. In 1795 the interdenominational London Missionary Society was founded and sent a band of workers to the South Sea Islands. The following year the Scottish Presbyterians formed two societies: the Church of Scotland Foreign Missions and the Glasgow Missionary Society. In 1799 the evangelicals of the Church of England formed the Society for Missions to Africa and the East, afterwards to become the Church Missionary Society. And in 1813, the same year in which Parliament removed the East India Company's restrictions on missionary work in India, the Methodists founded the Wesleyan Missionary Society.

The foreign missionary work of the early years of the nineteenth century was pursued with enthusiasm but within a generation this enthusiasm once again languished. Half a century after its foundation, for instance, the Church Missionary Society could count only 172 European missionaries at work in foreign lands.[2] Missionary work continued throughout the century: missionaries were sent out individually or in small groups to risk their lives in heathen lands and their reports and exhortations to greater effort were circulated by hand and by missionary magazines to the missionary groups of children and adults which met regularly in churches. But the great expansion of foreign missionary work occurred only in the last third of the century. This period of enthusiastic missionary effort, which began in approximately 1870, coincided with two other revivals in England: the first was the revival of popular evangelical religion characterized by the visits of Moody and Sankey; the second was the popular revival of imperialism.

The enthusiasm of the religious revival led to a great expenditure of lives, money, and effort in missionary work abroad. By the time of the Centenary of the Church Missionary Society in 1899, that society alone was maintaining 1,096 European missionaries, 343 native clergy, 5,747 other native teachers, 2,257 schools, and 30 hospitals.[3] By 1887 British missionary societies were annually spending approximately £1 1/4 million on foreign missions, a sum which had steadily increased for fifteen years.[4] Hymnbooks for the use of heathen or newly converted congregations had been translated into 150 languages and dialects by 1892.[5] By 1890 the British and Foreign Bible Society had circulated the Scriptures in 291 languages.[6]

We are not, however, primarily concerned here with the work of foreign missionaries, but with the attitudes of Englishmen toward those missions, and specifically, the attitudes which Englishmen voiced in their hymns. These attitudes underwent a great change during the nineteenth century. At the beginning of the century, most missionary hymns were extremely limited in vision—salvation was restricted to the few. Those people excluded from God's grace, those carelessly labeled "the heathen," "men benighted," or "the rude barbarian," were considered the rightful object of Christian mission by an elect people. Missionary effort, by its very nature, implies a position of superiority of the missionary. If the Briton abroad did not consider his product, whether it was religion, politics, medicine, or industrial production, to be superior, he would have little reason to urge it on others. For approximately the first three-quarters of the century this attitude of superiority dominated missionary hymns. It was only at the end of the century that prophetic and wrathful voices were raised in hymns against the vanity, boastfulness, and lack of Christian humility and brotherhood of the Christian missions.

In the early years of the century an attitude of pity and condescension for inferior nonChristian folk was unabashedly voiced in missionary hymns.

O'er the realms of pagan darkness,
  Let the eye of pity gaze;
See the kindreds of the people,
  Lost in sin's bewild'ring maze:
Darkness brooding on the face of all the earth.

. . . .

Let the Heathen, now adoring
  Idol-gods of wood and stone,

Come, and, worshipping before Thee,
Serve the Living God alone:
Let thy glory fill the earth, as floods the sea.[7]

This attitude was not limited to hymns, of course. In the *Missionary Book for the Young*, the central character, Mrs. Darnley, explained Chinese customs to her children's missionary group in terms of opprobrium:

"You once told us, Mrs. Darnley, that the Chinese were a clever and an educated people; but this custom of feeding ghosts is silly and childish. How can they be so foolish?"

"The Bible says that the heathen 'are vain in their imaginations, and their foolish hearts are darkened'; for, 'professing themselves to be wise, they become fools,' Rom. i. 21, 22: this explains all the foolish and wicked things the heathen are guilty of through all the world."[8]

The customs of other lands were viewed with incomprehension and horror and children in the Sunday Schools and missionary groups were spared none of the details of these horrors. We have the distinct impression, in fact, that these scare tactics were purposefully used to encourage enthusiastic participation in the missionary effort. When, in one of her later sessions, Mrs. Darnley shows her class a picture of an Indian widow being burned on her husband's funeral pyre, the narrator comments, "It was a painful scene, and the kind lady would have gladly spared the feelings of her young friends; but she was anxious that they should feel that heathenism is a system of misery and cruelty."[9] In another publication of the Religious Tract Society, this one for Sunday Schools, the child is asked to imagine what his life would be like if he had been born in a foreign land:

Suppose that you had been born in some of those distant lands, how miserable you would have been! There mothers leave their children by the side of a river, from which large alligators come and devour them, or they murder them with their own hands, or treat them with the utmost cruelty. There the people throw themselves down in the middle of the roads, that the immense heavy car, which contains their idol, may be dragged over them, by which they may be crushed to death; and all this they do that they may please their god. Oh! do you not pity them? Will you not pray for them? Are you not very thankful to God that you are not so ignorant and deluded as they?[10]

English children were taught to sing hymns of England's superiority. They were told to be thankful for their superior God as well as for their earthly blessings, a gift of their God.

I thank the goodness and the grace
  Which on my birth have smiled,
And made me, in these Christian days,
  A happy English child.

I was not born, as thousands are,
  Where God was never known;
And taught to pray a useless prayer
  To blocks of wood and stone.

I was not born a little slave,
  Beneath a burning sun,
To wish I were but in the grave,
  And all my labour done.

I was not born without a home,
  Or in some broken shed,
A gipsy baby, taught to roam,
  And steal my daily bread.

My God, I thank Thee, who hast planned
  A better lot for me,
And placed me in this happy land,
  Where I may hear of Thee.[11]

In one of his best-known, and to this day one of the most frequently reprinted, missionary hymns, Reginald Heber, later Bishop of Calcutta, voiced the same attitude of Christian superiority to the "benighted" heathens:

From Greenland's icy mountains,
  From India's coral strand,
Where Afric's sunny fountains
  Roll down their golden sand,
From many an ancient river,
  From many a palmy plain,
They call us to deliver
  Their land from error's chain.

What though the spicy breezes
Blow soft o'er Ceylon's isle;
Though every prospect pleases,
And only man is vile:
In vain with lavish kindness
The gifts of God are strown;
The heathen in his blindness
Bows down to wood and stone.

Can we, whose souls are lighted
With wisdom from on high,
Can we to men benighted
The lamp of life deny?
Salvation! O salvation!
The joyful sound proclaim,
Till each remotest nation
Has learned Messiah's Name.[12]

Heber skillfully contrasted the natural beauty and abundance of the nonChristian lands to the "vile," "blind," and "benighted" heathens. His attitude, while condescending, was one of pity. Other missionary hymns were not so gentle:

Look down, O God, with pitying eye,
And view the desolations round;
See what wide realms in darkness lie,
And hurl their idols to the ground![13]

The assumption of British superiority in missionary hymns was applied not only to the uncivilized "barbarians" but also to the religions of civilized nations:

Arm of the Lord, thy power extend,
Let Mahomet's imposture end;
Break Superstition's Papal chain,
And the proud scoffer's rage restrain.[14]

This feeling of superiority came to the British from several sources. An awareness of the separate and distinct character of the culture of the "island race" has been a theme of British literature since its earliest period. Since the fifteenth century English patriotism has been a common boast of Englishmen abroad. By 1815 British empire and British industry had obviously outstripped its continental rivals. This secular superiority was reinforced in religion by English protestantism's Calvinist heritage. Calvin's doctrine of election, the predestined salvation only of God's elect few, was accepted by most seventeenth- and eighteenth-century English protestant churches. Calvinist hymns filled seventeenth- and eighteenth-century English hymnbooks. One such hymn published in a hymnbook as late as 1891 reads:

All the elected train
  Were chosen in their Head,
To all eternal good,
  Before the worlds were made;
Chosen to know the Prince of Peace,
And taste the riches of His grace.

Chosen to faith and hope,
  To purity and love,
To all the life of God,
  To all the things above;
Chosen to prove salvation sure;
Chosen to reign for evermore.[15]

Although not all Calvinist hymns stated the doctrine of election this baldly, the sentiments were recognized as valid by many protestants. August Toplady's starkly Calvinistic hymn, *Rock of Ages, cleft for me*, was one of the most popular hymns of the nineteenth century; its popularity extended to nonCalvinists as well as Calvinists. It remained a favorite of Gladstone long after he espoused high-Church views and it was sung at his funeral. Although Calvinist theology holds terrifying prospects for religious men unconvinced of their own election, it serves as a liberating force for those who feel they have been saved. (Considering that Calvinist theology dictates that only a few will be saved, the number of Calvin's followers who counted themselves among the few is amazing.) The elect are assured of the rightness of their beliefs; they can, therefore, embark upon mission without questioning their right to do so. Although the Methodists in the eighteenth century rejected the rigid predestination of Calvinism in their theology, the feeling of superiority in their belief, which Calvinism had helped to establish in English religion over a period of three centuries, lingered on for most Englishmen.

If feelings of security and superiority came from the Calvinist heritage, the imperative to mission came from the evangelical heritage. The evangelicals aimed at a personal inward conversion experience for their converts. According to several psychological studies, a frequent result of the conversion experience is the urge to spread that experience.[16] Almost immediately after his conversion, John Wesley felt impelled to carry the good news to those less fortunate. It was Wesley's and Whitefield's field preaching to the unchurched, more than anything else, that alienated the establishment from the evangelical revival. "Enthusiasm," one aspect of which is the compulsion to evangelize, has typically been an embarrassment to the staid organizational church. It is no coincidence that the missionary societies were founded largely by evangelicals. They felt an imperative to mission among the heathen which is prominently displayed in the missionary hymns.

Let the Indian, let the Negro,
  Let the rude barbarian see
That divine and glorious conquest,
  Once obtained on Calvary;
    Let the gospel
  Loud resound from pole to pole.[17]

The ebullience of this urge to mission could not be contained;

Tell it out among the heathen that
  the Saviour reigns! Tell it out!
  Tell it out!
Tell it out among the nations, bid
  them burst their chains! Tell
  it out! Tell it out![18]

Another reason for the compulsion to mission was the conviction that those who were outside the church would be eternally damned. The eighteenth-century poet and hymn writer, William Cowper, had denied that the heathen were automatically condemned to hell:

Ten thousand sages lost in endless woe
For ignorance of what they could not know!
That speech betrays at once a bigot's tongue;
Charge not a God with such outrageous wrong.[19]

But early nineteenth-century foreign mission hymns for the most part took a different attitude. They considered all non-Christian lands to be the dwelling place of the devil:

Set up thy throne where Satan reigns,
On Afric's shore, on India's plains;
On wilds and continents unknown!
And make the universe Thine own.[20]

Heathen gods are equated with the Antichrist, who must be vanquished by the word of the Christian God:

Then shall the heathen, fill'd with awe,
Learn the bless'd knowledge of thy law;
And Antichrist, on every shore,
Fall from his throne to rise no more.[21]

The hymns taught that eternal life was possible only for Christians, that death was the fate of unbaptised heathens.

Hark! hark, the voice of numbers,
  Whose number no man knows,
Awakes the Church's slumbers
  And stirs her long repose:
The wail of men and mothers,
  The children's piteous cry,
"Come, help us, we are brothers;
  Come help us, ere we die."

. . . .

There no baptismal blessing
  Rests on the infant brow;
No lips, our God confessing,
  Pledge there the holy vow;
No ear enraptured listens
  To Jesus' words of grace;
No eye with longing glistens
  To see Him face to face.

Still onward to the river,
  Which all must cross, they move,
And meet the dread Forever,
  Unweeting, "God is love."
And yet the Sun has risen
  Of everlasting day;
The bars of death's dark prison
  Our life has borne away.[22]

There is an urgency to this missionary message; sinful heathen souls must be snatched from the gates of hell:

Awake! arise! the Heathen fall
  Before the power of sin and death;
Go sound the Gospel's trumpet call,
  And rescue them from hell beneath.[23]

The third motive of mission was a sense of British Christian patriotism. Many English Christians believed that their nation was especially covenanted to God. In a personal testimony to Sunday School children, a man who had traveled widely urged English children to stay in England if they wanted to remain good Christians: "Never was I more glad than when I again put my foot in old England. Say what you will, there is no place like it. If you wish to forget God, go abroad; but if you like bibles, sabbaths, and sunday schools, stay at home."[24] Even after the religious census of 1851 clearly indicated that a large part of the population did not attend a church regularly, many Britons continued to think of themselves as a singularly Christian nation. In their hymns they exhibited at times an Old Testament assurance that they were the Chosen People of God:

While Britain, favour'd of the skies,
Recalls the wonders God hath wrought;
Let grateful joy adoring rise,
And warm to rapture ev'ry thought.

When wicked men combined their power,
And doom'd these Isles their certain prey,
Thy hand forbad the fatal hour;
Their evil plots in ruin lay.

Again our restless cruel foes,
Resumed, avow'd, a fresh design;
Again to save us God arose,
And Britain owns the hand divine.

Such great deliv'rance God has wrought!
And still the care of heaven
Has down to us salvation brought!
All praise to God be giv'n.[25]

The hymns tell the hymn singer that the British are specially covenanted by God. He protects the island race from their enemies—"and Britain owns the hand divine."

As Christians, and particularly as God's chosen people, the British were responsible for spreading the gospel to "souls in heathen darkness lying." As E. W. Benson, Archbishop of Canterbury at the end of the century, expressed it, the Church of England was "charged with the world's Christianity."[26] Jesus' sacrifice had bought all heathen souls; it was the duty of the first-saved to teach all other nations. Failure to meet this responsibility would be judged against them:

> Haste, oh, haste, and spread the tidings
>   Wide to earth's remotest strand;
> Let no brother's bitter chidings
>   Rise against us,—when we stand
>   In the judgment,—
>   From some far, forgotten land.[27]

The hymns repeatedly stressed the urgency of mission. The task must be undertaken regardless of the difficulties.

> 'Neath many a toil by land and sea
>   An English life is bending;
> Lord, grant that they who onward press
>   To tasks of Thy creation,
> May onward bear through toil and stress
>   The faith that made their nation.[28]

This was the White Man's Burden, particularly the English white man's burden: honor, decency, and Christian responsibility compelled the English to accept the burden of mission, regardless of the hardships it imposed.

By the end of the century patriotic pride knew few bounds. At the Diamond Jubilee Service in 1897, Queen Victoria chose the hymn, *The day thou gavest, Lord, is ended.* In this hymn, the expanding Christian British Empire becomes synonymous with the Kingdom of God.

> We thank Thee that Thy Church unsleeping,
>   While earth rolls onward into light,

Through all the world her watch is keeping,
And rests not now by day or night.

As o'er each continent and island
The dawn leads on another day,
The voice of prayer is never silent,
Nor dies the strain of praise away.

The sun that bids us rest is waking
Our brethren 'neath the western sky,
And hour by hour fresh lips are making
Thy wondrous doings heard on high.

So be it, Lord; Thy Throne shall never,
Like earth's proud empires, pass away;
Thy Kingdom stands, and grows for ever,
Till all Thy creatures own Thy sway.[29]

John Ellerton, the author, mentions in the last stanza that earthly empires are ephemeral, but there is no mistaking the pride in British missionary accomplishment.

Two years later, at the centenary celebration of the Anglican Church Missionary Society, patriotic pride in a century of successful foreign mission was effusive.

The years brought life and blessing
To many a tribe and tongue,
All kindreds of the peoples
Unite with ours their song;
Redeemed from out the nations,
His servants shout and say,—
"The Lord hath done great things for us
We praise His Name to-day!"[30]

The conquest of heathens for Christ and Empire was a latter-day crusade for many Christians. Conversions were counted as trophies.

Great God, we bless Thy Name
For all Thy grace has done,
Thy Gospel's growing fame,
The trophies it has won.[31]

Surprisingly, military imagery was scarce in hymns specifically for foreign mission, but there were some hymns which likened foreign mission to military conquest.

See, o'er the world, wide open doors inviting;
Soldiers of Christ, arise and enter in!
Christians, awake! your forces all uniting,
  Send forth the Gospel, break the chains of sin.[32]

One special missionary conquest must be mentioned here. During the nineteenth century the British made a determined effort to convert the Jews. Six separate societies were formed in Britain, the sole purpose of which was to evangelize Jews both at home and in foreign lands. This movement to convert the Jews was not limited to Britain. *The Missionary Year-Book for 1889* lists forty-three worldwide societies which were founded during the nineteenth century exclusively for this purpose. Most Victorian hymnbooks which contain hymns of foreign mission, also contain at least one hymn of "Mission to the Jews." Edward Bickersteth's *Christian Psalmody* contains seven! The hymns speak of the Jews as "outcasts," "soul-blind," "who from Thy favour fell." *Hymns Ancient and Modern* (1904) contains one hymn which declares the Jews guilty of Jesus' betrayal, asks for their forgiveness, but at the same time demands their repentance:

Though the Blood, betray'd and spilt,
  On the race entail'd a doom,
Let its virtue cleanse the guilt,
  Melt the hardness, chase the gloom;
Lift the veil from off their heart,
  Make them Israelites indeed,
Meet once more for lot and part
  With Thy household's genuine seed.

Thou that didst Thy dews outpour,
  Crowning alien grafts with fruit,
Soon the native growths restore,
  Making glad the parent root:
Ah! but let not pride ensnare
  Souls that need to mourn their sin;
Still the boughs adopted spare,
  And the outcasts—graft them in![33]

The assurance of superiority of Christians over Jews is blatant in the hymns. God is no longer the God of the Jews, but the exclusive God of the English Christians, who invite "Abra'am's seed" to share their God:

Great God of Abra'm! hear our prayer;
Let Abra'am's seed thy mercy share:
O may they now at length return,
And look on Him they pierced, and mourn.

Remember Jacob's flock of old:
Bring home the wand'rers to thy fold:
Remember too thy promised word,
"Israel at last shall seek the Lord."

Lord, put thy law within their hearts,
And write it in their inward parts:
The veil of darkness rend in two,
Which hides Messiah from their view.

Oh haste the day, foretold so long,
When Jew and Greek, (a glorious throng,)
One House shall seek, one prayer shall pour,
And one Redeemer shall adore.[34]

This is not to say that all missionary hymns were arrogant hymns exhibiting a zenophobic racial or national superiority. There have always been some hymns of worldwide Christian brotherhood. In a plea for Christian unity in the eighteenth century, for instance, Benjamin Beddome wrote,

Let party names no more
The Christian world o'erspread;
Gentile and Jew, and bond and free,
Are one in Christ their Head.[35]

James Montgomery, the Sheffield newspaper publisher who suffered for his revolutionary social and political views, and whose hymns on social justice we quoted before, wrote a number of hymns urging worldwide Christian mission without mentioning ethnic or national superiority.

People of many a tribe and tongue,
  Men of strange colours, climates, lands,
Have heard Thy truth, Thy glory sung.
  And offer'd prayer with holy hands.

. . . .

From east to west, the sun survey'd
  From north to south, adoring throngs;
And still, where evening stretch'd her shade,
  The stars came forth to hear their songs.

. . . .

Yet one prayer more—and be it one
  In which both heaven and earth accord;
Fulfil Thy promise to Thy Son,
  Let all that breathe call Jesus Lord![36]

There were great missionary hymns written during the nineteenth century which asked simply and humbly for God's help in leading "the erring children" to God. Such a one is Frances Ridley Havergal's *Lord, speak to me, that I may speak* (1872).

But a survey of the nineteenth-century hymns of foreign mission shows that the majority are not of this type. Most speak in terms of a condescending paternalism—"heathens," "rude barbarians," and "sin-darkened creatures" are phrases casually used to describe the subjects of foreign mission. By the end of the century, however, there is an indication in the hymnbooks that these attitudes were beginning to change. Certainly, it can be no coincidence that by the end of the Victorian era a number of events were casting doubts on the British Christian's assumption of superiority. Uncertainty marked much British thinking, both within and without the church, by the end of the century. By mid-century most church people were beginning to realize that many Englishmen at home were in as great need of missionary persuasion as dark-skinned non-Englishmen. Novelists had a heyday portraying the religious ignorance of the lower classes. Benjamin Disraeli, in *Sybil*, for instance, characterized the religious state of the metal-workers of Wodgate in the most satirical terms:

"And what is your name, my good fellow?"
"They call me Tummas, but I ayn't got no second name; but now I'm

married I mean to take my wife's, for she has been baptized, and so has got two."

"Yes, sir," said the girl . . . ; "I be a reg'lar born Christian and my mother afore me, and that's what few gals in the Yard can say. Thomas will take to it himself when work is slack; and he believes now in our Lord and Saviour Pontius Pilate, who was crucified to save our sins; and in Moses, Goliath, and the rest of the Apostles."

"Ah! me," thought Morley, "and could not they spare one Missionary from Tahiti for their fellowcountrymen at Wodgate?"[37]

The church at home was placed under attack also by the new biological and archeological discoveries and German Biblical criticism. In the case of Bishop Colenso of Natal, the attack originated from the missionary church abroad. By the end of the century British economic expansion was being challenged by German and American competition; the slowing of economic expansion which occurred in the last three decades of the century created a mood of uncertainty in some quarters. The Boer War raised questions about the morality of international conquest and dominance.

With the faltering confidence of the last years of the century, came a new type of missionary hymn, urging world peace and brotherhood and warning against arrogance. At the turn of the century the voices were few, but they were strong in their objection to the proud and arrogant attitudes with which the British viewed their Empire. Rudyard Kipling's powerful "Recessional," written for the London *Times* in the year of Queen Victoria's Diamond Jubilee, makes an ironic contrast to Ellerton's *The day thou gavest, Lord, is ended.* It warns, with the doomsaying voice of an Old Testament prophet, that the Kingdom of God will endure long after the British Empire, with its human qualities of military force, pomp, glorification of power, boasting, and reliance on earthly science, is gone:

God of our fathers, known of old,
Lord of our far-flung battle line,
Beneath whose awful hand we hold
Dominion over palm and pine:
Lord God of hosts, be with us yet
Lest we forget, lest we forget.

The tumult and the shouting dies;
The captains and the kings depart;
Still stands thine ancient sacrifice,

An humble and a contrite heart:
Lord God of hosts, be with us yet,
Lest we forget, lest we forget.

Far-called our navies melt away,
On dune and headland sinks the fire;
Lo, all pomp of yesterday
Is one with Nineveh and Tyre!
Judge of the nations, spare us yet,
Lest we forget, lest we forget.

If drunk with sight of power we loose
Wild tongues that have not thee in awe,
Such boasting as the Gentiles use
Or lesser breeds without the law:
Lord God of hosts, be with us yet,
Lest we forget, lest we forget.

For heathen heart that puts her trust
In reeking tube and iron shard;
All valiant dust that builds on dust,
And guarding, calls not thee to guard;
For frantic boast and foolish word,
Thy mercy on thy people, Lord![38]

For the London Missionary Society's exhibition of 1908 John Oxenham wrote a hymn of brotherhood of all races which would help to point the way to a new attitude toward foreign mission:

In Christ there is no East or West,
  In Him no South or North;
But one great fellowship of love
  Throughout the whole wide earth.

In Him shall true hearts everywhere
  Their high communion find,
His service is the golden cord
  Close binding all mankind.

Join hands then, brothers of the faith,
  Whate're your race may be.
Who serves my Father as a son
  Is surely kin to me.

In Christ now meet both East and West
  In Him meet South and North;
All Christly souls are one in Him
  Throughout the whole wide earth.[39]

John Addington Symonds' *These things shall be! A loftier race* sang of scientific progress and world brotherhood:

Nation with nation, land with land,
Unarmed shall live as comrades free;
In every heart and brain shall throb
The pulse of one fraternity.[40]

This change in attitude toward foreign mission and toward foreigners is seen at approximately the same time that the popular enthusiasm for empire began to wane—at the turn of the century, during the Boer War. It would be several decades before these hymns urging Christian world brotherhood became a noticeable quantity in the denominational hymnals—social attitudes change slowly. But by the end of the century we see a beginning of a new attitude.

CHAPTER VII

IMAGERY

THE language that a society uses reveals much about that society's conscious and unconscious ideals; the images* that it uses are chosen because of its occupations and preoccupations. The imagery of the Lord's Prayer, which varies slightly in different churches, is a pertinent example. The Anglican Church has traditionally been the church of the establishment; its language is the language of a landowning class in an agricultural age. It naturally uses images of the land: "Forgive us our trespasses as we forgive those who trespass against us." The nonconformist churches, on the other hand, originated largely among the urban middle class. Their language is, just as naturally, the language of commerce: "Forgive us our debts as we forgive our debtors." Although the imagery in Christian hymns is determined by scriptural imagery to a great extent, the choice of which of these biblical images to use is determined by the hymn writer and, indirectly, by the culture of which he is a part.

This chapter is not an exhaustive study of the images employed in nineteenth-century English hymns; such an inquiry would require a separate volume. However, certain prominent images in the hymns have forcibly struck the author because of their repeated use. It seems worthwhile to note here some outstanding examples of Victorian attitudes that are indicated by hymn imagery and to hope that further

* I use "images" here in the literary sense of a word-picture.

research in this area might be encouraged. We will look at only four groups of images here: the evangelical images of blood and wounds associated with the crucifixion; sentimental images as exemplified by the idealization of the family and the figure of the mother; rural images of an agricultural society; and military images of wrath and war.

The most prominent single group of images in nineteenth-century hymns is, perhaps, that associated with the crucifixion. Images of wounds, blood, and pain are particularly frequent in the early evangelical hymn books because of the evangelical emphasis on the individual's personal relationship to God through the mediation of Christ's sacrifice. But these introspective, physically intimate hymns are not limited to the evangelicals—they are included to some extent in all of the early hymn books. The four most prominent, prolific, and enduring hymn writers of the eighteenth century, Isaac Watts, William Cowper, John Newton, and Charles Wesley, each wrote a large number of hymns on the subject of the crucifixion and its redemptive significance for man. Man could be saved through Christ and the "through" becomes literal as well as figurative in many of these hymns. They speak freely and repeatedly of bowels, cavities, blood, incisions, and flesh. The singer yearns to "fly to the bosom of Jesus," to "drink the living water," to "wash in the fountain of blood."

During the course of the nineteenth century the vivid images of washing-in-the-fountain-of-blood or hiding-in-wounds-of-Christ decreased in frequency in the denominational hymnals. The blood imagery of the eighteenth-century hymns, the reference to bathing in Christ's blood or crawling into his wounds, proved unacceptable to many late-Victorians—the intimate anatomical details were disapproved by a proper middle class that insisted on calling a "leg" a "limb" or that covered table legs. Some of these hymns have been retained in modern denominational hymnals, although in many cases the most extreme of the intimate images have been deleted.

Revival hymns, on the other hand, continued to give a prominent place to these introspective and intimate details. This general trend may be a social-class distinction—revivals were aimed primarily at the lower classes, which were not thoroughly indoctrinated with middle class ideas of proper behavior. The attitude of the churches toward these hymns may also be an indication of the perennial tendency of any church to become more concerned with corporate worship and liturgy and less concerned with individual pietism as the church becomes established in the social scheme. At the same time, revival religions tend to return to an emphasis of the intimate details of Christ's sacrifice because of the introspective, pietistic nature of most religious revivals.

B. F. Crawford's study of nineteenth-century American Methodist hymnbooks indicates that the American Methodist hymnbooks followed this pattern. In Crawford's words,

> . . . it is evident that there is a growing emphasis on worship, that it is becoming more formal and stately, more ritualistic, and that its function and value in life has greatly broadened. The trend in worship is away from an evangelistic emphasis with its individualistic function to that of a corporate and social emphasis with a function to release for life all the divine resources that may be available through the grace and goodness of God.[1]

The images of most nineteenth-century hymns about the crucifixion were blander and more objective, less enthusiastic, less intimate, and thus, more acceptable to churches which had become staid and were accepted into the social order.

Although nineteenth-century hymns were less embarrassingly intimate in physical detail than eighteenth-century hymns, they tended to be more mawkishly sentimental. When the Congregational Union published a Supplement to its denominational hymnbook in 1874 to meet the new demands of congregations, the new hymnal was criticized largely because of "the number of hysterically-sentimental hymns."[2] But sentimentality was acceptable to many late-Victorians, particularly if it served a didactic function. We have only to look at the literary and visual arts of the period to see that many late-Victorians considered a good wallow in morally uplifting sentimentality a valid function of the arts. Victorian literature abounds in deathbed scenes, particularly deaths of innocent children or moral and earnest individuals who have been wronged. When Charles Dickens allowed Little Nell to die a heartrending death in *The Old Curiosity Shop*, the public reaction was enormous; although some of Dickens' readers objected to the injustice of Little Nell's end, we can imagine the satisfaction of many more families as they, like Gladstone, shed sympathetic tears over Little Nell's untimely but edifying end. A survey of church literature for children reveals an abundance of stories about the lives of children whose early and pious deaths are expected to set a good example for the reader. *The Child's Companion; or Sunday Scholar's Reward*, a magazine produced by the Religious Tract Society from 1824 and continuing well into the twentieth century, and *The Child's*

Own Magazine, published by the Sunday School Union from 1852 to 1871, contained such stories in almost every issue. The reason for late Victorian love of sentimentality in art and literature was, perhaps, that it was one of the few emotional outlets for people who were expected to be earnest, sober, brave, strong, bold, and righteous.

Hymnbooks of the late nineteenth century abound in sentimental hymns. Hymnbooks for children and for revivals are the most sentimental, but by the end of the century even the staid *English Hymnal* and *Hymns Ancient and Modern* had been invaded by melodramatic and sentimental hymns. We will discuss only one of these sentimental and melodramatic late nineteenth-century images here: family life and, especially, motherhood.

In Victorian hymns, Christianity is oftened explained in terms of the family, which is a haven of peace and security and source of Christian learning. God, of course, is the father. Jesus becomes the brother or the friend. But the central role in the Victorian Christian family belongs to the mother. She is the source of wisdom and it is she who leads her children to Christianity. For the most part, however, the mother is not an active figure, but a passive symbol.

To late Victorians, motherhood represented all that was best in the idealized Christian life: peace, selfless love, gentleness, patience, forgiveness, simplicity, and virtue. She was responsible for teaching Christian morality to the children. The image of motherhood is one of extreme quietism, acceptance of one's earthly lot, and anticipation of heaven. As one hymn from the Torrey-Alexander revival put it:

Oft within a little cottage,
As the shadows gently fall,
While the sunlight touches softly
One sweet face upon the wall,
There the lonely loved ones gather
And in hushed and tender tone
Ask each other's full forgiveness
For the wrong that each had done.
Chorus: As I wondered why this custom,
At the closing of the day,
"Tis because," they sweetly answered
"It was once our mother's way."

If our home be bright and cheery,
If it holds a welcome true,
Op'ning wide its door of greeting

To the many—not the few;
If we share our Father's bounty,
With the needy day by day,
'Tis because our hearts remember,
"This was ever mother's way."

Chorus: Gentle mother, loving mother,
Sainted mother, fond and true;
Resting now in peace with Jesus,
Loving hearts remember you.

Sometimes when our hearts grow weary,
Or our task seems very long,
When our burdens look too heavy,
And we deem the right all wrong,
Then we gain anew fresh courage,
As once more we rise to say,
"Let us do our duty bravely,
This was our dear mother's way."

O, how oft it comes before us
That sweet face upon the wall!
And her mem'ry seems more precious,
As we on her Saviour call:
That at last, when ev'ning shadows
Mark the closing of life's day,
They may find us calmly waiting
To go home our mother's way.[3]

While the mother is the symbol of spiritual Christian purity, the child is often, like the prodigal son, the symbol of physical lust and the evil temptations of the mundane world. He disobeys his mother's directions, wanders from the strait and narrow path, and is punished by his mother's death. This sentimentalized, objectified mother image is used as a reward or punishment for the child's behavior.

When I was but a little child,
How well I recollect
How I would grieve my mother
With my folly and neglect;
And now that she has gone to heav'n,
I miss her tender care:
O Saviour, tell my mother I'll be there.

Chorus: Tell mother I'll be there,
In answer to her pray'r;
This message, blessed Saviour, to her bear;
Tell mother I'll be there,
Heav'n's joys with her to share;
Yes, tell my darling mother I'll be there.

Tho' I was often wayward,
She was always kind and good—
So patient, gentle, loving,
When I acted rough and rude;
My childhood griefs and trials
She would gladly with me share:
O Saviour, tell my mother I'll be there.

When I became a prodigal,
And left the old roof-tree,
She almost broke her loving heart
In mourning after me;
And day and night she pray'd to God
To keep me in his care:
O Saviour, tell my mother I'll be there.

One day a message came to me—
It bade me quickly come,
If I would see my mother
Ere the Saviour took her home—
I promised her before she died,
For heaven to prepare:
O Saviour, tell my mother I'll be there.[4]

This theme of the death of a mother as a result of the child's waywardness is a prominent one, not only in hymns but in Victorian popular secular songs and literature as well. The threat of the loss of his parents, but particularly of his mother, is repeatedly used in children's literature to urge good behavior. It plays upon a child's natural fears of loss and his egotism in thinking that he is responsible for the events which take place in his world. This use of the image of mother was probably very effective.

The portrayals of family life and motherhood are not realistic—they are idealized, romantic images. The mother was portrayed as an object, not as a person: she was the personification of the passive Christian virtues. It is interesting to note that the most common setting for this image of mother is a simple rural cottage; she is poor but honest, admonishing her children to be pious and respectable. The family unit, particularly the lower class rural family, was idealized at the very time that family ties were dissolving among the lower classes. During the nineteenth century, population shifted from rural to urban areas; industrial labor imposed new patterns of life on many families. The New Poor Law of 1834 divided impoverished families. The factory system encouraged women and children to work outside of the home. Urban living provided greater possibilities for entertainment and socialization outside of the home. Housing conditions in many urban slums were so unattractive that life in the home was unbearably grim for many. At the very time, then, that family life was becoming less cohesive for the urban lower classes and that many lower class mothers were spending less time in the household, hymns present an image of close-knit family life that was an anachronism. It was an ideal which became a standard for middle class life and which colored the bourgeois conception of what the lower classes should be. This depersonification of woman and the idealization of the family were not, of course, the special province of hymns. They are attitudes which are reflected in most Victorian literature; hymns here simply adopt contemporary social conventions in their imagery.

If the hymn image of family life was an anachronistic middle class ideal, another set of images—those of a rural, agricultural society—just as anachronistically portrayed the middle class conception of the lower classes. At the beginning of the century, Robert Southey bemoaned the passing of the simple but noble cottager who was surrounded by rural beauty and who taught his children the yeoman virtues. In one of his colloquies Southey described the pre-industrial countryside in romantic terms:

> The old cottages are such as the poet and the painter equally delight in beholding. Substantially built of the native stone without mortar, dirtied with no white-lime, and their long low roofs covered with slate, if they had been raised by the magic of some indigenous Amphion's music, the materials could not have adjusted themselves more beautifully in accord with the surrounding scene; and time has still farther harmonized them with weather stains, lichens and moss, short grasses and short fern, and stone plants of various kinds; . . . the hedge of clipt box beneath the windows, the rose bushes beside the door, the little patch of flower ground with its tall hollyhocks in front, the garden beside, the beehives, and the orchard with its bank of daffodils and snowdrops . . . indicate in the owners some portion of ease and leisure, some regard to neatness

> and comfort, some sense of natural and innocent and healthful environment.[5]

Many nineteenth-century Englishmen refused to recognize the change from a rural, agricultural society to an urban, industrial society. The popularity of the Romantic movement in literature, Gothicism in art and architecture, and the Young England philosophy in politics are indications of a nostalgic flight to fantasy. This romantic yearning for the past retarded the formulation of a social philosophy which could realistically cope with industrial conditions.

The Anglican Church was, of course, tied to a parochial system which belonged to a rural, pre-industrial era; the psychological and economic difficulties of accommodating this system to rapidly growing cities were enormous.[6] In 1867 the Church of England reported that 70% of the total population of the country lived in towns and cities.[7] In 1871, however, almost 70% of the clergy were in country livings and approximately 75% of the church endowments were tied to these country livings.[8] It was not just the Anglican Church, however, which was tied to the ideal of a rural society. To understand the extent of the rural bias throughout society we can look at the Salvation Army, a group which dealt entirely with the plight of the "submerged tenth" of urban destitute. In his book, *Darkest England*, William Booth, the founder and General of the Army, described his plan which relied heavily on returning the poor to the farm. A City Colony would "gather, relieve, employ and uplift the destitute." Those who were found to be "sincere, industrious and honest" would go on to the Farm Colony, from which, after training, "some will go home, some will get work outside, some will be settled in cottages or on co-operative farms, and most will sail to the third community, the Oversea Colony—a vast tract of land in one of the British colonies, governed by the Army."[9] Booth's solution to the problem of urban poverty was to put the poor back in the country.

That Englishmen thought of themselves as a rural, agricultural people long after they had become predominantly urban and industrial, is well documented by a perusal of nineteenth-century hymnbooks. Agricultural images abound. By far the most popular of these images is the metaphorical sowing and reaping of the missionary:

> Thrust in your sharpened sickle,
> And gather in the grain;
> The night is fast approaching,

And soon will come again;
The Master calls for reapers,
And shall He call in vain?
Shall sheaves lie there ungathered,
And waste upon the plain?[10]

In a rather confusing metaphor, Christopher Wordsworth has the Christian grain rising from the grave:

Christ is risen, Christ the first-fruits
Of the holy harvest-field,
Which with all its full abundance
  At his second coming yield;
Then the golden ears of harvest
  Will their heads before Him wave,
Ripened by His glorious sunshine,
  From the furrows of the grave.[11]

Also popular was the image of Christ as the sheperd and mortal sinners as the sheep. One of the most popular of the melodramatic mission hymns of the last quarter of the century, *There were ninety and nine that safely lay*, used this image:

There were ninety and nine that safely lay
In the shelter of the fold,
But one was out on the hills away,
Far from the gates of gold.
Away on the mountains wild and bare,
Away from the tender Shepherd's care,
Away from the tender Shepherd's care.

"Lord, Thou hast here Thy ninety and nine;
Are they not enough for Thee?"
But the Shepherd made answer: "This of mine
Has wandered away from me;
And although the road be rough and stony
I go to the desert to find my sheep."

But none of the ransomed ever knew
How deep were the waters crossed;
Nor how dark was the night that the Lord passed through
Ere He found His sheep that was lost.
Out in the desert He heard its cry—
Sick and helpless, and ready to die.

"Lord, whence are those blood-drops all the way
That mark out the mountain's track?"
"They were shed for one who had gone astray
Ere the Shepherd could bring him back."
"Lord, whence are Thy hands so rent and torn?"
"They are pierced to-night by many a thorn."

And all thro' the mountains, thunder-riven,
And up from the rocky steep,
There rose a cry to the gate of heaven,
"Rejoice! I have found my sheep!"
And the angels echoed around the throne,
"Rejoice, for the Lord brings back his own."[12]

In 1842, in thanksgiving for a bountiful harvest after a year of scarcity, a Harvest Home festival was instituted in the Church of England. The popularity of this celebration continued throughout the century and it occasioned the writing of a multitude of harvest hymns.

It seems that as Englishmen were further removed from the countryside, they embraced it more in their hymns. When Thomas Toke Lynch published *The Rivulet* in 1855, his use of nature images was condemned as freethinking, undoctrinal, and deistic by a number of fellow clergymen. By the end of the century, however, hymns extolling nature were readily accepted in the denominational hymnbooks.

One explanation for this predominance of rural imagery is, of course, that scriptural imagery is agrarian and pastoral. We would expect to meet references to sheep and pastures and agricultural fertility. But the impression of scriptural imagery upon the hymns does not adequately explain the almost total absence of urban imagery in Victorian hymns. During the nineteenth century England became increasingly urbanized and industrialized. And yet, in my search of Victorian hymnbooks, I found only two hymns written during the nineteenth century which were based on contemporary secular images of industry or city, and then the use was very self-conscious. One was an unsuccessful attempt to use the railroad as a symbol for the pilgrim's progress to heaven:

The line to heav'n by Christ was made,
With heav'nly truths the rails were laid;
From earth to heaven the line extends,
To life eternal, where it ends.

Repentance is the station then
Where passengers are taken in;
No fee is there for them to pay,
For Jesus is Himself the way.

The Bible is the engineer,
It points the way to heaven so clear;
Through tunnels dark and dreary here,
It doth the way to heaven steer.

In first, and second, and third class
Repentance, faith and holiness,
You must the way to glory gain.
Or you with Christ can never reign.

Come, now, poor sinners, now's the time,
At any station on the line,
If you'll repent and turn from sin,
The train will stop and take you in.[13]

The second hymn is an adaptation from an American poet, William Cullen Bryant, in which the poet criticizes the rural emphasis of the churches:

  Not in the solitude
Alone may man commune with Heaven, or see
  Only in savage wood
And sunny vale the present Deity;
  Or only hear his voice
Where the winds whisper and the waves rejoice.

  Even here do I behold
Thy steps, Almighty!—here amidst the crowd
  Through the great city rolled,
With everlasting murmur deep and loud,
  Choking the ways that wind
'Mongst the proud piles, the work of human-kind.

. . . .

  Thy Spirit is around,
Quickening the restless mass that sweeps along;
  And this eternal sound,

Voices and footfalls of the numberless throng,
Like the resounding sea,
Or like the rainy tempest, speaks of Thee.[14]

Throughout the nineteenth century, literature in general and hymns in particular equated the countryside with an idealized society. The landed aristocracy continued to dominate many aspects of English life well into the twentieth century, long after the economic reasons for this dominance had disappeared. This romantic yearning for a return to an agricultural society is evident in the hymn imagery into our own time. Contemporary hymnbooks contain very few hymns about cities, or machinery, or overpopulation; we sing instead of the country or village church, of sheep, and of unpopulated hills.

The quietistic and sentimental images of motherhood and the serene images of a romantic countryside jar strangely with another prominent set of images in nineteenth-century hymns—military images. After 1815, English troops, as opposed to colonial troops, fought only two wars: in the Crimea at mid-century and in South Africa at the end of the century. Although the nineteenth century was a relatively peaceful era, the number of military images in nineteenth-century English hymns is truly amazing. One can pick up any hymn book of the Victorian era, even those of the most pietistic and introspective churches, and find stirring military marches like *Onward Christian Soldiers*.[15] The Oxford movement, which emphasized largely stately liturgical hymns, gave a fresh impulse to translation of older hymns and from these translations came one of the most militant Anglican battle hymns of the century—Philip Pusey's *Lord of our life, and God of our salvation.*[16] Bishop Christopher Wordsworth speaks of the ascension in military terms:

Lord of battles, God of armies,
He has gained the victory.[17]

The Salvation Army hymnbook published in 1890, contains nineteen hymns in which the central image is military battle. In fact, the very names of two of the most prominent missionary movements of the end of the century, William Booth's Salvation Army and the Church of England's Church Army, indicate the Victorian penchant for military imagery.

This love of military imagery derives from several sources: the Old Testament tradition of wrath and war, the medieval glorification of the military, the puritan and evangelical tradition of struggle against the forces of evil, and the Victorian emphasis on the "manly" virtues. English hymnody received its earliest thread of military imagery from the Hebrew songs of war of the Old Testament. The Old Testament ideas of the sixteenth- and seventeenth-century Calvinist puritans were spread in England by psalmody which, until the eighteenth century, was the only acceptable form of congregational singing. The psalms are generally characterized by a warlike spirit and in many of the psalms war is portrayed with vicious enthusiasm. It was, in fact, this viciousness which occasioned much of the eighteenth- and nineteenth-century criticism of both the Old and New Versions of psalmody. Nevertheless, until the end of the nineteenth century the Psalter continued to play an important part, in some churches the only part, in church praise.

The medieval church continued the military imagery, dividing the church into three parts: the church penitent, the church militant, and the church triumphant. It is from medieval warfare that many of the military images of the hymns are taken: they speak of swords, shields, spears, and armor.

Another source of military imagery is the Manichaean concept of struggle between good and evil, a concept which informed much puritan thought. This struggle is often voiced in dualistic, military terms:

God hath two families of love,
In earth below and heaven above:
One is in battle, sharp and sore;
And one is happy evermore.[18]

Life on earth is a constant battle which engages all Christians:

We are soldiers every one,
And the fight is just begun,
  And the Captain ever stands hard by,
For He sees our every need,
And our inmost thoughts doth read,
  As we Satan's host defy.[19]

The army of God will conquer the world, and it is every Christian's duty to enlist in the Christian army:

Stand up! stand up for Jesus!
  Ye soldiers of the Cross;

Lift high His royal banner,
  It must not suffer loss:
From victory unto victory
  His army shall He lead,
Till every foe is vanquished,
  And Christ is Lord indeed.[20]

Still another source of military imagery was the nineteenth-century emphasis on manly virtues. As we have noted, the Victorians viewed life as a constant struggle in which the individual was responsible for his own actions. Boys were best prepared for the struggle if they developed strong bodies and a competitive spirit; this was the reasoning behind the cult of games and sports at the public schools. Tom Brown's attitude represents his generation's ideas about fighting:

> After all, what would life be without fighting, I should like to know? From the cradle to the grave, fighting, rightly understood, is the business, the real, highest, honestest business of every son of man. . . .
>
> It is no good for Quakers, or any other body of men to uplift their voices against fighting. Human nature is too strong for them, and they don't follow their own precepts. Every soul of them is doing his own piece of fighting, somehow and somewhere. The world might be a better world without fighting, for anything I know, but it wouldn't be our world; and therefore I am dead against crying peace when there is no peace, and isn't meant to be. I am sorry as any man to see folk fighting the wrong people and the wrong things, but I'd deal sooner see them doing that, than that they should have no fight in them.[21]

One of the most popular children's books at the end of the century, Mrs. Ewing's *Jackanapes* (published by the Society for Promoting Christian Knowledge, 220,000 copies of the book were sold by 1900), is a glorification of military valor. After the young hero's death in a foreign war, the story ends with the narrator's comment:

> A sorrowful story, and ending badly?
>
> Nay. . . . There is a heritage of heroic example and noble obligation, not reckoned in the Wealth of Nations, but essential to a nation's life; the contempt of which, in any people, may, not slowly, mean even its commercial downfall.[22]

We can see this attitude reflected in hymns; the Christian is urged to "fight like a man":

Fight the good fight with all thy might!
Christ is thy strength, and Christ thy right;
Lay hold on life, and it shall be
Thy joy and crown eternally.

Run the straight race through God's good grace,
Lift up thine eyes, and seek his face;
Life with its way before us lies.
Christ is the path, and Christ the prize.[23]

This struggle is often couched in military images in the Victorian hymns:

Stout-hearted like a soldier,
Who never leaves the fight,
But meets the foe-man face to face
And meets him with his might;
So bear thee in thy battles
Until the war be past,
Stand fast for Christ thy Savior!
Stand faithful to the last.[24]

There were some prominent Victorians, individuals like the Unitarian Mrs. Gaskell or the Congregationalists Edward Williams, John Pye Smith, and Henry Richards, as well as the Quakers, who declared that war of any kind was wrong and that Christianity was a religion of pacifism because it was a religion of real forgiveness. And the mid-century democratic movements of the laboring classes early gave voice to antimilitarism, as in this hymn from *Democratic Hymns and Songs* (1849):

The warrior grasps the battle brand
  And seeks the field of fight,
And madly lifts his daring hand
  Against all human right.
He goeth with unholy wrath,
To scatter death along his path,
  While nations mourn his night;
But tho' he win the world's acclaim,
This is not glory—is not fame.[25]

In one of his short stories, Kipling pointed out that although most chapels officially took an antimilitary attitude, this was a superficial and hypocritical attempt at "respectability." Kipling's young protagonist Learoyd notices:

> And now I come to think on it, one at strangest things I know is 'at they couldn't abide th' thought o' soldiering. There's a vast o' fightin' i' th' Bible, and there's a deal of Methodists i' th' army; but to hear chapel folk talk yo'd think that soldierin' were next door, an' t' other side, to hangin'. I' their meetin's all their talk is o' fightin'.[26]

For most Victorians of the last half of the century, war was accepted and even welcomed if it could be proved to be "just and necessary." It was in the name of God that Carlyle declared that "might is right." After the Indian Mutiny of 1858, the Congregational Union considered that, despite the losses, the rebellion and its consequent repression was a good thing:

> It has shown the natives the power of the British arms, and crushed thereby the hopes they have ever entertained of destroying the British and restoring the native rule. It has awakened attention and solicitude among British patriots respecting the future administration of India, and has led to measures which will ameliorate the social condition of the Hindoos; and, still more than all, has roused the entire church of God to prayer and effort for the salvation of the idolatrous millions that people those distant presidencies of our Empire.[27]

E. E. Kellett reports that when Alexandria was bombarded in 1882, "A Christian minister I knew remarked that the bombardment was a good thing—it taught the barbarians not to despise the British navy."[28]

This militant attitude is reflected in many Victorian hymns.

> Sound the battle cry!
> See, the foe is nigh,
> Raise the standard high
> For the Lord;
> Gird your armour on,
> Stand firm ev'ry one;
> Rest your cause upon His holy word.
>
> Chorus: Rouse then, soldiers!
> Rally round the banner!
> Onward, forward, shout a loud hosanna!
> Christ is Captain of the mighty throng.[29]

In the hymns of the Church Militant, Jesus becomes the "captain"; the Gospel becomes the "banner," the "trumpet," and the "armour"; the Holy Spirit becomes the "sword." The images are, in fact, those of ancient warfare. In an industrial age, the church sang of fighting a medieval crusade or an Old Testament battle.

This brief review of four hymn images will not allow us to make any sweeping conclusions about Victorian society. It does indicate something about Victorian thinking, however; in their hymns there is a strong thread of conservatism and romanticism. The images which they used were not those of contemporary reality, but of an idealized past.

Thus far we have looked at hymn imagery as a reflection of social values. We must say something about the effect of hymn imagery on those who experience it. As mentioned in the introduction above, it is difficult if not impossible at the present time to evaluate quantitatively this effect, but our inability to quantify the effect does not deny that imagery affects the personality. Our perception of reality is formed by the images in our minds.* The images we carry with us locate us in time and space, they make the unknown concrete, they express symbolically our affective experiences—they are the materials out of which our "imaginations" construct our expectations of the world in which we live. Insofar as human beings are rational creatures, their behavior is directed by the complex of images carried within the mind. The sources of these images are many and various and probably for no two individuals will the combination be quite the same. But inasmuch as individuals share in a common and popular culture, they also share sets of images, or mindsets, which guide their expectations and orient their behavior.

We have attempted to show the widespread popularity of hymns in Victorian England; in individual instances we have indicated the profound psychic impact of hymns. We have also attempted to show that the images contained in hymns were, for the most part, consistent with the images presented in other types of popular culture—art, literature, political rhetoric, and interpersonal communications. Taken altogether, these images formed a recipe-book knowledge of the world for those who shared the culture. Insofar as we can comprehend and understand this total culture, we can understand the "inward thoughts" of the Victorians.

* I use the word "images" here in the phenomenological sense of the consciousness of the meaning of an intentional object.

CONCLUSION

THE major influence on early nineteenth-century hymns was the evangelical revival which began in the eighteenth century and continued through the nineteenth and which deeply impressed most nonconformist churches as well as a considerable part of the Anglican church. The evangelicals tended to be "other-worldly"; their emphasis on individual salvation through Christ diminished their concern for the corporate aspects of society and their puritanical rejection of the mundane as impure and ungodly meant that the main thrust of evangelical hymns throughout most of the nineteenth century would be toward heaven above and not toward building a heaven on earth in their own contemporary situation. This situation was one of rapid change; during the nineteenth century the face of England was transformed. Industrialization and urbanization put great strains on the social fabric. But evangelical hymns largely ignored the changes and the conflicts which those changes created. The hymns urged good Christians to "bear the load and murmur not."

At the same time, the nonevangelical majority of the Anglican church was so tied by tradition, by fear of attack on established privilege, and by their connections to rural and aristocratic dominance that they were forced to fight a largely defensive battle to maintain the social, political, economic, and theological *status quo*. Bishop Reginald Heber wrote a hymn warning against change during the early decades of the century:

From blinded zeal by faction led;
From giddy change by fancy bred;
From poisonous error's serpent head,
Good Lord, preserve us free![1]

A hymn translated during the 1830s, when the Church was fighting against disestablishment, reflects the intensity of the Church's defensive battle:

See round Thine ark the hungry billows curling,
See how Thy foes their banners are unfurling;
Lord, while their darts envenomed they are hurling,
Thou canst preserve us.[2]

Change is often frightening; a leap into the unknown produces anxiety in individuals. In their collective organizations or institutions, individuals tend to resist change because it threatens their emotional well-being as well as their economic and social status. The church is a particularly conservative institution because it is the embodiment and guarantor of one of man's greatest concerns—eternal life. The church represents security in an anxiety-filled world. In the words of an early nineteenth-century hymn,

Change is our portion here!
Yet midst our changing lot,
Midst withering flowers and tempests drear
There is that changes not;
Unchangeable Jehovah's word,
"I will be with thee," saith the Lord.[3]

Because familiar hymns make a special appeal to the memory, hymns are one of the most conservative components of an already conservative institution. It is the old hymn, the hymn of childhood, which comforts most and thus is most readily sung. Thus, hymns not only reflect conservative attitudes but also help to perpetuate them.

Any institution which resists change entirely, however, atrophies and becomes useless. During the nineteenth century the British churches realized this: the religious census of 1851 rudely awakened even the most conservative to the fact that many Englishmen, particularly the urban working class, were rejecting the churches. If the fact of nonattendance didn't alert the faithful, popular literature made the working class's rejection of both the denominational churches and Christianity itself flagrantly obvious. Disraeli's Wodgate and Dicken's city slums were peopled by many who had never learned their catechism because the church never touched their lives. Worse, there were numerous fictional (and real) characters like Ned in Tirebuck's *Miss Grace of All Souls* who purposefully rejected the church because of its support of the established social and economic order. And so the churches were forced to make changes, but they acted with painful slowness. Hymns reflect both the inertia of the institutional churches and the changes in attitudes which gradually developed.

During the first half of the century the demands for change in the churches' attitudes toward the social, economic, and political structure came largely from outside of the denominational churches—from the Chartists and other similar dissident groups. The hymns which demanded change were published largely in newspapers, tracts, or private hymnbooks. They were published by Ethical Societies, Societies for Rational Religion and dissident radical individuals rather than by the institutional churches. It is only in the last decades of the century that hymns of social protest appear in the denominational hymnals. By 1904 the editors of *Hymns Ancient and Modern* expressed a desire to publish more hymns concerning social justice; the dearth of hymns on the subject in that edition, they declared, was due to the fact that few good hymns had been written.

We have traced other changes in nineteenth-century hymns: in the field of foreign mission we saw a change from the belief that since non-Christians were eternally damned, the Christian had an imperative to mission, to an earnest questioning of the British motives and methods of foreign mission by the end of the century. We have, in fact, emphasized change in our review of hymns because change is the basis of historical study. The distinctive characteristics of a period of civilization, the changes which it undergoes, allow the historian to distinguish one period from another. And yet, in the study of cultural history, particularly the study of popular culture, there is much that remains the same because man's basic needs change relatively little from epoch to epoch. Hymns must always respond to man's basic religious needs—his need for liturgical ritual, for an ethical law, and his hope for eternal life. There is, therefore, a large part of hymn literature which remains unchanging and which defies a sociological study. This inertia, then, produces a constant state of conflict with the forces of change. This perennial dilemma between the old and the new, between what Ernst Troeltsch has called the "church" and "sect," creates tension within the church and society. In Victorian society the tension erupted in conflicts on several fronts.

A study of nineteenth-century English hymns reveals that Victorian society, even the part of society which could be classed as churchgoing, was not a monolithic culture. Victorian social ideals often conflicted: for instance, the world-rejection of the evangelicals would ultimately come into direct conflict with their own humanitarian instincts and with the humanistic "churches" which organized in the later years of the century; the ideal of Christian submissiveness contradicted the ideals of individualism, striving, and self-help; the value of competition was called into question by the ideal of Christian equality and sharing; English Christian patriotism collided, in the period of imperial expansion, with the Christian ideal of world brotherhood. During the century some of these value conflicts became apparent to English Christians and an attempt was made to resolve them; the challenges and the changes are apparent in the hymns. Some of the ambivalences, however, were not consciously realized and continued as dichotomous sources of unease into the present century. The changes that were made and the changes that were not made help the historian to define the social attitudes of a period and hymns are one index of these attitudes.

In conclusion, there are few ideas in this study which are entirely new. Students of the Victorian era have already noted the influence of evangelicalism on nineteenth-century British society. The slowness with which the churches accepted demands for social justice has been observed and railed at by a number of historians. The churches' didactic role in the area of ethics and morality has been investigated by sociologists and historians. What is new in this study is the evidence which is explored.

Hymns are a particularly valuable source of study of popular culture. They were sung by the churchgoing and nonchurchgoing alike. The form of the hymns was a familiar medium through which secular social values of all kinds could be expressed. While the denominational hymns reveal the conservative attitudes of the churches, many of the hymns first printed in nondenominational publications, or nonchurch publications, reveal the dissident view of Christian purpose. As these dissident hymns were accepted in the denominational hymnals, we can trace the change of attitudes of the churches. Hymns, in other words, reflect many of the ideas and attitudes of Victorian society.

BIBLIOGRAPHY

I. GENERAL WORKS

Allen, Peter R. "F. D. Maurice and J. M. Ludlow: A Reassessment of the Leaders of Christian Socialism," *Victorian Studies*, XI (June, 1968), 461-482.

Altholz, Josef L. *The Churches in the Nineteenth Century*. Indianapolis: The Bobbs-Merrill Company, 1967.

———. *Victorian England 1837-1901*. Cambridge: University Press, 1970.

Anderson, William K. (ed.). *Christian World Mission*. Nashville, Tenn.: Commission on Ministerial Training, 1946.

Argyle, Michael. *Religious Behavior*. Glencoe, Illinois: The Free Press, 1959.

Ariès, Philippe. *Centuries of Childhood, A Social History of Family Life*, trans. by Robert Baldick. New York: Alfred A. Knopf, 1962.

Arnstein, Walter L. "The Myth of the Triumphant Victorian Middle Class," *The Historian*, XXXVII (Feb., 1975), 205-221.

Backstrom, Philip N., Jr. "The Practical Side of Christian Socialism in Victorian England," *Victorian Studies*, VI (June, 1963), 305-324.

Balleine, G. R. *A History of the Evangelical Party in the Church of England*. London: Longmans, Green and Co., 1908.

Baring-Gould, S. *The Evangelical Revival*. London: Methuen and Co., 1920.

Bax, Ernest Belfort. *Reminiscences and Reflexions of a Mid and Late Victorian*. London: George Allen & Unwin, Ltd., 1918.

Bowen, Desmond. *The Idea of the Victorian Church: A Study of the Church of England 1833-1889*. Montreal: McGill University Press, 1968.

Bready, J. Wesley. *England: Before and After Wesley, The Evangelical Revival and Social Reform*. London: Harper and Brothers, 1938.

Brebner, J. Bartlet. "Laissez Faire and State Intervention in Nineteenth-Century Britain," *The Journal of Economic History*, VIII (1948), 59-73.

Briggs, Asa. *The Age of Improvement*. London: Longmans, Green and Company, 1959.

———. *Victorian People, A Reassessment of Persons and Themes, 1851-67*. Rev. ed. Chicago: University of Chicago Press, 1972.

Brontë, Charlotte. *Villette*. New York: Derby & Jackson, 1859.

Brose, Olive. "F. D. Maurice and the Victorian Crisis of Belief," *Victorian Studies*, III (March, 1960), 227-248.

Burn, W. L. *The Age of Equipoise, A Study of the Mid-Victorian Generation*. New York: W. W. Norton and Company, 1964.

Carus-Wilson, Mrs. Ashley. *The Expansion of Christendom, A Study in Religious History*. London: Hodder and Stoughton, 1910.

Cazamian, Louis. *The Social Novel in England, 1830-1850: Dickens, Disraeli, Mrs. Gaskell, Kingsley*, trans. by Martin Fido. London: Routledge & Kegan Paul, 1973.

Chadwick, Owen. *The Victorian Church*. 2 vols. New York: Oxford University Press, 1966.

Chapman, Raymond. *The Victorian Debate: English Literature and Society, 1832-1901*. New York: Basic Books, 1968.

Churchill, Winston S. *My Early Life, A Roving Commission*. New York: Charles Scribner's Sons, 1930.

Clark, G. Kitson. *An Expanding Society: Britain, 1830-1900*. Melbourne, 1967.

———. *Churchmen and the Condition of England, 1832-1885, A study in the development of social ideas and practice from the Old Regime to the Modern State*. London: Methuen & Co., 1973.

———. *The Making of Victorian England*. Cambridge, Mass.: Harvard University Press, 1962.

Cockshut, A. O. J. *Anglican Attitudes, A Study of Victorian Religious Controversies*, London: Collins, 1959.

Cornish, Francis Warre. *The English Church in the Nineteenth Century*. 2 vols. London: Macmillan and Company, 1910.

Courtney, Janet E. *Freethinkers of the Nineteenth Century*. Freeport, New York: Books for Libraries Press, Inc., 1967.

Cowherd, Raymond G. *The Politics of Dissent: The Religious Aspects of Liberal and Humanitarian Reform Movements from 1815 to 1848*. New York: New York University Press, 1956.

Crowther, M. A. *Church Embattled: Religious Controversy in Mid-Victorian England*. Newton Abbot, England: David and Charles, 1970.

Cruse, Amy. *The Victorians and Their Reading*. Boston: Houghton Mifflin Company, 1935.

Daiches, David. *Some Late Victorian Attitudes*. New York: W. W. Norton & Co., Inc., 1969.

Davenport, Frederick Morgan. *Primitive Traits in Religious Revivals: A Study in Mental and Social Evolution.* New York: The Macmillan Company, 1906.

Davies, Horton. *Worship and Theology in England from Newman to Martineau, 1850-1900.* Princeton: Princeton University Press, 1962.

———. *Worship and Theology in England from Watts and Wesley to Maurice, 1690-1850.* Princeton: Princeton University Press, 1961.

Dodds, John W. *The Age of Paradox: A Biography of England, 1841-1851.* New York: Rinehart and Co., 1952.

Edwards, David L. *Religion and Change.* New York: Harper & Row, 1969.

Elliott-Binns, L. E. *Religion In the Victorian Era.* 2nd ed. London: Lutterworth Press, 1964.

Ensor, R. C. K. *England, 1870-1914.* Oxford: The Clarendon Press, 1936.

Fletcher, Peter (pseud. A. B. W. Fletcher). *The Long Sunday.* London: Faber and Faber, 1958.

Glover, Willis B. *Evangelical Nonconformists and Higher Criticism in the Nineteenth Century.* London: Independent Press, 1954.

Goddard, Burton L. (ed.). *The Encyclopedia of Modern Christian Missions, The Agencies.* Camden, New Jersey: Thomas Nelson & Sons, 1967.

Gosse, Edmund. *Father and Son, A Study of Two Temperaments.* New York: Oxford University Press, 1907.

Grounds, Vernon C. *Evangelicalism and Social Responsibility.* Scottsdale, Pa.: Herald Press, 1969.

Halévy, Elie. *The Birth of Methodism in England,* trans. and ed. by Bernard Semmel. Chicago: University of Chicago Press, 1971.

———. *England in 1815,* trans. by E. I. Watkin and D. A. Barker. London: Ernest Benn, 1949.

Hall, Thomas C. *The Social Meaning of Modern Religious Movements in England.* New York: Charles Scribner's Sons, 1900.

Harding, F. A. J. *The Social Impact of the Evangelical Revival.* London: The Epworth Press, 1947.

Haroutunian, Joseph. *Piety Versus Moralism: The Passing of the New England Theology.* Hamden, Connecticut: Archon Books, 1964.

Hart, Jenifer. "Nineteenth-Century Social Reform: A Tory Interpretation of History," *Past and Present,* XXXI (July, 1965), 39-61.

Heasman, Kathleen. *Evangelicals in Action: An Appraisal of their Social Work in the Victorian Era.* London: Geoffrey Bles, 1962.

Hill, Michael. *A Sociology of Religion.* New York: Basic Books, 1973.

Himmelfarb, Gertrude. "The Writing of Social History," *The Journal of British Studies,* XI (November, 1971).

Houghton, Walter E. *The Victorian Frame of Mind, 1830-1870.* New Haven: Yale University Press, 1957.

Hughes, Thomas. *Tom Brown's School-Days.* 6th ed. New York: Harper and Brothers, 1911.

Hutchins, B. L. and Harrison, A. *A History of Factory Legislation*. 3rd ed. New York: Augustus M. Kelley, 1968.

Inglis, K. S. *Churches and the Working Classes in Victorian England*. London: Routledge and Kegan Paul, 1963.

Inskip, James Theodore. *Evangelical Influence in English Life*. London: Macmillan and Company, 1933.

Itzkin, Elissa S. "The Halévy Thesis—a Working Hypothesis? English Revivalism: Antidote for Revolution and Radicalism 1789-1815," *Church History*, (March, 1975), 47-56.

Jackman, Sydney W. (ed.). *The English Reform Tradition, 1790-1910*. Englewood Cliffs, N.J.: Prentice Hall, 1965.

James, Louis. *Fiction for the Working Man, 1830-1850*. London: Oxford University Press, 1963.

Jevons, W. Stanley. *Methods of Social Reform and Other Papers*. London: Macmillan and Co., 1883.

Johnson, Benton. "Church and Sect Revisited," *Journal for the Scientific Study of Religion*, X (Summer, 1971), 124-137.

Jones, Gareth Stedman. "Working-Class Culture and Working-Class Politics in London, 1870-1900; Notes on the Remaking of the Working Class," *Journal of Social History*, VII (Summer, 1974), 460-508.

Jones, Henry. *The Working Faith of the Social Reformer and Other Essays*. London: Macmillan and Co., 1910.

Jones, R. Tudur. *Congregationalism in England, 1662-1962*. London: Independent Press, 1962.

Kauvar, Gerald B. and Sorensen, Gerald C. (eds.). *The Victorian Mind*. New York: Capricorn Books, 1969.

Keating, P. J. *The Working Classes in Victorian Fiction*. New York: Barnes & Noble, Inc., 1971.

Kellett, E. E. *Religion and Life in the Early Victorian Age*. London: The Epworth Press, 1938.

Kent, John. "The Victorian Resistance: Comments on Religious Life and Culture, 1840-80," *Victorian Studies*, XII (December, 1968), 145-154.

Knoepflmacher, U. C. *Religious Humanism and the Victorian Novel: George Eliot, Walter Pater, and Samuel Butler*. Princeton: Princeton University Press, 1965.

Latourette, Kenneth Scott. *The Great Century in Europe and the United States of America, A. D. 1800–A. D. 1914*. Vol. IV of *A History of the Expansion of Christianity*. New York: Harper & Brothers, 1941.

LeRoy, Gaylord C. *Perplexed Prophets: Six Nineteenth-Century British Authors*. Philadelphia: University of Pennsylvania Press, 1953.

Levine, George (ed.). *The Emergence of Victorian Consciousness, The Spirit of the Age*. New York: The Free Press, 1967.

MacDonagh, Oliver. *A Pattern of Government Growth, 1800-60: The Passenger Acts and Their Enforcement*. London: MacGibbon and Kee, 1961.

———. "The Nineteenth-Century Revolution in Government: A Reappraisal," *The Historical Journal*, I (1958), 52-67.

MacDonald, D. F. *The Age of Transition: Britain in the Nineteenth and Twentieth Centuries.* London: Macmillan Company, 1967.

McCulloch, Samuel Clyde. *British Humanitarianism, Essays Honoring Frank J. Klingberg.* Philadelphia: The Church Historical Society, 1950.

Maison, Margaret M. *The Victorian Vision: Studies in the Religious Novel.* New York: Sheed and Ward, 1961.

Martin, David. *A Sociology of English Religion.* New York: Basic Books, 1967.

Missionary Book for the Young. New ed. London: The Religious Tract Society, [c. 1850].

The Missionary Year-Book for 1889. London: The Religious Tract Society, n.d.

Moule, H. C. G. *The Evangelical School in the Church of England, Its men and its work in the nineteenth century.* London: James Nisbet and Company, 1901.

Oliver, John. *The Church and Social Order, Social Thought in the Church of England,* 1918-1939. London: A. R. Mowbray & Co., 1968.

O'Neill, James E. "The Victorian Background to the British Welfare State," *The South Atlantic Quarterly,* LXVI (Spring, 1967), 204-217.

Orr, J. Edwin. *The Second Evangelical Awakening.* London: Marshall, Morgan and Scott, 1949.

Overton, John H. *The English Church in the Nineteenth Century (1800-1833).* London: Longmans, Green & Co., 1894.

Pearsall, Ronald. *Victorian Popular Music.* Detroit, Michigan: Gale Research Co., 1973.

———. *The Worm in the Bud: The World of Victorian Sexuality.* New York: Macmillan Company, 1969.

Peckham, Morse. "Can 'Victorian' Have a Useful Meaning?" *Victorian Studies,* X (March, 1967), 273-277.

Peel, Albert. *These Hundred Years: A History of the Congregational Union of England and Wales, 1831-1931.* London: Congregational Union of England and Wales, 1931.

Petrie, Sir Charles. *The Victorians.* New York: David McKay Co., 1962.

Polanyi, Karl. *The Great Transformation.* New York: Rinehart & Co., 1944.

Poole-Connor, E. J. *Evangelicalism in England.* London: Fellowship of Independent Evangelical Churches, 1951.

Rice, Edwin Wilbur. *The Sunday-School Movement (1780-1917)* and *The American Sunday-School Union (1817-1917).* New York: Arno Press and the *New York Times,* 1971.

Richter, Melvin. *The Politics of Conscience: T. H. Green and His Age.* Cambridge, Mass.: Harvard University Press, 1964.

Roberts, David. "Tory Paternalism and Social Reform in Early Victorian England," *American Historical Review,* LXIII (January, 1958), 323-337.

———. *Victorian Origins of the British Welfare State.* New Haven: Yale University Press, 1960.

Shepherd, Ambrose. *The Gospel and Social Questions*. 2nd ed. London: Hodder & Stoughton, 1902.

Simeral, Isabel. *Reform Movements in Behalf of Children in England of the Early Nineteenth Century, and the Agents of those Reforms*. New York, 1916.

Smith, Paul. *Disraelian Conservatism and Social Reform*. London: Routledge and Kegan Paul, 1967.

Soloway, Richard A. "Church and Society: Recent Trends in Nineteenth Century Religious History," *The Journal of British Studies*, XI (May, 1972), 142-159.

———. *Prelates and People: Ecclesiastical Social Thought in England, 1783-1852*. London: Routledge & Kegan Paul, 1969.

Starbuck, Edwin Diller. *The Psychology of Religion: An Empirical Study of the Growth of Religious Consciousness*. London: The Walter Scott Publishing Co., [1914].

Stark, Werner. *The Sociology of Religion: A Study of Christendom*. New York: Fordham University Press, 1966.

Stoughton, John. *Religion in England from 1800 to 1850*. 2 vols. London: Hodder and Stoughton, 1884.

Taine, Hippolyte. *Taine's Notes on England*, trans. by Edward Hyams. Fair Lawn, N.J.: Essential Books, 1958.

Taylor, Gordon Rattray. *The Angel-Makers: A Study in the Psychological Origins of Historical Change, 1750-1850*. London: Heinemann, 1958.

Thomas, George F. *Christian Ethics and Moral Philosophy*. New York: Charles Scribner's Sons, 1955.

Thompson, David M. (ed.). *Nonconformity in the Nineteenth Century*. London: Routledge and Kegan Paul, 1972.

———. *England in the Nineteenth Century, 1815-1914*. Baltimore: Penguin Books, 1950.

Thompson, E. P. *The Making of the English Working Class*. New York: Pantheon Books, 1964.

Thouless, Robert H. *An Introduction to the Psychology of Religion*. New York: The Macmillan Company, 1931.

Toynbee, Arnold. *An Historian's Approach to Religion*. London: Oxford University Press, 1956.

Trevelyan, G. M. *The Nineteenth Century*. Vol. IV of *Illustrated English Social History*. London: Longmans, Green and Company, 1942.

Troeltsch, Ernst. *The Social Teachings of the Christian Churches*, trans. by Olive Wyon. 2 Vols. Glencoe, Ill.: The Free Press, 1949.

Trollope, Anthony. *Barchester Towers*. New York: Bantam Books, 1959.

Vicinus, Martha. *The Industrial Muse: A Study of Nineteenth Century British Working-Class Literature*. New York: Harper and Row, 1974.

Wagner, Donald O. *The Church of England and Social Reform Since 1854*. New York: Columbia University Press, 1930.

Walker, Williston. *A History of the Christian Church*. Rev. ed. New York: Charles Scribner's Sons, 1959.

Ward, Mrs. Humphry. *Robert Elsmere*. London: Smith, Elder & Co., 1914.

Ward, W. R. *Religion and Society in England, 1790-1850*. London: B. T. Batsford, Ltd., 1972.

Watson, David. *Social Problems and the Church's Duty*. London: A. & C. Black, 1908.

Wearmouth, Robert F. *Methodism and the Working-Class Movements of England, 1800-1850*. London: The Epworth Press, 1937.

Webb, Beatrice. *My Apprenticeship*. New York: Longmans, Green and Co., 1926.

Weber, Max. *The Sociology of Religion*, trans. by Ephraim Fischoff. Boston: Beacon Press, 1964.

Whitley, Oliver R. *Religious Behavior: Where Sociology and Religion Meet*. Englewood Cliffs, N.J.: Prentice-Hall, 1964.

Wickham, E. R. *Church and People In an Industrial City*. London: Lutterworth Press, 1957.

Willey, Basil. *More Nineteenth Century Studies, A Group of Honest Doubters*. New York: Columbia University Press, 1956.

———. *Nineteenth Century Studies, Coleridge to Matthew Arnold*. New York: Columbia University Press, 1949.

Wirt, Sherwood Eliot. *The Social Conscience of the Evangelical*. New York: Harper and Row, 1968.

Yinger, J. Milton. *Religion in the Struggle for Power: A Study in the Sociology of Religion*. New York: Russell & Russell, 1961.

Young, G. M. *Victorian England, Portrait of an Age*. 2nd ed. London: Oxford University Press, 1953.

Young, Kenneth. *Chapel*. London: Eyre Methuen, 1972.

II. WORKS ABOUT HYMNS

Adams, Mrs. Crosby. *Studies in Hymnology*. Richmond, Va.: Onward Press, 1929.

Alexander, William Lindsay. "Lectures on the Public Psalmody of the Church," *The Scottish Congregational Magazine* (April, 1848; June, 1848; July, 1848; August, 1848; September, 1848; October, 1848).

Appleby, David P. *History of Church Music*. Chicago: Moody Press, 1965.

Bailey, Albert Edward. *The Gospel in Hymns, Backgrounds and Interpretations*. New York: Charles Scribner's Sons, 1950.

Barr, W. W. "The Psalms and their Use, or the Matter and Manner of Praise," *Evangelical Repository*, LVI (November, 1879), 161-166.

Benson, Louis F. *The Best Church Hymns*. Philadelphia: Westminster Press, 1898.

———. *The English Hymn, Its Development and Use In Worship*. Philadelphia: The Presbyterian Board of Publication, 1915.

———. *Studies of Familiar Hymns*. Philadelphia: The Westminster Press, 1926.

Bett, Henry. *The Hymns of Methodism in their Literary Relations*. London: The Epworth Press, 1913.

Biggs, Louis Coutier. *English Hymnology*. London: Mozleys, 1873.

Blew, William John. *Hymns and Hymn-Books, with a Few Words on anthems: A Letter to the Rev. William Upton Richards, M. A. from William John Blew*. London: Rivingtons, 1858.

Box, Charles. *Church Music in the Metropolis, Its Past and Present Condition*. London: William Reeves, 1884.

Brawley, Benjamin. *History of the English Hymn*. New York: The Abingdon Press, 1932.

Breed, David R. *The History and Use of Hymns and Hymn-Tunes*. New York: Fleming H. Revell, 1903.

Brown, Theron and Butterworth, Hezekiah. *The Story of the Hymns and Tunes*. New York: American Tract Society, 1906.

Brownlie, John. *The Hymns and Hymn Writers of the Church Hymnary*. London: Henry Frowde, 1899.

Bultmann, Phyllis Wetherell. "Everybody Sing: The Social Significance of the Eighteenth-Century Hymn." Unpublished Ph.D. dissertation, University of California at Los Angeles, 1950.

Bunn, L. H. *Seventy Years of English Presbyterian Praise*. London: Presbyterian Historical Society of England, 1959.

Burgess, William Penington. *Wesleyan Hymnology: or, A Companion to the Wesleyan Hymn Book*. 2nd ed. London: John Snow, 1846.

Burrage, Henry S. *Baptist Hymn Writers and Their Hymns*. Portland, Maine: Brown Thurston, 1888.

Chappell, Paul. *Music and Worship in the Anglican Church, 597-1967*. London: The Faith Press, 1968.

Christophers, S. W. *Hymn-Writers and Their Hymns*. London: S. W. Partridge & Co., [c. 1870].

Clarke, W. K. Lother. *A Hundred Years of Hymns Ancient and Modern*. London: William Clowes and Sons, 1960.

Claybaugh, J. *The Ordinance of Praise, or An Argument in Favor of the Exclusive Use of the Book of Psalms, in Singing Praises to God*. 2nd ed. Rossville, Ohio: J. M. Christy, 1843.

Crawford, Benjamin Franklin. *Religious Trends in a Century of Hymns*. Carnegie, Pa.: Carnegie Church Press, 1938.

Creamer, David. *Methodist Hymnology, Comprehending Notices of the Poetical Works of John and Charles Wesley*. New York: Joseph Longking, 1848.

Dearmer, Percy. *Songs of Praise Discussed: A Handbook to the Best-Known Hymns and to Others Recently Introduced*. Oxford: Oxford University Press, 1933.

Duffield, Samuel Willoughby. *English Hymns: Their Authors and History*. New York: Funk and Wagnalls, 1886.

Escott, Harry. *Isaac Watts, Hymnographer: A Study of the Beginnings, Development, and Philosophy of the English Hymn*. London: Independent Press, 1962.

Hamilton, James. *The Psalter and Hymn Book: Three Lectures*. London: James Nisbet and Co., 1865.

Hunter, Stanley Armstrong (ed.). *The Music of the Gospel*. New York: The Abingdon Press, 1932.

"Hymn Makers and Hymn Menders," *Presbyterian Quarterly Review* (March 1858), 605-636.

Jefferson, H. A. L. *Hymns in Christian Worship*. London: Rockliff Publishing Corporation, 1950.

Julian, John. *A Dictionary of Hymnology*. New York: Charles Scribner's Sons, 1892.

King, James. *Anglican Hymnology*. London: Hatchards, 1885.

Laufer, Calvin W. *Hymn Lore*. Philadelphia: The Westminster Press, 1932.

Leask, G. A. *Hymn-Writers of the Nineteenth Century*. London: Elliot Stock, 1902.

Lorenz, Edmund S. *The Singing Church: The Hymns It Wrote and Sang*. Nashville: Cokesbury Press, 1938.

Manning, Bernard L. *The Hymns of Wesley and Watts, Five Informal Papers*. London: The Epworth Press, 1942.

Marks, Harvey B. *The Rise and Growth of English Hymnody*. New York: Fleming H. Revell Company, 1937.

Nutter, Charles S. and Tillett, Wilbur F. *The Hymns and Hymn Writers of the Church, An Annotated Edition of the Methodist Hymnal*. New York: Eaton and Mains, 1911.

Phillips, C. S. *Hymnody Past and Present*. London: Society for Promoting Christian Knowledge, 1937.

Reeves, Jeremiah Bascom. *The Hymn as Literature*. New York: The Century Company, 1924.

Routley, Erik. *Hymns and Human Life*. London: John Murray, 1952.

———. *Hymns Today and Tomorrow*. London: Darton Longman & Todd, 1966.

Sankey, Ira D. *My Life and the Story of the Gospel Hymns, and of Sacred Songs and Solos*. Philadelphia: P. W. Ziegler, 1907.

A Short Commentary on The Hymnal Noted, from Ancient Sources, Intended Chiefly for the Use of the Poor. London: Joseph Masters, 1812.

Sims, Henry Upson. *150 Great Hymns in the English Language*. Richmond, Va.: The Dietz Press, 1949.

Smith, Eva Mudson (ed.). *Woman in Sacred Song, A Library of Hymns, Religious Poems, and Sacred Music by Woman*. Boston: D. Lothrop and Company, 1885.

Smith, J. Augustine. *Lyric Religion, The Romance of Immortal Hymns*. New York: The Century Company. 1931.

Stead, W. T. *Hymns That Have Helped, Being a Collection of Hymns which Have Been Found Most Useful to the Children of Men*. New York: Doubleday, Page & Company, 1904.

Sutherland, Allan. *Famous Hymns of the World, Their Origin and Their Romance*. Rev. ed. New York: Frederick A. Stokes Company, 1923.

Sydnor, James Rawlings (ed.). *A Short Bibliography for the Study of Hymns.* The Papers of the Hymn Society, Vol. XXV. New York: The Hymn Society of America, 1964.

Taggart, R. B. "The Psalms—the Voice of Christ and the Church," *Evangelical Repository*, LVI (September, 1879), 105-110.

Thomson, Ronald W. *Who's Who of Hymn Writers.* London: Epworth Press, 1967.

III. HYMNBOOKS

A. L. O. E. [Charlotte Maria Tucker]. *Hymns and Poems.* London: T. Nelson and Sons, 1868.

Aitken, W. Hay M. H. (ed.). *Hymns for a Parochial Mission with Accompanying Tunes.* Rev. ed. London: The Church Parochial Mission Society, n.d.

The Albion Sunday School Hymn Book. Southampton: Albion Chapel, 1867.

Alexander, Cecil Frances. *Narrative Hymns for Village Schools.* London: Joseph Masters, 1861.

———. *Hymns for Little Children.* London: Joseph Masters, 1848.

Alexander, Charles. *Alexander's New Revival Hymns.* London: Morgan and Scott, n.d.

Alexander, J[ames] (ed.). *The Beauties of Sacred Melody for the Voice, Piano Forte or Organ.* London: J. Alexander, [ca.1830].

Allen, John. *The Penny Hymnbook.* London: George Routledge and Sons, 1860.

Allon, Henry. *Children's Worship: A Book of Sacred Song for Home and School.* London: Hodder and Stoughton, 1887.

Aspland, Robert. *A Selection of Psalms and Hymns for Unitarian Worship.* London: Johnson and Co., 1810.

Barrett, George S. (ed.). *Congregational Church Hymnal.* London: Congregational Union of England and Wales, [1883].

———. *The Congregational Mission Hymnal and Weeknight Service Book.* London: Congregational Union of England and Wales, 1890.

[Barry, D. T. (ed.)]. *The Parish Hymn Book for the Church, School, and Home.* Edition B. London: Frederick Warne and Co., [1871].

[Bateman, Henry]. *Sunday Sunshine, New Hymns and Poems for the Young.* London: James Nisbet and Co., 1858.

Bathurst, W. H. *Psalms and Hymns for Public and Private Worship.* London: Hatchard and Sons, 1831.

Baynes, R. H. *Lyra Anglicana, Hymns and Sacred Songs.* London: Noulston & Sons, 1873.

Beardsall, F. *Selection of Hymns and Songs Suitable for Public and Social Temperance Meetings.* 5th ed. Manchester: George Hesketh, [1850].

Bennett, Thomas. *Sacred Melodies.* London: Chappell & Co., [after 1825].

Bennett, William Sterndale and Goldschmidt, Otto (eds.). *The Chorale Book for England.* London: Longman, Green, Longman, Roberts, and Green, 1863.

Bickersteth, Edward. *Christian Psalmody: A Collection of Above 700 Psalms, Hymns And Spiritual Songs.* London: L. B. Seeley and Sons, 1833.

Body, George (ed.). *The Durham Mission Hymn-Book with Supplement.* London: Charles Taylor, [1885].

Bonar, Horatius. *Hymns of Faith and Hope.* London: James Nisbet & Co., 1857.

Booth, George (ed.). *The Primitive Methodist Hymnal.* London: Edwin Dalton, [1889].

Booth, William (ed.). *Salvaion Army Music.* London: Salvation Army, 1890.

[Bradbury, Thomas]. *Psalms and Hymns and Spiritual Songs for the Elect of God.* 3rd ed. Brighton: A. M. Robinson & Son, 1891.

Braithwaite, Martha. *The Fireside Hymn-Book.* London: Hamilton, Adams and Co., 1865.

Bridge, Sir Frederick (ed.). *The Methodist Hymn-Book with Tunes.* London: Wesleyan Conference Office, [1904].

Brooke, Stopford A. (ed.). *Christian Hymns.* London: Women's Printing Society, 1881.

Carpenter, Lant. *Collection of Hymns for Public Worship, and for the Private Exercise of the Religious Affections.* Bristol: Philp and Evans, 1838.

Chapman, W. *Teetotal Hymns.* London: William Tweedie, 1859.

The Children's Hymn Book. Rev. ed. London: Society for Promoting Christian Knowledge, n.d.

Children's Hymn and Chant Book. London: John Marshall & Co., 1873.

Chope, R. R. *Congregational Hymn and Tune Book.* Bristol: J. Wright & Co. Steam Press, [1859].

The Church Mission Hymn-Book. Rev. ed. London: Sampson Low, Marston, Searle, and Rivington, 1883.

The Church Mission Hymn Book with Mission Liturgies. London: Robert Scott, 1913.

The Church Missionary Hymn Book. London: Church Missionary Society, [1899].

Church of England Temperance Society, *Hymns and Songs to Be Used at Meetings of the Society.* New ed. London: Church of England Temperance Society, n.d.

[Coit, Stanton]. *Ethical Hymn Book with Music.* Rev. ed. London: Oppenheimer Brothers, 1905.

Committee of the Presbyterian Church of England. *Church Praise.* London: James Nisbet & Co., 1885.

Cooke, William and Webb, Benjamin (eds.). *The Hymnary, A Book of Church Song.* 2nd ed. London: Novello, Ewer and Co., 1872.

Dearmer, Percy, Williams, Ralph Vaughn, and Shaw, Martin (eds.). *Songs of Praise, with Music.* London: Oxford University Press, 1926.

Democratic Hymns and Songs. Wortley: J. Barker, 1849.

Edmeston, James. *Sacred Lyrics*. London: B. J. Holdsworh, 1820.

The English Hymnal. New ed. London: Oxford University Press, 1906.

Farquharson, James. *A Selection of Sacred Music Suitable for Public & Private Devotion*. Edinburgh: Waugh and Innes Booksellers, 1824.

Foster, John (ed.). *Psalms and Hymns Adapted to the Services of Church of England*. London: Rivingtons, 1863.

[Hall, William John (ed.)]. *Psalms and Hymns Adapted to the Services of the Church of England*. London: Henry Wix, 1842.

[Hollis, B. S. (ed.)]. *The One Book of Psalms and Hymns*. London: Partridge & Oakey, 1849.

Hood, Paxton (ed.). *The Children's Choir and Little Service of Sacred Song*. Brighton: Queen Square Chapel, 1870.

Hymns Ancient and Modern. 4th ed. London: William Clowes and Sons, 1904.

Hymns and Tunes for the Use of Clifton College. 3rd ed. Bristol: Taylor Brothers, 1885.

Hymns Composed and Selected for the Use of the Sunday School Union Prayer Meetings. Portsmouth: Lea and Son, 1816.

Hymns for Sunday Schools. 2nd ed. Nottingham: J. Dunn, 1821.

Hymns for the Chapel of Harrow School. Harrow: Crossley and Clarke, 1860.

Hymns for the Poor of the Flock. London: Central Tract Depot, 1841.

Hymns for the Church Army. London: The Church Army Publishing Office, [1894].

Hymns for the Little Ones in Sunday Schools. London: The Church Sunday School Union, n.d.

Hymns for use at United Prayer Meetings and Other Devotional Services. London: Alliance House, 1886.

Hymns for Use During 1897, Being the Sixtieth Year of the Reign of Queen Victoria. London: Skeffington & Son, [1897].

The Invalid's Hymn-Book. 2nd ed. Dublin: John Robertson, 1841.

Jackson, A. G. (ed.). *The Missioner's Hymnal*. London: Rivingtons, 1884.

Jones, Robert Crompton (ed.). *Hymns of Duty and Faith*. London: E. T. Whitfield, 1872.

[Keble, John]. *The Christian Year: Thoughts in Verse for the Sundays and Holydays Throughout the Year*. 23rd ed. Oxford: J. H. Parker, 1843.

Lane, S. *Spiritual Songs, for Heaven-Bound Travellers*. 3rd ed. Hull: T. Chapman, 1846.

Leifchild, J. (ed.). *Original Hymns, Adapted to General Worship and Special Occasions*. London: Ward and Co., 1856.

[Little, R. (ed.)]. *A Collection of Hymns for Those Who Follow the Faith and Practice of the Primitive Christians*. Birmingham: J. Belcher and Son, 1807.

Lynch, Thomas T. *The Rivulet, A Contribution to Sacred Song*. 4th ed. London: Strahan & Co., 1871.

Martineau, James (ed.). *Hymns for the Christian Church and Home*. London: John Green, 1840.

Mason, Gerard M. (ed.). *Church Militant Hymns*. London: The Church Printing Company, [1885].

McGranahan, James, *Hymn, Psalm and Gospel Song Selections*. London: Morgan and Scott, [c.1904].

The Methodist Sunday-School Hymn-Book. [London]: Wesleyan-Methodist Sunday-School Union, 1879.

Missionary Hymns: Composed and Selected for the Public Services at the Annual Meetings of the London Missionary Society. New ed. London: London Missionary Society, 1830.

Missionary Hymns for Children. Sheffield: George Ridge, [1851].

Missionary Hymns Selected for the Use of Meetings for the Propagation of the Gospel among Jews and Gentiles. Reading: E. Blackwell, 1837.

The Mission Hymnal of the Church Pastoral-Aid Society, with Tunes. London: Nisbet and Co., 1887.

Monsell, John S. B. *Hymns of Love and Praise for the Church's Year*. London: Bell and Daldy, 1863.

Montgomery, James. *Original Hymns for Public, Private, and Social Devotion*. London: Longman, Brown, Green, and Longmans, 1853.

Mussey, Mabel Hay Barrows. *Social Hymns of Brotherhood and Aspiration*. New York: The A. S. Barnes Company, 1914.

Neale, J. M. *Hymns for Children*. 9th ed. London: J. Masters and Co., 1885.

The North of England Sunday School Hymn Book. 15th ed. Newcastle-on-Tyne: T. P. Barkas, [1862].

The Progressive League Hymnal. London: The League of Progressive Thought and Social Service, [1909].

Sankey, Ira D. *New Hymns and Solos*. London: Morgan and Scott, n.d.

Sankey, Ira D., McGranahan, James, and Stebbins, Geo. C. *Gospel Hymns, Nos. 5 and 6 Combined*. Cincinnati: The John Church Co., 1892.

Shipton, Anna. *The Brook in the Way, Original Hymns and Poems*, 2nd ed. London: Morgan and Chase, n.d.

———. *Whispers in the Palms, Hymns and Meditations*. London: Morgan and Chase, [1865].

Simple Hymns for Infants' Schools. London: Darnton and Harvey, 1835.

Singleton, Robert Corbet and Monk, Edwin George (eds.). *The Anglican Hymn Book*. London: Novello, Ewer and Co., 1868.

[Skinner, James (ed.)]. *The Daily Service Hymnal*. London: Rivingtons, [1863].

[Smith, W. Hind (ed.)]. *Hymns for the Use of Christian Associations, Evangelistic Services, etc.* 3rd ed. London: Hodder and Stoughton, 1880.

Snepp, Charles B. and Havergal, Frances Ridley (eds.). *Songs of Grace and Glory*. London: James Nisbet and Co., 1876.

Social Hymns, for the use of the Friends of the Rational System of Society. 2nd ed. Leeds: Central Board of the Universal Community Society of Rational Religionists, 1840.

Soldier's Hymn Book: Compiled for Use at the Aldersgate Mission Hall and Soldiers' Institute. London: Aldersgate Mission Hall, 1868.

Song of Moses and the Lamb, To Be Used by the Society of Christian Israelites. Gravesend: W. Deane, 1853.

Songs for Schools. Westminster: The National Society, 1851.

[South Place Ethical Society]. *Hymns and Anthems for the Use of the South Place Ethical Society*. London: South Place Chapel, 1889.

Spencer, Fanny M. *Thirty-two Hymns with Original Tunes*. London: Novello, Ewer and Co., 1893.

The Spiritual Songster, A Choice and Unique Collection of Song and Hymn for the Awakening of Spiritual and Progressive Ideas in the Mind of Humanity. Newcastle-on-Tyne: H. A. Kersey, [1893].

Spurgeon, C. H. (ed.). *Our Own Hymn-Book*. London: Passmore and Alabaster, 1866.

Stone, S. J. *Hymns*. n.p., n.d.

Sullivan, Arthur (ed.). *Church Hymns with Tunes*. London: Society for Promoting Christian Knowledge, [1874].

The Sunday School Teachers' Hymn-Book. London: The Sunday School Union, 1824.

Taylor, Ann and Jane. *Hymns for Infant Minds*. Rev. ed. London: Ward, Lock, and Tyler, 1876.

Taylor, Mrs. Clare. *Hymns Composed Chiefly on the Death and Sufferings of Christ, and Redemption through His Blood*. London, 1859.

Thring, Godfrey (ed.). *A Church of England Hymn Book*. London: W. Skeffington & Son, 1880.

———. *Hymns and Verses*. London: Rivingtons, 1866.

Troutbeck, John. *The Westminster Abbey Hymn-Book*. London: Novello, Ewer and Co., 1897.

Tuttiett, Rev. L. *Original Hymns for Younger Members of the Church*. 2nd ed. London: Wells Gardner, Darton, & Co., 1889.

The Union Hymn Book for Scholars. London: Sunday School Union, [1852].

Varley, Henry (ed.). *The Sacrifice of Praise, Hymns for Congregational Use and Gospel Meetings*. London: Hodder & Stoughton [1872].

Victorian Hymns, English Sacred Songs of Fifty Years. London: Kegan Paul, Trench & Co., 1887.

W.[aring], A.[nna] L. *Hymns and Meditations*. 11th ed. London: Strahan & Co., 1870.

I. Watts. *Divine and Moral Songs for the Use of Children*. London: W. Darton, 1812.

[Widdrington, Sidney Henry]. *A Collection of Psalms and Hymns for the Churches and Chapels Connected with the Rectory of Walcot*. 2nd ed. London: Hamilton, Adams, & Co., 1842.

[Williams, Isaac]. *Ancient Hymns for Children*. London: James Burns, 1842.

[Williamson, Mrs. J. (ed.)]. *Hymns for the Household of Faith and Lays of the Better Land*. London: Wertheim, MacIntosh, and Hunt, 1861.

Wither, George and Havergal, Henry E. (ed.). *Hymns and Songs of the Church*. Oxford: John Henry Parker, 1846.

[Yonge, Frances Mary]. *The Child's Christian Year: Hymns for Every Sunday and Holy-Day*. Oxford: John Henry Parker, 1841.

NOTES

INTRODUCTION

1. Walter E. Houghton, *The Victorian Frame of Mind, 1830-1870* (New Haven, 1957), p. xv.

2. Although a number of critics of the Victorians have denigrated Victorian religion because of its alleged hypocrisy, it is hard to deny the influence of the churches on the social life of the period. G. M. Trevelyan, *Illustrated English Social History*, Vol. IV (London, 1942), p. 29, notes that "the Victorian gentleman and his family were more religious in their habits and sober in their tone of thought than their predecessors in the lighthearted days of Horace Walpole and Charles Fox." Asa Briggs, *Victorian People, A Reassessment of Persons and Themes, 1851-67* (Chicago, 1972), p. 147, has characterized the mid-Victorian period as "an age when Christian values were the central values of society and all deep individual problems were related to Christian morals." R. C. K. Ensor, *England, 1870-1914* (Oxford, 1960), agrees: "No one will ever understand Victorian England who does not appreciate that among highly civilized . . . countries, it is one of the most religious the world has ever known." The census report of 1851-53 concluded that although many in the lower class were unchurched, "the middle classes have augmented rather than diminished that devotional sentiment and strictness of attention to religious services by which, for several centuries, they have so eminently been distinguished. With the upper classes, too, the subject of religion has obtained of late a marked degree of notice, and a regular church-attendance is now ranked among the recognized proprieties of life."

Raymond Chapman, *The Victorian Debate: English Literature, 1832-1901* (New York, 1968), p. 62, has noted the enormous market for religious books sold during the period: Marie Corelli's *The Master Christian* (1900) had a prepublication printing of 75,000 copies; in 1841 the Methodist Book Room issued 1,326,000 copies of tracts; the *Publishers' Circular* for 1880 listed 580 new novels but 975 volumes under the heading "theological, biblical, etc." Three years after the publication of *Robert Elsmere*, pundits suggested that the census of 1890 should include the question, "What do you think of

Robert Elsmere?" The crowds that gathered throughout the century to hear the famous preachers are further evidence of the widespread influence of Victorian religion; when Charles Haddon Spurgeon preached at the Surrey Gardens Music Hall, with a seating capacity of ten thousand, hundreds had to be turned away.

For a review of the recent research into nineteenth-century religion *see* Richard A. Soloway, "Church and Society: Recent Trends in Nineteenth Century Religious History," *The Journal of British Studies*, XI (May, 1972), pp. 145-159.

3. For the most part the songs of the church have been left largely to the theologian and churchmen. Albert Edward Bailey, *The Gospel in Hymns, Backgrounds and Interpretations* (New York, 1950), has attempted to illustrate history with hymns, but the chronological scope of his work is so broad that the nineteenth century receives only a brief perusal.

The hymns of the Moravians and the Wesleys and their successors in the puritan-evangelical tradition have been explored very briefly by Gordon Rattray Taylor, *The Angel-Makers*: *A Study in the Psychological Origins of Historical Change, 1750-1850* (London, 1958), pp. 165-167, and E. P. Thompson, *The Making of the English Working Class* (New York, 1964). Both of these authors stress the Freudian interpretations of the introspective evangelical hymns and both find in these hymns signs of regression to infantilism or flights from reality. (The reality that is being fled from is, for Thompson, the class struggle of the early nineteenth century; for Taylor, it is a threatening Oedipal father-figure.)

Novelists recognized the value of hymns to add color and depth to the social background of their work: Howard Spring, for instance, puts hymns of Wesley or Sankey in the mouths of down-and-out souls to illustrate the almost hysterical enthusiasm of a new convert (*see Fame Is the Spur* and *There Is No Armour*). George Eliot uses a Wesleyan hymn to ridicule, by contrast, high church formalism (*see Adam Bede*).

4. J. Edwin Orr, *The Second Evangelical Awakening* (London, 1949), p. 261.

5. Jeremiah Bascom Reeves, *The Hymn as Literature* (New York, 1924), pp. 216-217.

6. W. K. Lother Clarke, *A Hundred Years of Hymns Ancient and Modern* (London, 1960), p. 17.

7. *Taine's Notes on England*, trans. Edward Hyams (Fair Lawn, N.J., 1958), p. 191.

8. W. T. Stead, *Hymns That Have Helped* (New York, 1909), pp. 11-12.

9. Ibid., p. 16.

10. Johanna Spyri, *Heidi*, trans. by Helen B. Dole (New York, 1927), pp. 197-198. Although written by a Swiss woman about a Swiss girl, *Heidi*'s moral tone and *weltanschauung* reflect attitudes that were commonly held by the Victorian middle class.

11. Janet Courtney, *Freethinkers of the Nineteenth Century* (Freeport, N.Y., 1967; originally published in 1920), p. 4.

12. Horton Davies, *Worship and Theology in England from Newman to Martineau, 1850-1900* (Princeton, 1962), p. 169.

13. *The Salvation Army in Relation to the Church and State* (1883), p. 53.

14. William Pett Ridge, *A Story Teller: Forty Years in London* (London, 1923), p. 234.

15. L. E. Elliott-Binns, *Religion in the Victorian Era* (2nd ed.; London, 1964), p. 374.

16. W. L. Alexander, "Lectures on the Public Psalmody of the Church," *The Scottish Congregational Magazine* (August, 1848), p. 254.

17. Martin, *A Sociology of English Religion* (New York, 1967), p. 88.

18. Peter Burke (ed.), *A New Kind of History and Other Essays: Lucien Febvre*, trans. by K. Folca (New York, 1973), p. 2.

19. H. A. L. Jefferson, *Hymns in Christian Worship* (London, 1950), p.221.

20. Erik Routley, *Hymns and Human Life* (London, 1952), p.9.

21. Albert Peel, *These Hundred Years: A History of the Congregational Union of England and Wales, 1831-1931* (London, 1931), p.287.

22. Harry Escott, *Isaac Watts, Hymnographer: A Study of the Beginnings, Development, and Philosophy of the English Hymn* (London, 1962), p.111.

23. *See*, for instance, Lorenz, *Singing Church*, p. 32.

24. Benjamin Franklin Crawford, *Religious Trends in a Century of Hymns* (Carnegie, Pa., 1938).

25. Owen Chadwick, *The Victorian Church* (New York, 1966), I, p.518.

26. Ibid., II, pp. 397-398.

27. Louis F. Benson, *The Church Hymns* (Philadelphia, 1898); James King, *Anglican Hymnology* (London, 1885).

28. King, *Anglican Hymnology*.

29. Hymns will be footnoted in the following form: hymn author; hymn title (usually the first line of the hymn, in which case the title is italicized; if the title is not the same as the first line, as in the case of many "gospel hymns," the title will be put in quotation marks); date of composition; hymnbook in which the present writer found the hymn: author or editor, hymnbook title, followed by publication data. Where any of this information is unavailable, it will be omitted without so noting.

CHAPTER I

1. Mark 14:26.

2. Ephesians 5:19. *See* also Colossians 3:16 and Corinthians 14:26.

3. There is a vast literature on the subject. For a concise review for the layman see C. S. Phillips, *Hymnody Past and Present* (London, 1937), Chapter I.

4. H.A.L. Jefferson, *Hymns in Christian Worship* (London, 1930), p.161.

5. Ibid., p.163.

6. Cranmer's preface to the 1549 Prayer Book.

7. Phillips, *Hymnody Past and Present*, p.100.

8. Marot's psalms, 50 in number, together with those of Theodore Beza, were published in 1562 as *Les Psaumes mis en rime française par Clément Marot et Theodore de Beza*; this was the famed "Genevan Psalter."

9. Fuller, *Church History of Britain* (Oxford, 1845), IV, p.73.

10. Horton Davies, *Theology in England from Watts and Wesley to Maurice, 1690-1850* (Princeton, 1961), p.65.

11. Ibid. Phillips, *Hymnody Past and Present*, p.144, names Queen Victoria as the questioner.

12. Vivian de Sola Pinto, *Enthusiast in Wit, A Portrait of John Wilmot Earl of Rochester, 1647-1680* (Lincoln, Nebr., 1962), p.138.

13. Phillips, *Hymnody Past and Present*, p.157.

14. Davies, *Theology in England, 1690-1850*, p.127.

15. Phyllis Wetherell Bultmann, "Everybody Sing: The Social Significance of the Eighteenth-Century Hymn" (Unpublished Ph.D. dissertation, University of California at Los Angeles, 1950), p.86.

16. Jefferson, *Hymns in Christian Worship*, pp.44-45.

17. Isaac Watts, *Hymns in three books* (1707); quoted by Mrs. Crosby Adams, *Studies in Hymnology* (Richmond, Va., 1929), p. 36.

18. Bultmann, "Everybody Sing," p.145.

19. Percy Dearmer, *Songs of Praise Discussed* (Oxford, 1933), p.317.

20. Doddridge, *Hymns* (1755), p.205.

21. Ibid., p.188.

22. Davies, *Theology in England, 1690-1850*, p.100.

23. *Prayers and Meditations*, Easter day, 1764: *Works of Johnson* (Oxford, 1825), ix, 221; quoted by Louis F. Benson, *The English Hymn* (Philadelphia, 1915), p.v.

24. G. R. Balleine, *A History of the Evangelical Party in the Church of England* (London, 1933), p. 199.

25. Erik Routley, *Hymns and Human Life* (London, 1952), p.79.

26. "Letters," *The Gentleman's Magazine*, XIII (Nov., 1752), 250; quoted by Bultmann, "Everybody Sing," p.229.

27. *Considerations on Parochial Music*, pp.10 and 14; quoted by L. E. Elliott-Binns, *Religion In the Victorian Era* (2nd ed.; London, 1964), p.372.

28. Charles was the most prolific hymn writer, although John wrote some hymns; John's work in editing and revising has caused some confusion about authorship.

29. *Journal of John Wesley*, I, 385; quoted by Bultmann, "Everybody Sing," p.163.

30. J. Wesley, *Journal* (Standard ed. by Curnock), I, 475; quoted by Philips, *Hymnody Past and Present*, p.175.

31. Benson, *English Hymn*, p.258.

32. Ibid., p.244.

33. Sydney G. Dimond, *The Psychology of the Methodist Revival, an Empirical and Descriptive Study* (Oxford, 1926), p. 44.

34. Stanley Armstrong Hunter, *The Music of the Gospel* (New York, 1932), p.16.

35. Bernard L. Manning, *The Hymns of Wesley and Watts* (London, 1942), p.43. Manning continues, "Take one rough, and not exhaustive, test. Of the 769 hymns in one edition not fewer than 84 have as their first word the Name: Jesus, Christ, Saviour. One hymn in every nine *opens* so."

36. Elie Halévy, *The Birth of Methodism in England*, trans. by Bernard Semmel (Chicago, 1971). *See* also E. P. Thompson, *The Making of the English Working Class* (New York, 1964).

37. Robert Southey, *The Life of Wesley and the Rise and Progress of Methodism*, ed. by J. A. Atkinson (London and New York, 1889), pp.109-113. Wesley himself repudiated the Moravian hymnody, shocked by its extravagences.

38. *See*, for instance, Benson, *English Hymn*, p.267.

39. G. R. Taylor, *The Angel-Makers*: *A Study in the Psychological Origins of Historical Change, 1750-1850* (London, 1958), pp.165-167.

40. Thompson, *Making of the English Working Class*, pp.370-374.

41. Ibid., p.372.

42. Ibid., p.374.

43. Until his death Wesley insisted that the "Methodist Connexion" remain within the Church and urged his followers to attend parish churches for Sunday services and Communion. But after his death in 1791, the Methodists formed their own churches.

44. Many of the Wesleys' hymns were used in these hymnals, but Louis Benson, *English Hymn*, p. 259, writes that the Methodists were so disdained by the more conservative churches that, even after Wesleyan hymns were adopted by other denominational hymnals in the first half of the nineteenth century, "even where compilers have been careful to give the names of other authors, the hymns of the Wesleys are frequently printed as anonymous, or ascribed to some other author."

45. John Julian, *A Dictionary of Hymnology* (New York, 1892), pp.331-343. Jeremiah Bascom Reeves, *The Hymn as Literature* (New York, 1924), pp.216-217, writes that "between 1800 and 1820 there were nearly fifty different hymn-books in use in the Church of England alone."

46. W. K. Lother Clarke, *A Hundred Years of Hymns Ancient and Modern* (London, 1960), p.15.

47. Paul Chappell, *Music and Worship in the Anglican Church, 1597-1967* (London, 1968), pp.94-95.

48. Owen Chadwick, *The Victorian Church* (New York, 1966), I, 67.

49. Clarke, *Hundred Years*, pp.18-20. The author says that since all articles were anonymous, they may be taken as representing editorial policy.

50. *Barchester Towers* (New York, 1959), pp.39-40.

51. Jefferson, *Hymns in Christian Worship*, p.169. The bishop is not identified.

52. Prestige, *Life of Charles Gore*, p.295; quoted by Elliott-Binns, *Religion in the Victorian Era*, pp.372-373.

53. William Lindsay Alexander, "Lectures on the Public Psalmody of the Church," *The Scottish Congregational Magazine* (Sept. 1848), p.293.

54. W. W. Barr, "The Psalms and their Use, or the Matter and Manner of Praise," *Evangelical Repository*, LVI (Nov. 1879), pp.161-166.

55. Horton Davies, *Worship and Theology in England from Newman to Martineau, 1850-1900* (Princeton, 1962), p.107.

56. John Brownlie, *The Hymns and Hymn Writers of the Church Hymnary* (London, 1899), pp.98-105.

CHAPTER II

1. In *Knots Untied*; quoted by E. J. Poole-Connor, *Evangelicalism in England* (London, 1951), p.207. Willis Glover, *Evangelical Nonconformists and Higher Criticism in The Nineteenth Century* (London, 1954), Chapter I, believes that nineteenth-century evangelicals had become even more Biblicist than their sixteenth-century forebears.

2. James Theodore Inskip, *Evangelical Influence in English Life* (London, 1933), p.41.

3. H. C. G. Moule, *The Evangelical School in the Church of England, Its Men and Its Work in the Nineteenth Century* (London, 1901), pp.62-63.

4. Poole-Connor, *Evangelicalism in England*, p.207.

5. Inskip, *Evangelical Influence*, p.32.

6. Roland H. Bainton, *A Life of Martin Luther: Here I Stand* (New York, 1950), p.144.

7. Ibid., pp.48-49.

8. John H. Overton, *The English Church in the Nineteenth Century (1800-1833)* (London, 1894), pp.108-109. Overton was a severe critic of evangelical ideas; his notice and his praise, therefore, were not lightly given.

9. Both tracts quote by Poole-Connor, *Evangelicalism in England*, p.182.

10. Moule, *Evangelical School*, p.9.

11. Surprisingly, considering the importance of hymns in both regular church services and missionary revival services, there have been no thorough studies of the psychology of hymn-singing. Psychologists have mentioned in passing the effects of hymns in revival services. Frederick Morgan Davenport, in *Primitive Traits in Religious Revivals: A Study in Mental and Social Evolution* (New York, 1906), pp.228-233, indicated that in revival services the repetition of single ideas or images can produce a self-hypnotization which can remove rational inhibitions and thus make the audience receptive to "conversion." Robert H. Thouless, *An Introduction to the Psychology of Religion* (New York, 1931), pp.148-149, 159, pointed out that any action which is performed by the congregaton as a whole reinforces the herd instinct of the group, but that ritualistic actions are particularly effective in creating herd suggestion. Edwin Diller Starbuck, *The Psychology of Religion:*

An Empirical Study of the Growth of Religious Consciousness (London, 1914), gave a number of examples of hymn-singing preceding the experience of religious conversion.

12. J. Edwin Orr, *The Second Evangelical Awakening* (London, 1949), p.261, writes, "The British publishers have sold more than 90,000,000 Sankey hymn-books in less than eighty years. They have sold many millions more of Alexander's hymn-book." David P. Appleby, *History of Church Music* (Chicago, 1965), p.143, writes, "Sankey relates that on a trip through Egypt, while traveling on the Nile River he heard nationals singing his gospel songs. He had similar experiences in many other countries. Eighty million copies of one collection of Sankey's songs were sold in England alone, within fifty years after initial publication."

13. L. E. Elliott-Binns, *Religion in the Victorian Era* (2nd ed.; London, 1964), p.214.

14. William Booth (ed.), *Salvation Army Music* (London, 1890), Preface.

15. David R. Breed, *The History and Use of Hymns and Hymn-Tunes* (New York, 1903), p.336.

16. Ira Sankey, *O wonderful words of the gospel* (1887), stanza 1. Ira D. Sankey, James McGranahan, and Geo. C. Stebbins, *Gospel Hymns, Nos. 5 and 6 Combined* (Cincinnati, 1892), Hymn #10.

17. James McGranahan, *Preach the gospel, sound it forth* (1891), stanza 1. Sankey *et al.*, *Gospel Hymns*, Hymn #268.

18. *From utmost East to utmost West*, stanza 2. Quoted by Jeremiah Bascom Reeves, *The Hymn as Literature* (New York, 1924), p. 311.

19. Harry Escott, *Isaac Watts, Hymnographer: A Study of the Beginnings, Development, and Philosophy of the English Hymn* (London, 1962), p.56.

20. Isaac Watts, *Come all harmonious tongues* (1707), stanza 3. Dr. Rippon (ed.), *The Psalms and Hymns of Dr. Watts* (Philadelphia, 1838), Hymn #252.

21. William Cowper, *There is a fountain filled with blood* (1771), stanzas 1 and 2. John Allen, *The Penny Hymnbook* (London, [1860]), Hymn #102.

22. H. A. L. Jefferson, *Hymns in Christian Worship* (London, 1950), p.18. *See* also E. P. Thompson, *The Making of the English Working Class* (New York, 1964).

23. Horton Davies, *Worship and Theology in England from Newman to Martineau, 1850-1900* (Princeton, 1962), p. 86.

24. Taylor's interpretation of these hymns is found in *The Angel-Makers: A Study in the Psychological Origins of Historical Change, 1750-1850* (London, 1958), pp.185-187.

25. Ira Sankey, *Behold a Fountain deep and wide* (1887), stanzas 1 and 2. Sankey *et al.*, *Gospel Hymns*, Hymn #6. See Mrs. Clare Taylor, *Hymns Composed Chiefly on the Death and Sufferings of Christ, and Redemption through His Blood* (London, 1859). This entire hymnbook is devoted to the subject of the crucifixion and redemption.

26. *Exceeding precious is my Lord*, stanzas 3-5. [Thomas Bradbury], *Psalms and Hymns and Spiritual Songs for the Elect of God* (3rd ed.; Brighton, 1891), Hymn #108.

27. Horatius Bonar, *I heard the voice of Jesus say* (1846), stanza 1. [Bradbury], *Psalms and Hymns*, Hymn #204.

28. *Come, my soul, thy suit prepare*, stanzas 3 and 4. Allen, *Penny Hymnbook*, Hymn #20.

29. John Newton, *One there is, above all others* (1779), stanzas 1 and 3. *Olney Hymns* (1779), I, Hymn #53.

30. Escott, *Isaac Watts*, p. 114. "He presented his reform at the bar of the worshipper's experience. . . . Watts was really the first hymn-writer to give due place to the subjective aspect of worship-song, and to take into full consideration the psychology of the congregation in its praises."

31. Bernard L. Manning, *The Hymns of Wesley and Watts, Five Informal Papers* (London, 1942), p.43.

32. Ibid., p.44.

33. Charles Wesley, *Jesus, lover of my soul* (1740), stanzas 1 and 2. Allen, *Penny Hymnbook*, Hymn #54.

34. Augustus Toplady, *Rock of Ages, cleft for me* (1776), stanza 3. Committee of the Presbyterian Church of England, *Church Praise* (London, 1885).

35. Orr, *Second Evangelical Awakening*, pp.255-261. Max Weber, in *The Sociology of Religion*, trans., Ephraim Fischoff (Boston, 1964), pp.101-102, sees the rise in popularity of the subjective in religious revivals as a class function: when a religious movement directed toward salvation moves to the nonintellectual and disadvantaged masses, he says, the emphasis on a personal relationship to the Saviour is a sociological consequence.

36. C. C. Case, *Fountain of purity opened for sin* (1891), stanza 2. Sankey *et al.*, *Gospel Hymns*, Hymn #335.

37. Isaac Watts, *Lord, I am Thine, but Thou wilt prove* (1719), stanza 4. [Bradbury], *Psalms and Hymns*, Hymn #302.

38. Augustus Toplady, *Emptied of earth I fain would be* (1759), stanza 1. [Bradbury], *Psalms and Hymns*, Hymn #101.

39. William Cowper, *Far from the world, O Lord, I flee* (1765), stanza 1. Allen, *Penny Hymnbook*, Hymn #25.

40. W. Hay M. H. Aitken, *O leave we all for Jesus*, stanzas 1 and 2. *The Church Mission Hymn Book with Mission Liturgies* (London, 1913), Hymn #87.

41. T. R. Taylor, *I'm but a stranger here*, (1836), stanza 1. *Hymns for Use at United Prayer Meetings and Other Devotional Services* (London, 1886), Hymn #54.

42. *Jerusalem! my happy home!* (from the 16th century), stanza 1. Allen, *Penny Hymnbook*, Hymn #52.

43. *Beautiful land! so bright so fair*, stanza 1. William Booth (ed.), *Salvation Army Music* (London, 1890), Hymn #37.

44. Ira Sankey, "Onward, upward, homeward!" (1887), stanza 1. Sankey *et al.*, *Gospel Hymns*, Hymn #2.

45. Thompson, *Making of the English Working Class*, pp.373-374.

46. *Wesleyan Conference Minutes* (1855), pp.78, 182; quoted by K.S. In-

glis, *Churches and the Working Classes in Victorian England* (London, 1963), p.74. Many historians have noted the ascetic character of evangelicalism. Walter Houghton, *The Victorian Frame of Mind, 1830-1870* (New Haven, 1957), p. 171, writes that "the emphasis on moral character allowed little or no consideration for intellectual and aesthetic virtues." G. M. Trevelyan, *Illustrated English Social History* (London, 1942), IV, 29, ties evangelical self-denial to the rugged individualism of liberal economics. "The English of all classes formed in the Nineteenth Century a strongly Protestant nation; most of them were religious, and most of them (including the Utilitarians and Agnostics) were 'serious,' with that strong preoccupation about morality which is the merit and danger of the Puritan character. In their double anxiety to obey a given ethical code and to 'get on' in profitable business, the typical men of the new age overlooked some of the other possibilities of life. An individualist commercialism and an equally individualist type of religion combined to produce a breed of self-reliant and reliable men, good citizens in many respects—but 'Philistines' in the phrase popularized by their most famous critic in a later generation. Neither machine industry nor evangelical religion had any use for art or beauty, which were despised as effeminate by the makers of the great factory towns of the North."

47. Erik Routley, *Hymns and Human Life* (London, 1952), pp.118-119.

48. W. J. L. Sheppard, *Hear, my soul, the solemn word*, stanzas 2 and 3. *Church Mission Hymn Book*, Hymn #9.

49. Samuel Wesley, *The morning flowers display their sweets* (1726), stanzas 1 and 2. Allen, *Penny Hymnbook*, Hymn #101.

50. *Let us gather up the sunbeams*, stanzas 1 and 2. Booth, *Salvation Army Music*, Hymn #15.

51. Erik Routley, *Hymns and Human Life*, p. 117. Horton Davies, *Worship and Theology (1850-1900)*, p. 207, has called the episode "a storm in a teacup."

52. Owen Chadwick, *The Victorian Church* (New York, 1966), I, p.406. Chadwick says that the congregation numbered eighteen adults. Chadwick's description of Lynch rings of the bias of a participant: "Lynch was a tender effeminate aesthete who with hardly a vein of true poetry imagined himself a poet; strange pastor, with a refined congregation of eighteen adults. He described himself with pathetic accuracy as a bird's heart without a bird's wings."

53. Albert Peel, *These Hundred Years: A History of the Congregational Union of England and Wales, 1831-1931* (London, 1931), pp.221-235. Except where noted otherwise, the account that follows is taken from this book.

54. Jefferson, *Hymns in Christian Worship* p.117.

55. Peel, *These Hundred Years*, p.228.

56. Balleine, *History of the Evangelical Party*, pp.148-149.

57. Anne Steele, *Father, whate'er of earthly bliss* (1776) stanzas 1 and 2. Allen, *Penny Hymnbook*, Hymn #28.

58. *The Invalid's Hymn-Book* (2nd ed.; Dublin, 1841), Hymn #1, stanzas 1-3, 5, and 7. W. L. Burn, *The Age of Equipoise, A Study of the Mid-Victorian Generation* (New York, 1964), writes, "Prayers, sermons, psalms and hymns had bitten into mid-Victorian England the acceptance of privation, suffering,

pain and death as the expression of God's will and even of His mercy."

59. John Newton, *I asked the Lord, that I might grow* (1774), stanzas 1-5. Allen, *Penny Hymnbook*, Hymn #49.

60. Thompson, *Making of the English Working Class*, p. 372.

61. Peter Fletcher (pseud. A. B. W. Fletcher), *The Long Sunday* (London, 1958), p.22.

62. Balleine, *History of the Evangelical Party*, p.252.

63. Kenneth Young, *Chapel* (London, 1972), p. 136.

64. K. S. Inglis, *Churches and the Working Classes in Victorian England* (London, 1963), p. 76.

65. Bready, *England: Before and After Wesley*, p. 405. Among others who espouse this view are G. M. Trevelyan, *Illustrated English Social History*, Vol. 4; Kathleen Heasman, *Evangelicals in Action: An Appraisal of their Social Work in the Victorian Era* (London, 1962); G. R. Balleine, *History of the Evangelical Party*; and Isabel Simeral, *Reform Movements in Behalf of Children in England of the Early Nineteenth Century, and the Agents of Those Reforms* (New York, 1916).

66. Young, *Chapel*, p. 21.

67. Thomas Kelly, *Happy they who trust in Jesus* (1806), stanza 1. *Hymns for Use at United Prayer Meetings*, Hymn #38.

68. James McGranahan, *Sitting by the gateway of a palace fair* (1887), stanzas 1-4. Sankey *et al.*, *Gospel Hymns*, Hymn #124.

69. Altenburg, *Fear not, O little flock, the foe* (trans. by Winkworth, 1855), stanzas 1 and 2. [Bradbury], *Psalms and Hymns*, Hymn #122.

70. J. H. Evans, *Faint not, Christian!* (1833), stanza 2. *Hymns for Use at United Prayer Meetings*, Hymn #20.

71. William J. Kirkpatrick, *O troubled heart, there is a home*, stanzas 1 and 2. Sankey *et al.*, *Gospel Hymns*, Hymn #64.

72. Elie Halévy, *England in 1815*, trans. by E. I. Watkin and D. A. Barker (London, 1949), p.387.

CHAPTER III

1. Many critics have noted the hypocrisy of this use of religion to enforce social values. A Victorian, Ernest Belfort Bax, in *Reminiscences and Reflexions of a Mid and Late Victorian* (New York, 1967; originally published London, 1918), pp.17-18, called this hypocrisy unconscious: "That some of it was genuine and a good deal of it deliberate hypocrisy I have no doubt whatever, but I should attribute the bulk of it to something between these two extremes which I should term *unconscious hypocrisy*. By unconscious hypocrisy I understand an attitude of mind which succeeds in persuading itself that it believes or approves certain things as it professes to do, while really *in foro conscientiae* this profession is dictated by a sense of its own interests, real or supposed."

2. Those familiar with the differences between sheep and goats will recognize how apt and revealing such a metaphor is: sheep will be herded, will

follow the leader, are meek, stupid and productive; goats are individualists, aggressive, quite intelligent, and, perhaps most telling, sexually active (the horns and cloven hoofs ascribed to the devil are not accidental attributes). Rulers always prefer to sheep to goats.

3. Edward Hyams (trans.), *Taine's Notes on England* (Fair Lawn, N.J.: Essential Books, 1958), pp.99. Another example of the Victorian belief that lower class morality was different from upper class morality and potentially dangerous to social well-being can be seen in the attitude of Dr. William Acton, author of *The Functions and Disorders of the Reproductive Organs* (1857). Acton believed that women had few sexual feelings. The exception to this statement, Acton said, were the "low and vulgar women"—i.e., women of lower classes—who did experience sexual desires and who consequently tempted men to immoral depravity and probable eventual ruin and/or insanity. From Steven Marcus, *The Other Victorians, A Study of Sexuality and Pornography in Mid-Nineteenth-Century England* (New York, 1964). In 1907, St. Loe Strachey echoed this opinion when he predicted that the emergence of the working class Labour party in the elections of the previous year meant "the overthrow of the Christian moral code . . . and must end in free love and promiscuity." Quoted by Kenneth D. Brown, "Non-Conformity and The British Labour Movement: A Study," *Journal of Social History* (Winter, 1975), p.113.

Ernest Belfort Bax, in *Reminiscences and Reflexions*, pp.17-18, confirms this belief that religion was a vital support to order and property: ". . . in discussing Freethought in religion or Radicalism in politics, as a makeweight to the conventional arguments against such subversive doctrines, one often heard it thrown in, that if Freethought prevailed, or the political constitution were overthrown, there would be no security for property and its interests. Apart from the truth of theological doctrine or political theory, religion and the existing English constitution were necessary to keep the lower classes in order."

4. Hyams, *Taine's Notes*, p.158. Taine wrote about church services: "The ceremony is an ethical meeting [*sic*] at which the chairman does his talking from the pulpit instead of the platform.

"In the sermons, as in the religion itself, dogma always takes a back seat and attention is chiefly paid to the means and will required in order to live a good life. Religion as such, with its emotions and great visions is hardly more than the poetry which informs ethics or a background to morality."

5. Winston S. Churchill, *My Early Life, A Roving Commission* (New York, 1930), p.114.

6. *Simple Hymns for Infants' Schools* (London, 1835), p.v.

7. Thomas Bradbury, *Psalms and Hymns and Spiritual Songs for the Elect of God* (3rd ed.; Brighton, 1891), Hymn #121.

8. William Booth (ed.), *Salvation Army Music* (London, 1890), Hymn #108, stanzas 1 and 2.

9. W. Hay M. H. Aiken, *O leave we all for Jesus*, stanza 1. *The Church Mission Hymn-Book* (London, 1883), Hymn #87.

10. Mrs. Cecil Frances Alexander, *All things bright and beautiful* (1849),

stanza 3. Committee of the Presbyterian Church of England (eds.), *Church Praise* (London, 1885), Hymn #433.

11. John Ellerton, *O how fair that morning broke*, stanza 4. John Troutbeck (ed.), *The Westminster Abbey Hymn-Book* (London, 1897), Hymn #350.

12. *Miss Grace of All Souls* (1895), p.24. Quoted by P. J. Keating, *The Working Classes in Victorian Fiction* (New York, 1971), p.237.

13. Walter E. Houghton, *The Victorian Frame of Mind, 1830-1870* (New Haven, 1957), p.242.

14. Stanzas 3 and 5. *Hymns Ancient and Modern* (1875), Hymn #475.

15. J. T. Lightwood, *Their earthly task who fail to do*. Sir Frederick Bridge (ed.), *The Methodist Hymn-Book with Tunes* (London, 1904).

16. Horatius Bonar, *Make haste, O man, to live* (1857), stanzas 2 and 5. Horatius Bonar, *Hymns of Faith and Hope* (London, 1857).

17. Anna Walker, *Work for the night is coming*! (1868), stanza 2. Henry Allon, *Children's Worship: A Book of Sacred Song for Home and School* (London, 1887), Hymn #502.

18. *The Albion Sunday School Hymn Book* (Southampton, 1867), Hymn #225, stanza #1.

19. Stopford A. Brooke (ed.), *Christian Hymns* (London, 1881), Hymn #1.

20. John Samuel Bewley Monsell, *Fight the good fight with all thy might* (1863), stanzas 1 and 2. John S. B. Monsell, *Hymns of Love and Praise for the Church's Year* (London, 1863).

21. Thomas Hughes, *Tom Brown's School-Days* (6th ed.; New York, 1911), p.142. Hughes wrote several hymns; in *O God of Truth, whose living Word*, he wrote:

We fight for truth, *we* fight for God,
  Poor slaves of lies and sin!
He who would fight for Thee on earth
  Must first be true within.

Then God of Truth, for whom we long,
  Thou who wilt hear our prayer,
Do Thine own battle in our hearts,
  And slay the falsehood there.

From *The Progressive League Hymnal* (London, [1909]), Hymn. #59.

22. Garret Horder, *Once to every man and nation* (1894), stanza 1. *The English Hymnal* (London, 1906).

23. Ambrose Shepherd, *The Gospel and Social Questions* (2nd ed.; London, 1902), p.34. One of the most popular images of late nineteenth-century hymns was one which symbolized the individual's responsibility for his own choice—the image of Christ knocking at the door. The image was inspired by a brief biblical passage: "Behold, I stand at the door and knock; if anyone hears my voice and opens the door, I will come in and eat with him, and he with me." (Revelation, III, 20). In 1854 William Holman Hunt, a pre-Raphaelite painter, exhibited *The Light of the World*, a dramatic painting of Christ

knocking at the door. The novelty of subject and style shocked some critics, but the painting attracted large crowds when it was put on exhibition. By the end of the century the image of Christ knocking at the door appeared repeatedly in hymnbooks, especially mission hymnbooks; *The Church Mission Hymn Book* alone contains six different hymns all based on this image. One of the gloomier versions, W. W. Skeats's *With patient Heart, O soul,* begins with an invitation to open the door of the heart and ends with a threat of death if the invitation is ignored:

Day wanes: the sun hath almost set;
With dews of night My locks are wet;
  Ah! wilt thou hearken never?
Thy day of grace is almost o'er!
Except thou hear, and ope the door,
  I leave thee—and for ever!

24. H. R. Palmer, *Yield not to temptation* (1868), stanzas 1 and 2. Ira D. Sankey, James McGranahan, and Geo. C. Stebbins, *Gospel Hymns. Nos. 2 and 6 Combined* (Cincinnati, 1892), Hymn #166.

25. David Daiches, *Some Late Victorian Attitudes* (New York, 1969), pp. 14-15.

26. London, 1868. The author, A. L. O. E. (A Lady of England), was Charlotte Marie Tucker.

27. Ibid., Hymn #23.

28. Peter Fletcher, *The Long Sunday* (London, 1958), p.78.

29. F. Beardsall, *Selection of Hymns and Songs Suitable for Public and Social Temperance Meetings* (5th ed.; Manchester, [1850]), Hymn #5, stanzas 1 and 2.

30. G. M. Trevelyan, *The Nineteenth Century*, Vol. IV of *Illustrated English Social History* (London, 1942), p. 110.

31. Fletcher, *Long Sunday*, p. 44.

32. Beardsall, *Selection of Hymns and Songs*, Hymn #39, stanzas 1-3 and 5.

33. Church of England Temperance Society, *Hymns and Songs to be Used at Meetings of the Society* (London, n.d.), Hymn #24.

34. Kenneth Young, *Chapel* (London, 1972), p.82.

35. Erik Routley, *Hymns and Human Life* (London, 1952), pp.303-304.

36. Canon H. Twells, *Awake, O Lord, as in the days of old* (1904), stanzas 1 and 2. *Hymns Ancient and Modern* (4th ed.; London, 1904), Hymn #454.

37. Alfred Tennyson, *Strong Son of God, immortal love*. This hymn was adapted from Tennyson's poem, *In Memoriam*. H. A. L. Jefferson, *Hymns in Christian Worship* (London, 1950), pp.222-223.

38. Arthur James Mason, *Church of the living God* (1889), stanzas 1, 2, 5, and 8. *Hymns Ancient and Modern* (1904), Hymn #396.

39. Samuel John Stone, *The Church's one foundation* (1866), stanzas 3 and 6. *Hymns Ancient and Modern* (London, 1875), Hymn #320.

40. Mrs. Humphry Ward, *Robert Elsmere* (London, 1914), p. 410.

NOTES

CHAPTER IV

1. Philippe Aries, in *Centuries of Childhood, A Social History of Family Life*, trans. by Robert Baldick (New York, 1962), p. 32, calls childhood the "privileged age" of the nineteenth century, as adolescence is of the twentieth century.

2. New York, 1937, p.740.

3. Owen Chadwick, *The Victorian Church* (New York, 1966), II, 257.

4. *See*, for instance, Kenneth Young, *Chapel* (London, 1972) and Edwin Wilbur Rice, *The Sunday-School Movement, 1780-1917* (New York, 1971).

5. Young, *Chapel*, p. 50.

6. W. L. Alexander, "Lectures on the Public Psalmody of the Church," *The Scottish Congregational Magazine* (August, 1848), p. 254.

7. Charlotte Brontë, *Villette* (New York, 1859), p.25.

8. W. T. Stead, *Hymns That Have Helped* (New York, 1909), p.19.

9. Edmund Gosse, *Father and Son, A Study of Two Temperaments* (New York, 1907), p. 234. In children's books of the period the children often recite hymns to emphasize a lesson being taught by the parent or teacher. *See*, for instance, Esther Hewlet, *The Old Man's Head* (London, 1820), which is by no means an isolated instance.

10. Gosse, *Father and Son*, p.55.

11. Edwin Diller Starbuck, *The Psychology of Religion: An Empirical Study of the Growth of Religious Consciousness* (London, 1914). We might add that there were probably many other instances where hymns helped to precipitate a religious experience but where the respondent failed to specially note the hymn; hymns are an integral part of congregational religious services and, just because they are commonplace and expected, there is usually no special awareness of their presence.

12. Stead, *Hymns That Have Helped*, p. 19.

13. Starbuck, *Psychology of Religion*, p. 302.

14. Young, *Chapel*, p. 70. The original verse was,

Here we suffer grief and pain;
Here we meet to part again:
In heaven we part no more.
    Oh, that will be joyful!
    Joyful, joyful, joyful!
    Oh, that will be joyful,
When we meet to part no more.

The hymn was a favorite for memorization. In the evangelical literature for children several exemplary pious children who die at an early age repeat this hymn in their last moments. *See*, for instance, *Alice Gray* (London, 1855).

15. Harry Escott, *Isaac Watts, Hymnographer: A Study of the Beginnings, Development, and Philosophy of the English Hymn* (London, 1962), pp.201-202.

16. Rice, *The Sunday-School Movement*, p.148.

17. H.A.L. Jefferson, *Hymns in Christian Worship* (London, 1950), p.201.

Watts' hymns included warnings against specific sins, such as this one about lying:

. . . but ev'ry liar
Must have his portion in the lake
That burns with brimstone and with fire.

Then let me always watch my lips,
Lest I be struck to death and hell;
Since God a book of reck'ning keeps,
For ev'ry lie that children tell. (*Divine and Moral Songs*, #8)

Those who scoff and call names are told,

God quickly stopp'd their wicked breath,
And sent two raging bears,
That tore them limb from limb to death,
With blood and groans and tears. (*Divine and Moral Songs*, #21)

Those who disobey their parents are told,

What heavy guilt upon him lies!
How cursed is his name!
The ravens shall pick out his eyes,
And eagles eat the same. (*Divine and Moral Songs*, #20)

Escott, in *Isaac Watts*, Chapter 8, argues that Watts' hymns for children are unfairly criticized as harsh and puritanical in comparison to modern views of childhood. They should, instead, he says, be praised as more pleasant and bright than children's songs and hymns of his own and previous times.

18. Gordon Rattray Taylor, *The Angel-Makers: A Study in the Psychological Origins of Historical Change, 1750-1850* (London, 1958), pp.145-146.

19. Phyllis Wetherell Bultmann, "Everybody Sing: The Social Significance of the Eighteenth-Century Hymn," Unpublished Ph.D. dissertation, University of California at Los Angeles, 1950, p.145., writes that "between 1715 and 1880 there were over 68 separate editions of this work, not counting reprints, of which there were a great many."

20. Rice, *Sunday-School Movement*, p.149.

21. Gosse, *Father and Son*, pp.74-75. Gosse's reaction of terror may have been extreme, but his exhilaration at the working out of retributive justice was evidently widely shared. An adult observer of a Punch and Judy show wrote:

> Then the performance began, and how the children screamed with laughter, yet at times felt shocked and sorry too at the wickedness of bad old Punch. How pleased they were when Toby seized that very red nose, and snarling held it long enough between his little white teeth to give it a good bite, and, after passing through a time of great excitement . . . they all felt that the evil-doer richly deserved the terrible fate that befell him when he was swallowed up by the dreadful brass monster.

"The Punch and Judy Show," *Little Wide-Awake*, 1889, pp.12 and 14. Although the trend in children's literature during the nineteenth century was away from didacticism which inspired terror, it should be noted that there is little conclusive evidence about whether or not children like it. As G. K. Chesterton pointed out, "Nobody has ever told stories to children without realizing how particular they are about factual justice and a sort of domestic day of judgment."

22. Ernest Belfort Bax, *Reminiscences and Reflexions of a Mid and Late Victorian* (London, 1918), p.13.

23. *Child's Companion* I, 12, (December 1832), pp.378-379.

24. Mrs. Sherwood, *The History of the Fairchild Family* (London, 1818), p.119.

25. *Ibid.*, p.124.

26. *The Methodist Sunday-School Hymn-Book* (London, 1879), Hymns #266 (by J. A. Wallace) and #370 (by Isaac Watts).

27. Janet Courtney, *Freethinkers of the Nineteenth Century* (Freeport, New York, 1967), p.4.

28. Ann and Jane Taylor, *Hymns for Infant Minds* (Rev. ed.; London, 1876). The popularity of this collection can be surmised from the fact that the London Sunday School Union, which in 1903 reported having 2,252,497 scholars, issued an edition of *Hymns for Infant Minds.*

29. Ibid., "Sin Makes God Angry," pp.49-51, stanza 6.

30. Ibid., pp.60-61, stanzas 3-6.

31. *Hymns for the Chapel of Harrow School* (Harrow, 1860), Hymn #143, stanza 1.

32. Cecil Frances Alexander, *We are but little children weak* (1850), stanza 6. Henry Allon, *Children's Worship: A Book of Sacred Song for Home and School* (London, 1887), Hymn #426.

33. Cecil Frances Alexander, *Christian children must be holy* (1859), stanza 4. *Children's Hymn Book* (Rev. ed.; London, n.d.), Hymn #86.

34. Taylor, *Hymns for Infant Minds*, pp.16-17, stanzas 2 and 6.

35. Ibid., pp.37-38.

36. L. Tuttiett, *Original Hymns for Younger Members of the Church* (2nd ed.; London, 1889), p.24, stanza 2.

37. Alexander, *Hymns for Little Children*, Hymn #5, stanza 3. His Royal Highness, Prince Albert joined in the movement to lead English children from temptation by composing tunes for several children's hymns, one of which reads in part,

My faith is weak, my heart is proud,
And this world's love is strong within;
Youthful temptations round me crowd,
And urge my soul to youthful sin.

Children's Hymn Book, Hymn #180, stanza 3.

38. William Walsham How, *God of mercy and of love*, stanza 4. *Children's Hymn Book* Hymn #8.

39. Cecil Frances Alexander, *Little birds sleep sweetly*, stanzas 2 and 6. *Victorian Hymns, English Sacred Songs of Fifty Years* (London, 1887).

40. G. B. Blanchard, *Jesus the Friend of children*, stanza 2. *The Church Mission Hymn Book with Mission Liturgies* (London, 1913), Hymn #114.

41. Girls were expected to be passive rather than active, to cultivate the domestic virtues:

O maidens, live for Jesus,
Who was a maiden's Son;
Be patient, pure, and gentle,
And perfect grace begun.

Quoted by Erik Routley, *Hymns and Human Life* (London, 1952), p.301.

42. J. A. Todd, *Hark! the voice of Jesus crying*, stanza 2. Allon, *Children's Worship*, Hymn #496.

43. Allon, *Children's Worship*, Hymn #437, stanzas 2 and 3. We have only to look at other popular works of Victorian children's literature such as Thomas Hughes' novel, *Tom Brown's Schooldays*, to see the prominence of this image of struggle for truth and earnestness.

44. Rudyard Kipling, *Father in heaven, who lovest all* (1906). Albert Edward Bailey, *The Gospel in Hymns, Backgrounds and Interpretations* (New York, 1950), p.448

CHAPTER V

1. Gertrude Himmelfarb, in "The Writing of Social History," *The Journal of British Studies*, XI (Nov., 1971), 155, calls the Condition of England Question "the Victorian euphemism for the condition of the lower classes." The phrase was coined by Thomas Carlyle and was widely used in parliamentary debates and polite conversation.

2. *See*, for instance, K. S. Inglis, *Churches and the Working Classes in Victorian England* (London, 1963); E. R. Wickham, *Church and People in an Industrial City* (London, 1957); and M. A. Crowther, *Church Embattled: Religious Controversy in Mid-Victorian England* (Newton Abbot, Eng., 1970). *See* also Paul Smith, *Disraelian Conservatism and Social Reform* (London, 1967), p.32 and Jenifer Hart, "Nineteenth-Century Social Reform: A Tory Interpretation of History," *Past and Present*, XXXI (July, 1965), 53-57.

3. Phillip Doddridge, *O fount of good, to own Thy love.* William Cooke and Benjamin Webb (eds.), *The Hymnary, A Book of Church Song* (2nd ed.; London, 1872), Hymn #523. This hymn, incidentally, is the only one in this large collection which specifically urges secular service to one's fellow man.

4. Thomas Kelly, *We've no abiding city here* (1802), stanzas 1, 2, and 6. *Hymns Ancient and Modern* (4th ed.; London, 1904), Hymn #427.

5. E. Caswell (trans.), *O Holy Ghost, Who with the Son* (1872), stanza 4. Cooke and Webb, *Hymnary*, Hymn #418.

6. William Booth (ed.), *Salvation Army Music* (London, 1890), Hymn #176.

7. *Poor and needy through I be*, stanzas 1 and 4. *Simple Hymns for Infants' Schools* (London, 1835), Hymn #v.

8. *In this our low and poor estate*, stanza 1. *Simple Hymns for Infants' Schools*, Hymn #XI.

9. William Gaskell, *Though lowly here our lot may be*, stanzas 1 and 5. Henry Allon (ed.), *Children's Worship: A Book of Sacred Song for Home and School* (London, 1887), Hymn #512.

10. Mrs. Cecil Frances Alexander, *All things bright and beautiful* (1849), stanza 3. Committee, *Church Praise*, II, Hymn #433. This attitude of social complacence was expressed in much of children's literature. In a poem from *The Mother's Fables in Verse* (London, 1812), p.34, when a child questions why a poor girl has to work so hard, her mother answers:

> 'Tis proper, Sophy, to be sure,
> To pity and relieve the poor;
> But do not waste your pity here,
> Work is not hard to her, my dear;
> It makes her healthy, strong, and gay,
> And is as pleasant as your play.
> We've each our task; and they may boast
> The happiest life, who do the most.

11. William Cameron, *Behold what witnesses unseen* (1781), stanza 5. Committee, *Church Praise*, II, Hymn #52.

12. Josef L. Altholz, *The Churches in the Nineteenth Century* (New York, 1967), p.32.

13. John Newton, *How welcome to the saints when pressed* (1779). John Allen (ed.), *The Penny Hymnbook* (London, 1860), Hymn #48.

14. Jonathan Evans, *Come, Thou soul-transforming Spirit* (1784), stanza 1. *The Mission Hymnal of the Church Pastoral-Aid Society, with Tunes* (London, 1887), Hymn #30.

15. Elie Halévy, *The Birth of Methodism in England*, trans. by Bernard Sammel (Chicago, 1971) and *England in 1815*, trans. by E. I. Watkin and D. A. Barker (London, 1949).

16. Halévy, *Birth of Methodism*, p.76.

17. Robert F. Wearmouth, *Methodism and the Working Class Movements of England, 1800-1850* (London, 1937), p.50.

18. G. M. Young, *Victorian England, Portrait of an Age* (2nd ed.; London, 1953), pp.65-66.

19. Albert Peel, *These Hundred Years: A History of the Congregational Union of England and Wales, 1831-1931* (London, 1931), p.107.

20. R. Tudur Jones, *Congregationalism in England, 1662-1962* (London, 1962), p.191.

21. Inglis, *Churches and Working Classes*, p.306.

22. *See*, for instance, W. Stanley Jervons, *Methods of Social Reform and Other Papers* (London, 1883) and Ambrose Shepherd, *The Gospel and Social Questions* (2nd ed.; London, 1902).

23. Desmond Bowen, *The Idea of the Victorian Church: A Study of the Church of England 1833-1889* (Montreal, 1968), p.286.

24. Margaret M. Maison, *The Victorian Vision: Studies in The Religious Novel* (New York, 1961), p.22.

25. Edward Bickersteth, *Christian Psalmody* (London, 1833), Hymn #460.

26. Ann and Jane Taylor, *Hymns for Infant Minds* (Rev. ed.; London, 1876), pp.117-118.

27. William Walsham How, *We give Thee but Thine own* (1858), stanzas 1 and 4. Committee, *Church Praise*, Hymn #366.

28. James Boden, *Bright source of everlasting love*! (1801), stanzas 4-6. Bickersteth, *Christian Psalmody*, Hymn #455.

29. Eliza Sibbald Alderson, *Lord of Glory, Who hast bought us* (1864), stanza 4. *Hymns Ancient and Modern* (1904), Hymn #548.

30. Christopher Wordsworth, *O Lord of heaven, and earth, and sea* (1862), stanzas 7-9. Committee, *Church Praise*, Hymn #19.

31. Elliott-Binns, *Religion in the Victorian Era*, p.209.

32. *The Mother's Fables in Verse* (London, 1812), p.22.

33. *Yes, there are joys that cannot die. Missionary Hymns* (London, 1830), Hymn #113.

34. *The Child's Companion; or, Sunday Scholar's Reward* (London: June, 1832), I, 6, p.169.

35. *Oh, what can little hands do*, stanzas 1 and 2. Committee, *Church Praise*, Hymn #459.

36. Desmond Bowen, *Idea of the Victorian Church*, p.252.

37. Wearmouth, *Methodism and the Working Class*, pp.109-110. Martha Vicinus, *The Industrial Muse: A Study of Nineteenth Century British Working-Class Literature* (New York, 1974), p.99, quotes a similar hymn from W. J. Linton's "Hymns to the Unenfranchised" (1839):

We begged for peace—ye gave us toil and war;
We begged for quiet bread—and stones were given:—
Tyrants and priests! we will be scourged no more:
The chains of loyalty and faith are riven.

According to Linton's footnote, the "stones" referred to the taxes for building new churches, imposed in time of famine.

38. Ebenezer Elliott, *When wilt thou save the people*, (1832). E. Elliott, *More Verse and Prose* (London, 1850), p.80.

39. George Loveless, *God is our Guide!* (1834). Quoted by J. Wesley Bready, *England: Before and After Wesley, The Evangelical Revival and Social Reform* (London, 1938), p.390.

40. Edward Osler, *Come, let us search our hearts, and try* (1836). Allen, *Penny Hymnbook*, Hymn #19.

41. James Montgomery, *Hail to the Lord's Anointed*, stanzas 1-3. Committee, *Church Praise*, II, Hymn #194. For a more balanced view of Montgomery's hymns, *see* one of his collections, such as *Original Hymns for Public, Private, and Social Devotion* (London, 1853).

42. *O Thou who didst create us all*, stanzas 1-4. *Democratic Hymns and Songs* (Wortley, 1849), p.53.

43. *Man makes his brother mourn*, stanzas 6 and 7. *Democratic Hymns and Songs*, pp.42-43.

44. *Thou shalt not steal! 'tis God that speaks. Democratic Hymns and Songs*, p.41.

45. *National Chartist Hymn Book*; quoted by E. P. Thompson, *The Making of the English Working Class* (New York, 1964), p.399. In 1839 the Scottish moral-force Christian Chartists claimed in *An Appeal to the People of Scotland* that "the great question of national liberty is the people's charter. . . . The cause of liberty is the cause of mankind and of God." Quoted by Raymond G. Cowherd, *The Politics of Dissent: The Religious Aspects of Liberal and Humanitarian Reform Movements from 1815 to 1848* (New York, 1956), p.107.

46. Louis James, *Fiction for the Working Man, 1830-1850* (London, 1963), p.175.

47. Wearmouth, *Methodism and the Working Class*, pp.109-110.

48. E. Miall, *The British Churches and the British People* (1848), pp. 143-4; quoted by K. S. Inglis, *Churches and the Working Classes*, pp.18-19. Miall himself denounced the class distinctions among congregations: "The service concludes, and the worshippers retire. Communion with God has not disposed them to communion with each other, beyond the well-defined boundaries of class."

49. Elliott-Binns, *Religion in Victorian Era*, p.262.

50. Erik Routley, *Hymns and Human Life* (London, 1962).

51. Percy Dearmer, *Songs of Praise Discussed: A Handbook to the Best-Known Hymns and to Others Recently Introduced* (London, 1933), pp. 172-178; *see* also Benjamin Brawley, *History of the English Hymn* (New York, 1932), pp.122 ff., for a discussion of American hymns of social service.

52. *See* especially Crowther, *Church Embattled.*

53. Willis B. Glover, *Evangelical Nonconformists and Higher Criticism in the Nineteenth Century* (London, 1954), pp.263-282.

54. J. Edwin Orr, *The Second Evangelical Awakening* (London, 1949), p.9.

55. George S. Barrett (ed.), *The Congregational Mission Hymnal and Weeknight Service Book* (London, 1890).

56. *Mission Hymnal* (1887).

57. *The Church Mission Hymn-Book* (rev. ed.; London, 1883).

58. Horton Davies, *Worship and Theology in England from Newman to Martineau, 1850-1900* (Princeton, 1962), p.169.

59. Ira D. Sankey, James McGranahan and George Stebbins, *Gospel Hymns, Nos. 5 and 6 Combined* (Cincinnati, Ohio, 1892).

60. Watson, *Social Problems*, pp.vii-viii.

61. Elliott-Binns, *Religion in the Victorian Era*, p.268.

62. H. C. Shuttleworth, *Father of men, in whom are one*, stanzas 1 and 2. *The English Hymnal* (Rev. ed.; London, 1906), Hymn #528.

63. S. C. Lowry, *Son of God, Eternal Saviour*, stanza 2 in the 1904 edition of *Hymns Ancient and Modern*; interestingly, this stanza is omitted from the 1906 edition of the *English Hymnal.*

64. Godfrey Thring, *O God of mercy, God of might* (1877), stanzas 3-5. *English Hymnal*, Hymn #448.

65. Henry Scott Holland, *Judge eternal, throned in splendour* (1902). *English Hymnal*, Hymn #423.

66. Edward Carpenter, *England, arise! the long night is over* (1888), stanzas 1 and 4. Dearmer, *Songs of Praise Discussed*, p.178.

67. Gilbert Keith Chesterton, *O God of earth and altar* (first published in 1906, but was evidently written during or shortly after the Boer War). *English Hymnal*, Hymn #562.

68. Dearmer, *Songs of Praise Discussed*, p.172.

69. *Hymns Ancient and Modern* (1904), p.iv.

70. Elliott-Binns, *Religion in the Victorian Era*, p.269.

71. Francis Warre Cornish, *The English Church in the Nineteenth Century* (London, 1910).

72. Shepherd, *Gospel and Social Questions*, pp.15-16.

73. Inglis, *Churches and the Working Classes*, p.234. The same could be said of *Hymns and Anthems for the Use of the South Place Ethical Society* (London, 1889), which is entirely humanistic and secular in content.

74. [Stanton Coit (ed.)], *Ethical Hymn Book with Music* (Rev. ed.; London, 1905).

75. *Ibid.*, Hymn #75.

76. *The Spiritual Songster, A Choice and Unique Collection of Song and Hymn for the Awakening of Spiritual and Progressive Ideas in the Mind of Humanity* (Newcastle-on-Tyne, 1893), Hymn #100.

77. Beatrice Webb, *My Apprenticeship* (New York, 1926), p.145.

CHAPTER VI

1. Mrs. Ashley Carus-Wilson, *The Expansion of Christendom, A Study in Religious History* (London, 1910) p.110.

2. G. R. Balleine, *A History of the Evangelical Party in the Church of England* (London, 1908), p.255.

3. Ibid., p.309.

4. *The Missionary Year-Book for 1889* (London, n.d.), p.12.

5. John Julian, *A Dictionary of Hymnology* (New York, 1892), p.759.

6. Burton L. Goddard (ed.), *The Encyclopedia of Modern Christian Missions* (Camden, N.J., 1967), p.99.

7. Thomas Cotterill, *O'er the realms of pagan darkness* (1819), stanzas 1 and 3. Edward Bickersteth, *Christian Psalmody* (London, 1833), Hymn #412.

8. *Missionary Book for the Young* (New ed.; London [c.1850]), p.60.

9. Ibid., p.79.

10. *The Child's Companion; or, Sunday Scholar's Reward*, 65 (May, 1837), 131.

11. Ann and Jane Taylor, *Hymns for Infant Minds* (Rev. ed.; London, 1876), pp.11-12.

12. Reginald Heber, *From Greenland's icy mountains* (1819), stanzas 1-3. *The Church Missionary Hymn Book* (London, [1899]).

13. *Look down, O God, with pitying eye*, stanza 1. *Missionary Hymns: Composed and Selected for the Public Services at the Annual Meetings of the London Missionary Society* (New ed.; London, 1830), Hymn #14.

14. *Arm of the Lord, awake! awake!.* stanza 4. *Missionary Hymns* (1830), Hymn #20.

15. Richard Burnham (1749-1810), *All the elected train*, stanzas 1 and 2. [Thomas Bradbury], *Psalms and Hymns and Spiritual Songs for the Elect of God* (3rd ed.; Brighton, 1891), Hymn #10.

16. *See*, for instance, Edwin Diller Starbuck, *The Psychology of Religion: An Empirical Study of the Growth of Religious Consciousness* (London, [1914]).

17. William Williams, *O'er the gloomy hills of darkness* (1772), stanza 2. Henry Allon, *Children's Worship: A Book of Sacred Song for Home and School* (London, 1887), Hymn #527.

18. Frances Ridley Havergal, *Tell it out among the heathen* (1872), stanza 2. Committee of the Presbyterian Church of England (eds.), *Church Praise* (London, 1885), Hymn #189.

19. Quoted by Carus-Wilson, *Expansion of Christendom*, p.14.

20. *Bright as the sun's meridian blaze*, stanza 3. *Missionary Hymns* (1830), Hymn #44.

21. *Missionary Hymns Selected for the Use of Meetings for the Propagation of the Gospel among Jews and Gentiles* (Reading, 1837), Hymn #59, stanza 2.

22. Bishop Edward Henry Bickersteth, *Hark! hark, the voice of numbers*, stanzas 1, 3, and 4. *Church Missionary Hymn Book*, Hymn #10.

23. *Wesleyan Juvenile Offering: A Miscellany of Missionary Information* (August, 1848), p.88.

24. *Child's Companion*, I, 1 (Jan. 1832), p.7.

25. *While Britain favour'd of the skies*, stanza 4. Bickersteth, *Christian Psalmody*, Hymn #434.

26. David L. Edwards, *Religion and Change* (New York, 1969), p.39.

27. Cecil Francis Alexander, *Souls in heathen darkness lying* (1851), stanza 3. *Church Missionary Hymn Book*, Hymn #23.

28. J. E. Ellison, *O Living God, Whose voice of old,* stanza 3. *Hymns Ancient and Modern* (4th ed.; London, 1904) Hymn #531.

29. John Ellerton, *The day thou gavest, Lord, is ended* (1870), stanzas 2-5. *The English Hymnal* (New ed.; London, 1906.)

30. *Church Missionary Hymn Book*, Hymn #242, stanza 3.

31. Ibid., Hymn #239, stanza 1.

32. Ibid., Hymn #6, stanza 2.

33. *Hymns Ancient and Modern* (1904), Hymn #534.

34. Bickersteth, *Christian Psalmody*, Hymn #405.

35. Benjamin Beddome, *Let party names no more* (1769), stanza 1. *Hymns for use at United Prayer Meetings and Other Devotional Services* (London, 1886), Hymn #88.

36. James Montgomery, *Millions within Thy courts have met* (1841), stanzas 3, 5, and 10. Martha Braithwaite, *The Fireside Hymn-Book* (London, 1865), pp.133-134.

37. Benjamin Disraeli, *Sybil, or, The Two Nations*, Book III, Chapter V.

38. Rudyard Kipling, *God of our fathers, known of old* (1897). *English Hymnal* (1906).

39. John Oxenham, *In Christ there is no East or West* (1908). Quoted by Calvin W. Laufer, *Hymn Lore* (Philadelphia, 1932), pp.158-161. This hymn makes an interesting comparison to Kipling's "O East is East and West is West,/ And never the twain shall meet." *See* also H. Ernest Nichol's *We've a story to tell to the nations* (1896).

40. Symonds, *These things shall be! A loftier race* (1880), stanza 3. *The Methodist Hymn Book* (London, 1904). This hymn became especially popular in England during World War I.

CHAPTER VII

1. Benjamin Franklin Crawford, *Religious Trends in a Century of Hymns* (Carnegie, Pa., 1938), p.76.

2. Albert Peel, *These Hundred Years: A History of the Congregational Union of England and Wales*, 1831-1931 (London, 1931), p.287.

3. James McGranahan, "Our Mother's Way." Charles Alexander, *Alexander's New Revival Hymns* (London, n.d), Hymn #69. This hymnbook, which was used at the Torrey-Alexander meetings at the turn of the century, abounds in hymns of this type on the subject of motherhood.

4. Ibid., Hymn #13.

5. Robert Southey, *Sir Thomas More; or Colloquies on the Progress and Prospects of Society*, I (1829), pp.173-174.

6. *See* especially, K. S. Inglis, *Churches and the Working Classes in Victorian England* (London, 1963); E. R. Wickham, *Church and People in an Industrial City* (London, 1957); and G. Kitson Clark, *Churchmen and the Condition of England, 1832-1885* (London, 1973).

7. Desmond Bowen, *The Idea of the Victorian Church: A Study of the Church of England 1833-1889* (Montreal, 1968), p.270.

8. George B. Howard, *Future Supply of Clergy for the Service of the Church of England: Letter to Right Honorable W. E. Gladstone* (1875); quoted by Bowen, *Idea of the Victorian Church*, p.24.

9. Inglis, *Churches and the Working Classes*, p.200.

10. Ira D. Sankey, James McGranahan, and Geo. Stebbins, *Gospel Hymns, Nos. 5 & 6 Combined* (Cincinnati, 1892), p.374, stanza 2.

11. Christopher Wordsworth, *Hallelujah! Hallelujah!* (1862), stanza 2.

12. Elizabeth C. Clephane, *There were ninety and nine that safely lay* (1874). William Booth (ed.), *Salvation Army Music* (London, 1890), Hymn #480.

13. Booth, *Salvation Army Music*, Hymn #100. Ann and William Reeder pointed out to me that these lyrics appeared earlier as an epitaph to William Pickering and Richard Edger, in Ely Cathedral Cloisters. The use of the railroad as a religious metaphor has a long and interesting tradition in popular hymns and preaching in the United States, particularly in the southern states. It was used much less extensively in England.

14. Robert Crompton Jones (ed.), *Hymns of Duty and Faith* (London, 1872), pp.21-22, stanzas 1, 2, and 4.

15. Written in 1865 by an Anglican vicar, Sabine Baring-Gould, for a children's Whitmonday school festival.

16. Translated in 1834 from Lowenstern's *Christe du Beistand*, which was written during the Thirty Years' War. Erik Routley, *Hymns and Human Life* (London, 1952), pp.111-112, points out that, although Pusey intended the hymn as a defense against the nonconformist attempt at disestablishment, by the end of the century it was sung by both Anglicans and nonconformists.

17. Christopher Wordsworth, *See the Conqueror mounts in triumph* (1862), stanza 2. *Hymns Ancient and Modern* (1904), Hymn #173.

18. J. M. Neale, *Hymns for Children* (9th ed.; London, 1885), Hymn #14, stanza 1.

19. Norman Bennet, *We are soldiers every one,* stanza 1. *The Church Mission Hymn Book with Mission Liturgies* (London, 1913), Hymn #93.

20. George Duffield, *Stand up! stand up for Jesus* (1868), stanza 1. *Church Mission Hymn Book*, Hymn #98.

21. Thomas Hughes, *Tom Brown's School Days* (New York; 1911), Part II, Chapter 5.

22. Juliana Horatio Ewing, *Jackanapes* (London, 1884), p.46.

23. John Samuel Bewley Monsell, *Fight the good fight with all thy might* (1863), stanzas 1 and 2. John S. B. Monsell, *Hymns of Love and Praise for the Church's Year* (London, 1863).

24. Walter J. Mathams, *Stand fast for Christ thy Saviour* (1913), stanza 3. Quoted by Calvin Laufer, *Hymn Lore* (Philadelphia, 1932).

25. "What Is Glory? What Is Fame?" stanza 1. *Democratic Hymns and Songs* (Wortley, 1849), p.18.

26. "On Greenhow Hill" (1890). Quoted by P. J. Keating, *The Working Classes in Victorian Fiction* (New York, 1971), pp.146-147.

27. Quoted by Peel, *These Hundred Years*, pp.201-202.

28. E. E. Kellett, *Religion and Life in the Early Victorian Age* (London, 1938), p.168. Ernest Belfort Bax, in *Reminiscences and Reflexions of a Mid and Late Victorian* (New York, 1967; originally published London, 1918), pp.195-196, noted that as religious fervor declined in the late nineteenth century, patriotism increased: "One of the most striking phenomena of social

change in the present generation, the counterpart of the rise and domination of Imperialism in politics, is the installation of imperialistic or patriotic sentiment in the place of the old religious feeling. Patriotism, as it is called, had undoubtedly taken the place formerly occupied by Christian sentiment and aspiration in the mind of the average man."

29. William F. Sherwin, *Sound the battle cry!*, stanza 1. *Hymns for the Church Army* (London, [1894]), p.7.

CONCLUSION

1. Reginald Heber, *From foes that would the land devour* (1827), stanza 2. *The English Hymnal* (New ed.; London, 1906), Hymn #557.

2. Philip Pusey, *Lord of our life, and God of our salvation* (1834), stanza 2. William Cooke and Benjamin Webb (eds.), *The Hymnary, A Book of Church Song* (2nd ed.; London, 1872), Hymn #448. This was a translation of a seventeenth-century German hymn.

3. James Harrington Evans, *Change is our portion here!* (1818), stanza 3. Thomas Bradbury, *Psalms and Hymns and Spiritual Songs for the Elect of God* (3rd ed.; Brighton, 1891), Hymn #59.

INDEX

INDEX

INDEX OF HYMN TITLES